100 THINGS DUKE FANS SHOULD KNOW & DO BEFORE THEY DIE

100 THINGS DUKE FANS SHOULD KNOW & DO BEFORE THEY DIE

Johnny Moore

TRIUMPH
BOOKS

Library of Congress Cataloging-in-Publication Data

Moore, Johnny, 1955–
  100 things Duke fans should know & do before they die / Johnny Moore.
    pages cm
  ISBN 978-1-60078-980-9
1.   Duke University—Basketball—Miscellanea. 2.   Duke Blue Devils
(Basketball team)—Miscellanea. I. Title. II. Title: One hundred things Duke
fans should know and do before they die.
  GV885.43.D85M68 2015
  796.32309756'563—dc23
                                             2015015632

This book is available in quantity at special discounts for your group or organization. For further information, contact:
  Triumph Books LLC
  814 North Franklin Street
  Chicago, Illinois 60610
  (312) 337-0747
  www.triumphbooks.com

Printed in U.S.A.
ISBN: 978-1-60078-980-9
Design by Patricia Frey
Photos courtesy of Robert Crawford unless otherwise indicated

To my mom and dad, especially my dad, who took me to my first Duke basketball game when I was six years old and made me a Duke fan for life. And to the coaches, players, and fans who make it such fun to be a part of Duke basketball.

Contents

Foreword

My love affair with Duke began the moment I arrived on campus for my first visit. It was in the fall; the trees were alive with color and painted against the pristine gothic background of campus. It was everything you ever dreamed of in a college campus. I immediately became enamored with the school.

As a member of a basketball team, I realized I would have my basketball family, but what I didn't know when I arrived on campus for my freshman year at the age of 17 was I would have a student body family as well. It provided a great balance in my life—the relationships with the people in the basketball program and the friendships developed on campus and in town. Those experiences afforded me the ability to take in everything that Duke has to offer. The person I became was formed because of all those relationships, both on and off the basketball court.

I feel a little like Moses from the Bible. I am a link, a bridge to the past of Duke basketball. I have always told Coach Krzyzewski that I am the Old Testament, and he is the New Testament. I was a member of the teams of the late '70s that were able to make such a great impact on college basketball, linking the great teams of the '60s with the teams of the future. As a history major, I am very proud of the history of Duke basketball, and one of the things I like about this book is there are stories about Eddie Cameron, Dick Groat, and Vic Bubas, along with my coach, Bill Foster, and all the great things that have happened in the Krzyzewski era. The history of this program has always been very important to me.

As a representative of Duke, in my everyday life and on the air on television and radio, I am very proud of my university and how it has continued to evolve into one of the great universities not only in the country but in the world.

There was nothing better in my life than running out onto the floor of Cameron Indoor Stadium for a basketball game. The history, the energy from the student body, and the fans were euphoric. There is something very special about being a Duke basketball player, something that seeps into your soul and stays with you forever.

So for those of you who are old-school Bob Verga-era Duke fans, newer Grant Hill fans, or recent Jahlil Okafor and Tyus Jones fans, this book will give you a look at everything you should know about Duke basketball.

Let's Go Duke!

—Mike Gminski

Introduction

If you ever get the chance, you should walk into Cameron Indoor Stadium and head onto the playing floor at night with just the upper lights tossing enough glow to give the building a mystical feel. Stop, take a deep breath, and you will feel the essence of the building, the ghosts—because it is the spirit, the people, the special feeling that make Cameron Indoor Stadium and Duke basketball so incredible.

There is Eddie Cameron sitting on the bench coaching the first game in the building. Vic Bubas, Bucky Waters, and Bill Foster prowling the sidelines leading the Blue Devils to more great wins. A young Mike Krzyzewski fighting for respect, and a veteran Coach K looking up at the banners he and his players placed in the rafters.

There is Max Crowder, the redheaded Duke trainer with the scowl on his face directed at one of the guys in the striped shirts like Lou Bello, Lenny Wirtz, or John Clougherty, who are making another call that Krzyzewski doesn't like—and neither do the fans. A smile will come across your face and maybe a tear in your eye as you look up into the stands and look at the spot where your father, golf coach, or best friend sat for so many years and is no longer there. You chuckle when you remember all the people who have sat in the same seats in Cameron for so many years.

Those people make Duke basketball the greatest college basketball program ever—five national championships, 19 ACC titles, more than 2,000 wins. Yes, we've had great players and great coaches, but each one of those players and coaches will tell you that somehow Duke basketball is much more than just winning games and playing basketball. It is much more about being Duke, being a part of something as a fan, player, or coach that has meaning. You believe in what you stand for and who you are. You're not a big state school with hundreds of thousands of fans. You are Duke. Rival and non-Duke fans call it cockiness. It's not cocky; it's a confidence that you are Duke basketball and you know what you stand for—academics, character, and success. You are proud to be a Blue Devil.

In this book we have tried to go through the fabric of Duke basketball and find the 100 things that will give you an accurate feel for the program loved by so many. Most of the 100 things are people, players, and coaches who have collectively completed Duke basketball. I hope that if you are a newbie to the world of Duke basketball that you can learn about Dick Groat and Shane Battier as well as the great teams of the '60s, '70s, '80s, '90s, and all the championships. If you are a veteran of Blue Devils basketball reliving the careers of your heroes like Bob Verga, Jim Spanarkel, Christian Laettner, or Grant Hill, I hope this book will be a lot of fun and rekindle great memories.

1 Cameron Indoor Stadium

A classic venue and the crown jewel of college basketball, Cameron Indoor Stadium originally opened in 1940 as Duke Indoor Stadium. Heading into the 2015–16 season, it has been the site of 832 men's basketball victories. More than a few of those victories have been influenced by the electric atmosphere within its Gothic halls.

Well before $2 million renovations in the 1980s, legend has it that it all began with a book of matches. For a town and a school founded on local tobacco fortunes, that seems a fitting way to start. On the cover of a matchbook, Eddie Cameron and Wallace Wade first sketched out the plan for Duke Indoor Stadium in 1935. The story may be a myth (the matchbook has never been found), but then the Indoor Stadium that emerged from those first scribblings lends itself to the propagation of myths.

For seven decades, spectators, players, and coaches have understood the unique magic of the Indoor Stadium. The building was dedicated to longtime Duke athletic director and basketball coach Eddie Cameron, a legend in his own right, on January 22, 1972. Then an unranked Duke team upset third-ranked North Carolina 76–74 after Robby West drove the length of the court to hit a pull-up jumper to win the game.

It's the intimacy of the arena, the unique seating arrangement that puts the wildest fans right down on the floor with the players. It's the legends that were made there, the feeling of history being made with every game. And it's something indescribable that comes from the building itself. No one who has experienced it will ever forget it.

1

Whether or not the matchbook story is true, it is a fact that the official architectural plans for the stadium were drawn up by the Philadelphia firm of Horace Trumbauer, a self-made man, a poor boy who left school at 16 to apprentice himself as a draftsman to a local architect. In 1890, at the age of 21, he opened his own office and quickly rose to prominence in the Northeast. His designs for the mansions and estates of wealthy northeastern magnates brought him to the attention of James Buchanan Duke, the North Carolina tobacco baron. Duke commissioned the architect to design his New York town home during the early part of the century. In 1924 when Duke created the $40 million Duke Endowment that turned Trinity College into Duke University, he called on Trumbauer to design the new university campus. In recent years it has come to light that the plans for the campus, as well as designs for later buildings, including the stadium, were drawn up not by Trumbauer himself (although his name appeared on all the blueprints) but by his chief designer, Julian Abele, one of the nation's first African American architects.

The original design for the Indoor Stadium was significantly less grand than the one from which the building was actually constructed. That first plan called for 5,000 basketball "sittings," and even that number was considered extravagant, at least by Trumbauer, who originally had proposed 4,000 seats. In a letter to Duke president Dr. William P. Few, Trumbauer said: "For your information Yale has in its new gymnasium a basket ball [sic] court with settings for 1,600…I think the settings for 8,000 people is rather liberal…the Palestra at the University of Pennsylvania seats 9,000." The original building was a domed structure with 16-feet steel ceiling spans and a 90-foot by 45-foot playing court.

As important as the size of the stadium was its external appearance. It was vital that the building be aesthetically integrated with the original West Campus buildings. For this reason stone was taken from the Duke quarry in nearby Hillsborough, where all the stone for the original campus had been found. The stone had to be laid in temperate weather. (In extremely cold temperatures, the mortar would freeze.)

Building on the stadium proceeded quickly and finished in nine months before it was officially opened on January 6, 1940. The final cost was $400,000, which Duke finished paying after the football team won the Sugar Bowl in 1945. Touring the building before the evening ceremony and subsequent game, local city officials were "speechless." Said Chamber of Commerce president Col. Marion B. Fowler, "It is so colossal and so wonderful...This building will not only be an asset to the university but to the entire community as well." Chamber secretary Frank Pierson concurred, "There are no superlatives for it."

But Duke's Indoor Stadium was a structure of superlatives. The arena measured 262 feet long by 175 feet wide and was the East Coast's largest indoor stadium south of the Palestra in Philadelphia. Nine fixed steel frames spanned the ceiling at 26-foot intervals. Seating for 8,800 included 3,500 folding bleacher seats on the floor designated, then as today, for the exclusive use of undergraduates. Maximum capacity was 12,000. It was, according to the program issued the opening night, "one of the most modern and complete physical education buildings in the country."

The building was dedicated before a crowd of 8,000, the largest ever in the history of southern basketball. President William P. Few and Dean William H. Wannamaker presented the stadium to the university. Dean R.B. House of UNC-Chapel Hill, representing the Southern Conference, also spoke. Aware of the tensions his presence as a member of a rival institution might cause, House affirmed, "I am a Methodist. I aspire to religion, I endorse erudition and I use...tobacco...Hence, I claim to have good personal grounds for being a friend and well-wisher of Duke University... here will be on parade not only Duke University, but also... youth...education...[and] the values of a great and democratic people. Modern games preserve for us the athletic glory of Greece, the executive efficiency of Rome." To the greater glory of Greece, Rome, and particularly Duke University, the Blue Devils beat the visiting Princeton Tigers that night 36–27.

Originally the largest indoor arena in the South, Cameron is today one of the smallest in the nation. Nevertheless, its stature grows from year to year. Sold-out crowds, top 25 rankings, and championships of every variety have become the norm. The "creative harassment" of student spectators has given Duke the honor of being known as "one of the toughest road games in the USA," according to *USA TODAY* and any visiting team that has ever played in Cameron. In its June 7, 1999 issue, *Sports Illustrated* rated Cameron Indoor Stadium fourth on a list of the top 20 sporting venues in the world in the 20th century, ranking ahead of such notables as Wrigley Field, Fenway Park, and Pebble Beach.

2 Coach K

He stands as the first Division I college basketball coach to amass more than 1,000 wins and the winningest coach in the history of Division I men's college basketball. But when he first arrived on the Duke campus, Krzyzewski not only spelled his name to everyone in attendance at his first press conference, he also tried to teach everyone how to pronounce his name. Was it with a silent K, like "shu" or was it a hard K? He wouldn't be called "Coach K" for a number of years. "Special K" was the first promotional material put out on the former Army player and coach.

But the people within his inner circle at Duke came up with the most appropriate nickname available—Captain. Since he was a captain in the Army, Captain just fit him. So for years he was called "Captain" or "Mike." Being "Captain" or a leader has always been a natural fit for the kid from Chicago. "Growing up I was always the leader of my group. There were just instinctive things you do as a leader," he explained. "Looking back, the people I admired were leaders—whether it was my coach in high school or my college coach. I gravitated toward wanting to know what leaders did."

Krzyzewski also grew up with a love for the game of basketball. He played at all-boys Catholic Weber High School in Chicago. "I loved playing basketball from the time I was in the seventh grade," Krzyzewski said. "I fell in love with basketball and I played all day with my buddies. I shot a lot by myself and imagined that my team always won. My high school coach, Al Ostrowski, made me better. He pushed me to be a better player and he helped me to understand the nuances of the game."

During Kryzyzewski's junior season, Ostrowski had to light a fire under Krzyzewski to get him to shoot more in the game. He finally told him he would have to run laps every time he didn't shoot the ball, so in the next game, Krzyzewski lit up the scoreboard for 30 points and he ended up leading the Catholic League in scoring that year, getting an early taste of what leadership and belief can do for a player. "I always thought the basketball was my friend, and it would never let me down," he said. "It's been my friend my entire life."

After high school Krzyzewski headed off to the best leadership school in the world at West Point, the United States Military Academy. "You take that desire or instinct to lead and now you are taught how to lead," Krzyzewski explained. "After West Point being in the service you are around a lot of leaders—good leaders, medium leaders, and not-so-good leaders. So you start developing your own leadership style."

During his military service, he coached service teams and served for two years as head coach at the U.S. Military Academy

Prep School at Belvoir, Virginia. After resigning from the service with the rank of Captain in 1974, Krzyzewski worked as a graduate assistant to his old Army coach, Bob Knight, at Indiana University.

Krzyzewski always wanted to teach. His ambition in high school was to be a high school teacher and coach. "The thing I loved the most—and still love the most about teaching—is that you can connect with an individual or a group and see that individual or group exceed their limits," he explained. "You feel like you've been a part of them. You become something bigger than yourself."

He got his first head coaching job at his alma mater and served there from 1975–80, putting together a 73–59 record and one trip to the NIT. Those weren't very impressive credentials to take over a Duke basketball program that played for the national championship in 1978 and spent the majority of the next three years ranked among the top five teams in the nation. But here he was, working to recruit players to play against two of the top programs in the nation in UNC and N.C. State and not making much progress as he missed on several top recruits before hitting the jackpot with his freshman class that entered Duke in the fall of 1982 and included Johnny Dawkins.

In those days he wasn't known so much for being a leader, he was a defensive coach—a belly button-in-your-face, help-side defensive coach. This was a world of change for most of the players and all the fans who had gotten used to zone defenses in this area of the country. North Carolina was one of the top zone defensive teams in the country with their coach Dean Smith being one of the great teachers of zone defensive play.

It took time and a lot of mistakes to get this defense down, but following his first NCAA Tournament appearance in 1984, the Blue Devils' man-to-man defense was part of the fabric of college basketball. One of the strongest rules in teaching this man-to-man, help-side defense is belief, and Krzyzewski with his leadership

Mike Krzyzewski has built Duke into one of the greatest programs in college basketball.

background was able to use belief as the lightning rod that made his defense effective.

In taking that leadership and teaching mantra to heart, Krzyzewski has developed into one of the finest college basketball coaches in the history of the game. A 12-time National Coach of the Year, he has also been voted the ACC Coach of the Year five times, second on the all-time list. In 1991 he was inducted into the National Polish American Sports Hall of Fame. *The* (Raleigh) *News and Observer* named Krzyzewski the best coach in ACC history in celebration of the league's 50th anniversary in 2002–03. In a postgame ceremony on November 17, 2000, the Cameron Indoor Stadium court was named Coach K Court in Krzyzewski's honor.

As part of a joint venture, *Time* magazine and CNN named Krzyzewski "America's Best Coach" in 2001. "No college hoops coach has won more in the past two decades, and Krzyzewski has accomplished all this with a program that turns out real-deal scholar-athletes—kids who go to class, graduate, and don't mind telling everyone about it," *Time*'s Josh Tyrangiel wrote. On October 5, 2001, Krzyzewski was inducted into the Naismith Basketball Hall of Fame. He became the youngest recipient of the Distinguished Graduate Award at the United States Military Academy in 2005 and in September 2009 he was inducted into the Army Sports Hall of Fame. In 2011, along with Tennessee women's coach Pat Summitt, he was named the Sportsman of the Year by *Sports Illustrated*.

His success has also made him a very rich man—with reports of his salary exceeding the $10 million mark and annually averaging well over $7 million. Beginning in 2005, his success led to a slew of commercial endorsements, including spots for Chevrolet, an endorsement deal with GMC, Allstate and State Farm Insurance companies, and an American Express commercial shot in Cameron Indoor Stadium that looked more like a commercial for Duke than a spot for Amex. "I don't look at myself as a basketball coach," he said in the commercial. "I look at myself as a leader who coaches basketball."

The commercial was part of the "My Life, My Card" series, which has also featured Ellen DeGeneres, Tiger Woods, Robert DeNiro, and Laird Hamilton. American Express spokesperson Rosa Alfonso said the commercial was not a pitch for Duke, but rather that the university is a central part of Krzyzewski's story.

"It's the reflection of his life and the story he has to tell, as with all the individuals we feature," Alfonso said of the commercial. "The reality is that he is an inspiration to many people and he affects a lot of people personally off the court."

His leadership plan is simple. "The single most important quality to be a leader is to be trustworthy, he has to be believable," Krzyzewski said. "He has to have the courage of conviction and the courage to do the right thing at the right time—forget about the consequences—do the right thing. A leader has to have energy, you need to be enthusiastic, you can't show weakness, you have to be strong."

Blue Devils assistant coach Jon Scheyer, a senior on the 2010 national championship team, saw that firsthand. "When we were struggling my freshman year, we lost two in a row and we were really down," he said. "He told us in a team meeting that if we keep doing what we were doing we would win a national championship. And my senior year we did."

Scheyer's senior team represented Coach K's fourth national title team, including championships in 1991, 1992, and 2001. His fifth would come in 2015. "He has been able to adapt to so many different eras," former Duke guard J.J. Redick said. "His players feel he never has an off day or a bad day. You can feel it every day in practice, in games, in the huddle, or in meetings. You are getting his best."

"Every day I watched him attack life," Jay Williams said. "He was always proactive, not reactive." Added Gerald Henderson: "The biggest thing with him is strength. You never see a weak moment when things are going bad or not like you planned. He is always strong and thinking of ways to dig himself out of a hole."

But even with all the leadership accolades, Krzyzewski was still missing something and he needed help, help he couldn't find on the basketball court. "In my own sport, once you get to a certain level, people aren't going to share much with you," he explained. "You are the one that talks about basketball at clinics. Where do you get ideas from? How do you keep learning? So I have gone outside my field to keep learning from leaders in other fields." His mentors have become people like Wall Street tycoon John Mack, the former Chairman and CEO of Morgan Stanley; Las Vegas entertainment and hotel entrepreneur Steve Wynn; and one of his former players, a three-star general, Lt. General Bob Brown, commander of Combined Arms Center and Fort Leavenworth. "Since I was at Duke and we started winning, I was able to do speaking engagements to major companies and be around leaders in other fields," Krzyzewski explained. "If I am speaking to a company, I get to study that company and pick up some things they are doing in leadership. It's a bonus for me."

In 2004 the Fuqua/Coach K Center on Leadership & Ethics, a premier academic center, was established by Duke University's Fuqua School of Business in collaboration with Duke University Athletics and Kenan Institute for Ethics. Krzyzewski serves as an executive-in-residence at the center, teaching and writing on leadership during the basketball offseason. One of the areas he has developed within the graduate school is a Coach K Leadership Conference, which is annually held at the Fuqua School of Business bringing together top leaders from around the country.

The Polish kid from Chicago had used his leadership abilities to win national championships, gold medals, and become not only the basketball coach at one of the most prestigious universities in the country, but also part of the very fabric of the school as a professor and coach.

3 The Shot

Many a basketball fan believes the greatest game in the history of the NCAA Tournament was played on March 28, 1992 in Philadelphia, Pennsylvania, when Duke defeated Kentucky 104–103 in the East Regional Finals to win a spot in the 1992 Final Four, which the Blue Devils would win to complete back-to-back championships.

Prior to the East Regional Final in The Spectrum, the Blue Devils had to fight through a very emotional game with Seton Hall as brothers, Bobby Hurley and Danny Hurley, played against each other for the first time in a game that really counted. Bobby Hurley scored just four points with seven assists and six turnovers, but his teammates picked up the slack, and they rolled to an 81–69 win in the Elite Eight. "I'm just glad it's over and we won," said a relieved Hurley following the game.

The Blue Devils were favored against Kentucky, but the seniors on this Wildcats team were used to winning big games. The game was played at the highest level with Duke shooting 65.4 percent from the floor and Kentucky making 56.9 percent of their shots and forcing 20 turnovers.

The game also featured controversy as Christian Laettner put his foot squarely on the chest of a fallen Aminu Timberlake, who was lying on the floor after some aggressive play under the basket. Laettner received a technical but not ejected.

The outstanding play of Grant Hill in the first half gave the Blue Devils a 50–45 lead. Then Thomas Hill came to life in the second half and delivered two of the Blue Devils' last three field goals in regulation on running jumpers, his last coming at the 1:03 mark, making the score 93–93 and sending it to overtime.

It was the final 33 seconds of overtime that turned this game into a classic. First Laettner made an eight-footer in traffic to put Duke up 100–98. Then Jamal Mashburn drove inside, scored, was fouled, and added the free throw for a 101–100 Kentucky lead. With 14 seconds left, Mashburn fouled out, and Laettner hit two free throws to put Duke back up 102–101.

Kentucky head coach Rick Pitino called a timeout with 7.8 seconds left to set up the last play, which Sean Woods converted by penetrating past Hurley for a one-handed bank shot that gave the Wildcats a 103–102 lead. But it wasn't quite the last play as Hurley quickly called timeout with 2.1 seconds remaining so that Duke could organize a final attempt.

As the team came to the bench after the timeout, Duke's Mike Krzyzewski greeted his players with this positive response: "We're going to win this game, and this is how we are going to do it."

The inbounds would come from under the opponent's basket, a play the Blue Devils had tried early in the year at Wake Forest, only that time Grant Hill was defended and threw the ball out of bounds.

Unguarded this time on the throw-in, Grant Hill hurled a perfect 75-foot pass to Laettner, who was guarded by John Pelphrey and Deron Feldhaus. The latter backed off as Laettner caught the ball. Laettner caught it with his back to the basket, faked right, took one dribble to the left, and launched a 16-foot turnaround jumper that went through the rim as time expired.

Laettner finished with a perfect line in the box score: 10-of-10 from the field and 10-of-10 from the foul line for 31 points, capped off by one of the most famous shots in college basketball history.

The Philadelphia Spectrum was a madhouse. Krzyzewski immediately went to the Kentucky Radio Network with Hall of Fame

Part of his perfect game against Kentucky, Christian Laettner hits the game-winning shot with 2.1 seconds left to send Duke to the 1992 Final Four.
(AP Images)

Laettner's Game-Winner Against Uconn

Two years before he hit the "Shot Heard Round the World" against Kentucky in the 1992 East Regional Finals, Duke's Christian Laettner hit another big shot to send the Blue Devils to the 1990 Final Four in Denver. The setting was the Meadowlands Arena in East Rutherford, New Jersey. The Blue Devils had made their way to the regional finals with a victory against UCLA 90–81.

Duke used its superior size inside to take an 11-point lead late in the first half. Alaa Abdelnaby scored 27 points, and Laettner had 23 against the undersized Huskies. But Connecticut cut the lead to seven at the half and then outscored Duke 16–5 in the first 4:30 of the second half to take a 46–42 edge. Then Scott Burrell's consecutive baskets put the Huskies ahead 69–64 with 3:55 left. Duke answered with eight consecutive points before Chris Smith's three-point shot from beyond the key tied it at 72 with nine seconds to go. The game ended in a tie, and the two teams went to the first overtime period.

Connecticut's only senior, Tate George, who wrote a miracle ending two days before with his buzzer-beater against Clemson, had this game in his hands, too. With the shot clock running out and the Huskies up by one in the overtime period, it looked like George would be the savior once again. This time George launched a three-pointer from deep in the right corner. It missed with 10 seconds left, and Duke got the ball. Duke point guard Bobby Hurley threw a pass for Phil Henderson in front of the Blue Devils' bench, but George was playing it, though he lost control of the ball with it going out of bounds with 2.6 second left on the clock.

Coming out of the timeout, Krzyzewski could see that UConn had his inbound play defended very well, so he switched plays and called "Special." The call meant that after being inbounded, the ball immediately went back to the inbounder, who just happened to be Laettner.

When Krzyzewski called out "Special," Laettner knew the ball would be in his hands. "I got kind of an anxiety feeling in my stomach," the clutch 6'11" forward said. "Once the ref blew the whistle, it was gone."

The Connecticut defense did not have a man in Laettner's face, so he threw the ball to Brian Davis, who quickly returned it. Laettner dribbled once to get inside the three-point line, double-pumped in the air to avoid Connecticut's Lyman DePriest, and pulled the trigger. The ball passed through the net as the horn sounded.

Laettner's shot ended a dream season for the Huskies, who were just becoming a national power. The Blue Devils won 79–78 and were heading to Denver for the Final Four. "In our ecstasy in winning, it can't be complete because of the people you play against," said Krzyzewski, following the game. "Either team that lost would have been crying in the locker room. We were crying in victory. There were an incredible number of big plays, and we happened to make the last one."

announcer Cawood Ledford and praised the Wildcats for their play and spirit. According to *The Boston Globe* columnist Bob Ryan, "There have been noted upsets. There have been countless games played at a high level and for great stakes. But no other college game has ever combined, in one package, this much meaning, this much expertise, and this much drama. Duke-Kentucky was the greatest college game of them all."

"For a guy who loves the game for the game itself, you hope that someday you're part of something like this, and I was," Krzyzewski said. "I've just been standing around trying to figure out what a lucky son of a gun I am just to be involved. How many kids from each team made great plays tonight? You can't write enough about how many good plays there were."

4 Upsetting UNLV and K's First Title

From their first meeting in the locker room as a team in September, head coach Mike Krzyzewski made it very clear what the goal was for the 1990–91 Duke basketball team—a national championship. Leading up to the glory-filled 1990–91 season were many anxious moments, including a 30-point loss to UNLV at the 1990 NCAA Championship Game, Krzyzewski being wooed by the Boston Celtics, and a tiring summer, which had Coach K leading the USA team (with Christian Laettner and Bobby Hurley) to medal-winning performances at the Goodwill Games and the World Championships. All of those were memories and lessons as the 1990–91 schedule got underway at the Dodge NIT Tournament in mid-November.

Duke rushed out to two quick and decisive victories in Cameron Indoor Stadium. The Blue Devils then headed to the Big Apple and Madison Square Garden, where they faced fellow 1990 Final Four member Arkansas, whom the Blue Devils had defeated to earn a trip to the championship game. This time the Razorbacks turned back Duke and advanced to the title game with a 98–88 win.

The month of December featured a road loss to Georgetown in the ACC/Big East Challenge and a key road victory at No. 11 Oklahoma, which snapped the Sooners' long home court winning streak. The opener of the ACC slate had the Blue Devils traveling to No. 18 Virginia. The Cavaliers crushed Duke 81–64, making it time for a re-commitment to the season by the Blue Devils. Freshman Grant Hill broke his nose following the Virginia game, which caused him to miss the next three ACC games. Duke won all three of those games, thanks in part to the emergence of sophomore

Upsetting UNLV

UNLV seemed unstoppable. The Runnin' Rebels were 34–0 and on a 45-game winning streak. That included destroying Duke 103–73 in the 1990 National Championship. When the teams met again in the semifinals of the 1991 Final Four, most figured it would be more of the same. But Duke was better than the year before, toughened by playing a difficult schedule and bolstered by the addition of freshman Grant Hill.

UNLV was led by All-American Larry Johnson, a burly player who had dominated Duke the year before during the slaughter of a game, but as he often did, Christian Laettner raised his game against the toughest of players and in the highest of stages. The junior outplayed Johnson, scoring 28 points to Johnson's 13.

Because of Laettner's efforts, Duke trailed by just two at halftime, and the dominant Rebels had rarely been challenged all year, winning by an average of more than 27 points in its 30 games prior to the NCAA Tournament. The fight was on, and Duke kept the pressure up as the epic game featured 17 ties and 25 lead changes.

Finally, it came down to a little more than two minutes to play, and the Blue Devils down by a 76–71 count. Bobby Hurley, who struggled so badly in the 1990 contest, connected on a three-pointer when all seemed lost to make it 76–74 with 2:14 to play. Then Duke put on the defensive clamps, and the shot clock ran down without a UNLV shot being taken. Next, Brian Davis took charge with a driving layup and a foul shot to give Duke a 77–76 lead. After a Johnson free throw tied the score, the ball landed in Laettner's hands on the offensive side, and he was fouled with 12.7 seconds to play. He calmly converted the two charity tosses to give Duke a 79–77 lead.

As cool as Laettner seemed, the Rebels seemed rattled. After the foul shots, UNLV took a timeout to set up a play for either Johnson or Anderson Hunt, who scored a game-high 29 points. But their execution on the final play was less than sharp. After receiving the inbounds pass, Johnson brought the ball up, stopping just outside the three-point line on the right side. He faked a three-point shot, but Laettner didn't bite. Johnson passed to Hunt, who dribbled near the top of the key and launched a three-point shot, which bounced hard off the rim. Duke had shocked the world, advancing to play Kansas in the final.

Thomas Hill. The 6'4" guard/forward had 22 points in an 89–67 win against Wake Forest and then added 20 more against No. 5 North Carolina five days later in Duke's 74–60 victory over the Tar Heels.

The ACC regular season championship came down to the final game against the chief rival—North Carolina. The No. 8 Blue Devils hustled out to a 20-point margin in the early part of the second half. The Tar Heels came back but could never catch Duke as the Blue Devils posted an 83–77 victory. A week later, the two squads met again in the ACC Tournament championship game. This time Carolina triumphed 96–74 to hand Duke a decisive loss and leave the Blue Devils with a 26–7 record heading into the NCAA Tournament.

It was apparent early that the Blue Devils meant business in their chance to go to Indianapolis. Duke disposed of Northeast Louisiana, Iowa, and Connecticut with little resistance leading up to the Midwest Regional Final against Big East member St. John's. Pacing the victory, Hurley earned MVP honors in the region with 20 points in the title game and a remarkable 6.75:1 assist-turnover ratio in the four NCAA games.

Duke then stunned undefeated power UNLV 79–77 in the Final Four semifinal. Two nights later, Duke took the court against Kansas, which had defeated North Carolina in the semifinals, in the national championship. The fatigued Blue Devils never faltered as Hurley and Grant Hill teamed up for a spectacular alley-oop dunk in the opening minutes to set the tone, and Laettner proved steady with a record-setting 12-for-12 performance from the free throw line.

It was a crowning glory to the spectacular season as the Blue Devils brought home the title with a 72–65 victory against the Jayhawks, who were guided by future North Carolina coach Roy Williams. Laettner earned MVP honors, and Hurley averaged 12 points and eight assists in the two games. Sophomore Bill

McCaffrey added 16 points in the title game to also earn a slot on the All-Final Four team. As part of its fourth straight Final Four berth, Duke had won its first national championship.

5 Johnny Dawkins

Without a doubt, Johnny Dawkins was the most crucial player in the success of Mike Krzyzewski at Duke. After playing his high school ball at Mackin Catholic High School, Dawkins led the Blue Devils to three consecutive NCAA Tournament bids after a tough freshman season in 1982. He was part of the freshman class that included Mark Alarie, Jay Bilas, and David Henderson and laid the foundation for Duke basketball.

In his four years as a Blue Devil, Dawkins became the team's all-time leading scorer with 2,556 points, which stood until 2006 when J.J. Redick surpassed it. In Dawkins' senior year at Duke, the 1985–86 season, the Blue Devils attained a win-loss record of 37–3, which was an NCAA record for both games played and games won in a single season at the time. They reached the 1986 NCAA Championship Game, where they lost to Louisville 72–69. In his senior season, Dawkins averaged 20.2 points per game and won the Naismith College Player of the Year Award. His jersey number No. 24 was retired at the end of the year.

Dawkins was a Freshman All-American and second team All-ACC selection in 1983, scoring in double figures in 27 of 28 games. As a sophomore Dawkins averaged 19.4 points per game and was selected to the second team All-ACC and first team All-ACC Tournament. Dawkins earned first team All-American and first team All-ACC honors as a junior, averaging 18.8 points per game and was the team MVP for the third year in a row. As a senior in 1985–86, Dawkins led the team to the NCAA championship game as well as the ACC regular season title and ACC Tournament title. He was named the National Player of the Year, East Region MVP, All-Final Four, first team All-American, first team All-ACC, and ACC Tournament MVP. He led Duke in scoring for four consecutive years. He is Duke's all-time leader in field goals made and field goals attempted.

Dawkins was the 10th pick in the 1986 NBA Draft and subsequently played nine seasons in the NBA with the San Antonio Spurs (1986–89), Philadelphia 76ers (1989–94), and Detroit Pistons (1994–95). In his nine-year NBA career, he averaged 11.1 points, 5.5 assists, and 2.5 rebounds.

Following his NBA career, Dawkins went back to Duke University in 1996, where he worked as an administrative intern in the athletic department and was on the air as an analyst for Duke's home basketball games. He joined the Duke coaching staff in 1998, working alongside head coach Mike Krzyzewski. He was promoted to associate head coach in charge of player development in 1999. In April of 2008, he was named head coach at Stanford University.

6 1992 National Championship

The season preview in the 1991–92 Duke men's basketball media guide began this way: "When four starters return to any college basketball team, there is always cause for celebration. When the four starters return from a team that captured the national championship the year before, the possibilities seem endless." With a roster that included ACC Athlete of the Year Christian Laettner,

All-ACC guards Bobby Hurley and Thomas Hill, versatile sophomore Grant Hill, and four additional returning letterwinners, the Blue Devils were poised to defend their title and become the first back-to-back champions since UCLA in 1972–73.

On December 14, Duke faced future NCAA championship opponent Michigan in Ann Arbor. The Blue Devils were 6–0 heading into the night, having swept four of the five previous teams by at least a 25-point margin. After leading by as many as 17 points early in the second half, Duke came back from a two-point deficit when Hurley scored five points in the last two minutes of play to secure an 88–85 overtime victory.

The ACC season started strong with solid victories against Virginia, Florida State, Maryland, Georgia Tech, and N.C. State. On February 1, 1992, Duke celebrated its 500th win in Cameron Indoor Stadium with a 100–71 blowout against Notre Dame. The first real challenge of the ACC season came against rival North Carolina on its home court in Chapel Hill. Hurley broke his foot midway through the first half but played anyway as the No. 9-ranked Tar Heels posted a 75–73 upset victory against top-ranked Duke. Without Hurley, the 6'8" Hill filled in at point guard, even leading the team to a road victory against Shaquille O'Neal and LSU.

As tournament time approached, Duke had only suffered two losses: the one to North Carolina and a second against Wake Forest in late February when Duke squandered a 10-point lead in the game's final five minutes to fall to the Demon Deacons 72–68. Brian Davis and Laettner had won just about every prize imaginable in their four-year Duke careers except one, the ACC Tournament. Duke recorded wins against Maryland and Georgia Tech to reach the finals before crushing North Carolina 94–74 in the 1992 ACC final that brought redemption after the previous year's 22-point loss to UNC in the same game. Laettner left nothing to chance with 25 points, 10 rebounds, and seven steals.

Five others hit double figures, including Grant Hill who hit all eight of his shots and added seven assists.

Duke, the top seed in the East Region, posted wins against Campbell and Iowa in the NCAA Tournament. That set up a

7 Out of 9 Final Fours

From 1986 through the 1994 basketball season, the Duke Blue Devils went on a remarkable run of playing in seven out of nine years in the Final Four. Previously their best run of consecutive Final Four appearances had been in the mid-1960s when teams coached by Vic Bubas went to three out of four Final Fours in 1963, 1964, and 1966.

Even more remarkable is the fact that the Blue Devils played for the national championship in five of those seven years (1986, 1990, 1991, 1992, and 1994) and won the title back-to-back in 1991 and 1992. And the teams were made up of very different players, starting with Mike Krzyzewski's first big-time recruiting class led by Johnny Dawkins as Duke lost to Louisville in the '86 title game to the likes of Danny Ferry in 1988 and 1989 and then the national championship teams of the '90s led by Christian Laettner and the Grant Hill-led squad of 1994.

Here is the breakdown of that run:

Year	Site	Results	Record
1986	Dallas, Texas	Defeated Kansas 71–67, Lost to Louisville 72–69	37–3
1988	Kansas City, Missouri	Lost to Kansas 66–59	28–7
1989	Seattle, Washington	Lost to Seton Hall 95–78	28–8
1990	Denver, Colorado	Defeated Arkansas 97–83 Lost to UNLV 103–73	29–9
1991	Indianapolis, Indiana	Defeated UNLV 79–77, Defeated Kansas 72–65	32–7*
1992	Minneapolis, Minnesota	Defeated Indiana 81–78 Defeated Michigan 71–51	34–2*
1994	Charlotte, North Carolina	Defeated Florida 70–65, Lost to Arkansas 76–72	28–6

*=national championship season

meeting with Seton Hall, a team that featured Hurley's brother, Dan, at guard. Duke won 81–69 against the No. 4 seed Pirates, but Bobby Hurley struggled, scoring just four points in the sibling rivalry game. With the victory, however, Duke moved on to the Elite Eight.

Duke's Elite Eight matchup against Kentucky on March 28, 1992 saw two of the most storied programs in basketball history face each other. Kentucky did everything possible to dethrone the champions and appeared to have Duke right where it wanted them with 2.1 seconds to play in the overtime period after Sean Woods drove by Hurley and banked in a one-handed shot over Laettner for a one-point lead. Then, in a season equally filled with magical moments and overwhelming adversity, a miracle took place. Grant Hill hurled the undefended inbounds pass to Laettner, who leapt to catch the ball over John Pelphrey and Deron Feldhaus. Time seemed to stand still as Laettner faked to his right, turned to his left, and lofted an 18-footer that found nothing but net as time expired. The Spectrum crowd erupted as the Duke players jumped on Laettner to celebrate another trip to the Final Four and a 104–103 victory over Kentucky.

Up next was Indiana, an intriguing matchup between Coach K and his mentor, Hoosiers coach Bob Knight. Though the two would settled their differences years later and become close once again, the pupil and his one-time coach were no longer on speaking terms. The beginning of the second half against Indiana, which began with Duke trailing by five points, turned into one of Duke's finest moments of the season. The Blue Devils reeled off 13 straight points and then made it a 21–3 surge to open the first 10 minutes of the frame to make the score 58–45 in favor of Duke. Free throws by Antonio Lang and Cherokee Parks closed out the 81–78 victory as the Blue Devils headed to the NCAA championship game for the third consecutive season.

The April 6 national championship between Michigan and Duke was hyped as The Fab Five meets The Victory Tour. Grant Hill made his first start since February when he was inserted for an injured Davis, scoring 18 points and grabbing 10 rebounds as Duke stumbled out of the blocks but hung tough in trailing by just one at the half 31–30. Perhaps drained from his heroic effort against Kentucky, Laettner, in particular, was in a funk. But he and the Blue Devils rebounded in the second half, turning up the defensive pressure in the second frame, forcing Michigan into 29 percent shooting from the field and just 20 second-half points. With 13.5 seconds remaining and a comfortable 20-point cushion, Coach K gave his starters one last curtain call to an incredible season-long journey. A roar echoed through the dome as players exchanged high-fives and hugs to start the celebration of the 71–51 victory.

7 Cameron Crazies

Famous for painting their bodies blue and white or wearing outrageous outfits, the Cameron Crazies have been the most publicized student group for many years. They start their cheering as soon as warm-ups begin. Throughout the game they jump up and down when the opposing team has possession of the ball and yell cheers in unison at focal points of the game.

They got their name from the colorful and crazy antics they perform during the Blue Devils home games in Cameron Indoor Stadium.

Although the Cameron Crazies are very dynamic today, it was in the early years that this student body gained their name. In the early '70s, Maryland forward Jim O'Brien, a dead ringer for Bozo

The Cameron Crazies help give Duke one of the best home-court advantages in sports.

the Clown, had bright red hair. In a game at Cameron, several of the Duke students showed up in clown uniforms with floppy shoes and red wigs. While the Maryland players were doing a layup drill, one of the imitators actually jumped into the line behind O'Brien, who apparently got a kick out of the attention.

Just a few years later, Maryland sharpshooter Brian Magid had a habit of coming out early to practice. This was before the three-point line but just about every shot Magid took would have been well beyond the NBA stripe. One of the Crazies came out of the stands and placed a $20 bill on the floor outside—what would now be the three-point line—and indicated to Magid to shoot from there. Magid came over, took the shot from behind the bill, made the bucket, picked up the money, and placed it in his warm-up pants.

Other Terrapins have been part of the Crazies legacy with long-time Terps coach and former Duke basketball player Lefty Driesell receiving attention numerous times for his bald head. One year, after breaking his ankle kicking a chair, Driesell came to the Duke game with his foot in a cast. Sure enough, three Crazies showed up with their legs in a cast and skull caps on. Being a Duke alum himself, Lefty graciously signed their skull caps with a big X.

One of the more vile displays by the students came at the expense of Maryland's Herman Veal in 1984, a year after he had been accused of some sexual improprieties. *The Washington Post* ripped the "several thousand Duke students majoring in smartass and chanting close to the ultimate in filth" at Veal. They cleaned up their act but didn't forget the criticism. The next time N.C. State came to town, a placard declaring, "If you can't go to college, got to State," had an addendum: "If you can't got to State, write for *The Washington Post*."

University president Terry Sanford admonished the student body in a letter, his second to the students, the first coming in 1979 prior to Senior Night against UNC. In the letter he asked them to clean up their act. "We can cheer and taunt with style. That should be the Duke tradition." He signed the letter "Uncle Terry."

When the Crazies protested an official's call during the ensuing game, they chanted, "We beg to differ." There was a banner that read "We're sorry, Uncle Terry. The Devil made us do it." The students wore aluminum halos and yelled "Go to Heck Carolina, Go to Heck." When the Tar Heels shot free throws, instead of arms waving behind the basket, there was a sign that read "Please miss."

Both State and Carolina have provided fodder for the Crazies' hijinks. During the 1970s and 1980s, it became habitual for students to throw items on the floor during pregame introductions. Someone threw a potato on the court when Wolfpack player Spud Webb was announced. Other players who had been linked to pilfering aspirin, pizza, and underwear had those things tossed in their direction. When Chris Washburn was accused of stealing a stereo, the Blue Devil mascot wheeled a shopping cart filled with stereo components onto the floor. One time a student dressed in drag showed up on the court during the national anthem and lip-synched part of the song, mimicking N.C. State coach Norm Sloan's wife who sang the anthem at Wolfpack home games.

After all these incidents, Clyde Austin from N.C. State showed up in Cameron for a game with the Blue Devils. There were current investigations into a yellow Cadillac, which Austin was driving in Raleigh. The Crazies had the Duke administration on edge, not knowing what they had planned for Austin.

During pregame there was…nothing. During introductions, again the Crazies were eerily quiet.

In the middle of the first half, Austin was fouled and when he went to the line to shoot his free throws, the student body pulled their keys out of their pockets and began rattling them at Austin, who, after holding back a smile, missed the free throw.

Other pranks included tossing bags of uncooked noodles at Georgia Tech's skinny Craig Neal, who was 6'5" and weighed 160 pounds, during warm-ups and conversely throwing Twinkies at Georgia Tech's Dennis Scott, an overweight scorer.

The "Air Ball" chant was a Cameron Crazy original in 1979 when North Carolina's only two shots in a 7–0 first half against Duke missed the rim. UNC's Steve Hale, suffering from a collapsed lung, heard "In-Hale, Ex-Hale." Tar Heels guard Jeff McInnis heard much worse after an altercation with reserve guard Jay Heaps late in a game in 1996. The students thundered vulgarity, which ignited some pointed public comments from Dean Smith and a rebuttal from Mike Krzyzewski. In 2004 with former Kansas coach

Roy Williams making his first trip to Duke as UNC's head coach, several students dressed as characters from *The Wizard of Oz* set up a makeshift yellow brick road outside the opponents' locker room and let Williams know that he wasn't in Kansas anymore.

Nobody is quite certain when the Cameron Crazies, the most famous student body cheering section in all of college basketball got their name, but the beginnings of the Cameron Carzies may well have been a living group on campus in the '70s and '80s. The BOG (Bunch of Guys) sat right behind the visitors bench and caused havoc on the opposition, even having South Carolina players toss cups of water on them. BOG was eventually disbanded as a living group.

Television has a love-hate relationship with the Crazies. Because of their outrageous antics, directors and producers have to be very careful what they put on the air. When C.D. Chesley owned and produced the *ACC Game of the Week*, he instructed his director not to put the Duke students on the air because of an incident with a sign that read "The ACC and Pilot Life" (an insurance company that was the major sponsor of ACC TV), and when the red light came on from the handheld camera, the student dropped a sign from the bottom that said "suck."

But ESPN and Dick Vitale were a marriage made in heaven for the Crazies. Vitale fell in love with the Crazies with their incredible support for the game of basketball. Vitale would often show up early for games and visit with the students, even to the point of them body surfing him through the crowd.

But Vitale wasn't the first to try and tame the Crazies. With NBC in town former Marquette coach and analyst Al McGuire came to a game with a pith helmet, whip, and a large bag of peanuts that he passed out to the Crazies along with Dick Enberg calling them the "zoo."

8 2015 National Championship

This one was different. This national championship was captured by a team made up mostly of freshmen, who even as a very young team set a national championship as its goal for the season and accomplished that objective with a 68–63 victory again Wisconsin at Lucas Oil Stadium in Indianapolis. It was the third national championship won by the Blue Devils in Indianapolis. The team had just eight scholarship players—following the transfer of Semi Ojeleye and the dismissal of Rasheed Sulaimon—and four of them were freshmen.

Even with three freshmen in control of the team, it wasn't any surprise that Duke was there to win the title—especially once the undefeated favorite, Kentucky, lost its first game of the season in the national semifinals to Wisconsin. The Blue Devils spent the entire season ranked among the top five teams in the nation, spending most of the season as either the No. 2 or No. 4-ranked team.

The season began with a focus to establish themselves as a team ready to win a national title and on capturing head coach Mike Krzyzewski's 1,000[th] win, the first Division I men's college basketball coach to ever accomplish that feat. Early season wins over No. 19 Michigan State in the State Farm Champions Classic 81–71 and No. 2 Wisconsin on the Badgers' home court quickly established the Blue Devils as a team ready to take the national championship trophy to Durham.

Strong play by the freshman trio of Jahlil Okafor, Justise Winslow, and Tyus Jones, along with the maturation of senior guard Quinn Cook keyed their success. Okafor's strong inside play gave the Blue Devils a dominant big man inside, Winslow's great play on the entire floor and athletic ability gave them immediate energy, and Jones' steadying play and clutch baskets added poise.

There were some stumbles during the year as the Blue Devils lost back-to-back games in the middle of January at N.C. State 87–75 and at home to Miami, in one of the worst home losses, 90–74, in Cameron Indoor Stadium. But the Blue Devils bounced back and on January 25 at Madison Square Garden in New York, captured a 77–68 win against St. John's to give their coach his 1,000th career victory. "It was tough to get involved with 1,000 wins, I was just trying to focus on the game," Krzyzewski said. "There was a little while there when it looked like we weren't gonna make it. I am glad it is over. I am honored, don't get me wrong. I am the lucky guy. I have been at two great institutions in Army and Duke."

Three days later the Blue Devils would lose a close game at No. 8 Notre Dame 77–73 and drop to No. 4 in the nation in the rankings. Ten days later they would play one of their best games of the year as they destroyed the Irish 90–60 in Cameron Indoor Stadium with the freshman troika of Okafor's 20 points, Winslow's 11 rebounds, and Jones' seven assists leading the way. The Irish would get their revenge in the ACC Tournament semifinals with a 74–64 win as Okafor scored 28 points.

But the Blue Devils were in good physical shape heading into the NCAA Tournament and rolled through their first two games in Charlotte with an 85–56 win against Robert Morris and a 68–49 victory against San Diego State to send them to the Sweet 16 in Houston. The Blue Devils won their Sweet 16 match with Utah 63–57 then faced No. 2 seed Gonzaga for the right to earn a trip to the Final Four. Shaking off an early ankle injury, freshman and Houston native Winslow finished with 16 points and five rebounds in the Blue Devils' 66–52 victory against Gonzaga in the NCAA South Regional Final Sunday at NRG Stadium. "Justise is a very special young man, not just a special young basketball player," said

A young but close-knit team, Duke's 2014–15 squad won the school's fifth men's basketball title.

Duke coach Mike Krzyzewski, who tied UCLA's John Wooden for the most Final Four appearances (12) in NCAA history.

In the Final Four semifinal game, the Blue Devils faced a Michigan State team that had become a much better team than the one it defeated in November. But Winslow once again made sure the Blue Devils advanced with a 19-point, nine-rebound performance as Duke won 81–61.

In the championship game against Wisconsin, the Blue Devils also faced a veteran Badgers team that it had defeated earlier in the year. After a couple of lead changes in the first half, the teams went to the locker room at halftime tied at 31.

Wisconsin, though, took control of the second half, taking a nine-point lead midway through the final frame. Suddenly the Blue Devils' backs were against the wall when up stepped their fourth freshman—Grayson Allen—who added a three-pointer, a steal, an and-one play, and free throws for eight straight points to keep the Blue Devils in the game. With 84 seconds left in the game Tyus Jones, who would be named the Final Four's Most Outstanding Player, hit a three-pointer, and the Blue Devils were on their way to their fifth national championship. Jones led the way scoring for the Blue Devils with 23 points. He and his freshmen teammates— Allen with 16, Winslow with 11, Okafor with 10—accounted for 60 of the Blue Devils' 68 points. Only freshmen scored for the Blue Devils in the second half. "I haven't loved a team any more than I've loved this team," Krzyzewski said after the Blue Devils beat Wisconsin 68–63 to claim the championship. "We have eight guys, and four of them are freshmen. For them to win 35 games and the national championship is incredible...They've been a joy. They've been an incredible joy."

Showing the unselfishness of the team, captain and senior Quinn Cook moved from point guard to shooting guard to accommodate Tyus Jones. "We believed we could do it and had faith. Coach K just helps everybody," Cook said. "He wasn't focused on getting his fifth championship. He was focused on getting our first. We are all blessed to be part of this Duke program." Added Coach K: "We had these four freshmen coming in, and they want to blend. They want to be led. They don't want it to be about them. They're good guys. They had the chemistry right away. It's been an incredible group."

Okafor, Winslow, and Jones announced they would be leaving for the NBA just 10 days after capturing the title. "As early as I can remember, I've fantasized and dreamed of the day that I could play professional basketball," said Okafor, who was named the ACC Rookie and Player of the Year along with being selected as a consensus All-American. "I recall at the age of six, promising my mom and dad that when I made it to the NBA I would buy them both different colored trucks. They would laugh with me in support and encouraged me to dream big and work hard. With that being said and now at the age of 19, my dream is still alive! My freshman year has been an amazing experience to say the least. It exceeded my expectations! I love Cameron and Duke University! I can't thank my coaches, teammates, and family enough for making this year so special and helping me grow on and off the court. With Coach K's and my family's blessing, I will be fulfilling my lifelong dream and proudly entering my name into the NBA draft."

Winslow echoed Okafor's statements. "I would like to thank Duke University for allowing me to be a part of such a prestigious institution where I have learned more about myself inside and outside of the classroom than I ever thought I could," Winslow said. "I would like to thank the students of Duke University for allowing me to develop my character and be myself without any judgment. You all have made this year extremely entertaining. I would like to thank Coach K and the rest of the coaching staff for helping me become a better player mentally and physically."

Tyus Jones was the last player to declare for the draft. "I want to say thank you to Duke University, the best university in the country for everything it has done for me," he said. "And lastly, thank you to this man [Coach K] who gave me a once-in-a-lifetime opportunity, who taught me so much on the court, but more than just basketball, he also taught me how to become a better man, brother, son, teammate, and much more. I'll forever be thankful and will always be a Duke Blue Devil!"

9 Christian Laettner

When it comes to players who wanted to win and did just that, there is none better than Christian Laettner. He is one of only four players to have ever played in four Final Fours and the only player to have ever started in four Final Fours. He holds the record for most games played in an NCAA Tournament career with 23, along with three more NCAA Tournament records and two NCAA national championship rings. He is perhaps most remembered for the two last-second shots that sent the Blue Devils to the Final Four. The first came in 1990 against Connecticut, and the second came in 1992 against Kentucky. Many consider "the Shot" against Kentucky to be the greatest play in NCAA Tournament history.

What made Laettner such a great player was his intense style of play on both ends of the court and his ability at 6'11" to be able to post up inside and make a strong move for a basket or step outside and hit jumpers from the perimeter. When overplayed he also had an uncanny ability to pass the ball to the open man for a score. His swagger and confidence gave him an edge that most college players did not have. His 407 total points in NCAA Tournament play will likely never be matched, considering the fact he played in 23 of the 24 games you can play in the NCAA Tournament and that college basketball has become such a transient sport with the best players staying just one season.

Born in Angola, New York, which is near Buffalo, Laettner played his high school ball at Nichols School, where he scored over 2,000 points, captured two state titles, and reached the state semifinals one other time. He took only three official visits—to Duke, North Carolina, and Virginia—before deciding to come to Durham. There he drew the ire of opponents and opposing fans to such an extent that ESPN aired a documentary prior to the 2015 Tournament entitled *I Hate Christian Laettner*. He received such acrimony in part because of his success. Over his four years at Duke, he became arguably the greatest player in school history and one of the best in the history of college basketball. In the 148 games he played in—128 of which he started—the Blue Devils were 122–26 and 21–2 in NCAA Tournament play.

As a freshman in 1988–89, he averaged 8.9 points per game and was named second team All-ACC Tournament and first team All-East Region. The latter was well-deserved after he outplayed star Georgetown big man Alonzo Mourning to help Duke advance to the Final Four.

In Laettner's sophomore season of 1989–90, he averaged 16.3 points and 9.6 rebounds and was named third team All-American, second team All-ACC, and MVP of the East Region.

The third trip to the Final Four was the charm for Laettner as the 1991 team captured Duke's first national championship. Laettner's awards mounted his junior year as he was named second team All-American, MVP of the Final Four, the McKevlin Award winner for ACC Athlete of the Year, first team All-ACC, and All-Midwest Region. Laettner averaged 19.8 points and 8.7 rebounds and had 75 steals, 44 blocked shots, and a 57.5 field goal percentage. Coming up biggest in the biggest moments like he always did, Laettner outplayed Larry Johnson to lead Duke to a monumental upset over UNLV in the semifinals of the Final Four.

As a senior in 1991–92, Laettner once again helped lead the Blue Devils to the national championship, the ACC regular season title, and the ACC Tournament championship as the squad compiled a 34–2 record and managed to hold the No. 1 position in the national rankings every week of the season. Laettner was the National Player of the Year, ACC Player of the Year, ACC Athlete of the Year, ACC Tournament MVP, and MVP of the East Region. With 2,460 points and 1,149 rebounds during his collegiate career,

Laettner ranks third in both categories in the Duke record books. His 713 free throws made at Duke are a school record.

Following his college career, Laettner was the lone college player on the famed Dream Team, the first U.S. Olympic team with NBA players and a squad that dominated opponents while capturing international adoration. The Minnesota Timberwolves drafted him with the third overall pick of the 1992 NBA Draft, following Shaquille O'Neal, who went first to the Orlando Magic, and Mourning, who was selected second by the Charlotte Hornets.

In his 13-year NBA career, Laettner played for the Timberwolves, Atlanta Hawks, Detroit Pistons, Dallas Mavericks, Washington Wizards, and Miami Heat. He was named to the All-Rookie team in his first season with the Timberwolves as he averaged 18.2 points per game and 8.7 rebounds in 81 starts. He averaged 16.6 points per game in his first six seasons, playing for the Timberwolves and Hawks, and made the 1997 All-Star Game when he had 18.1 points and 8.8 rebounds. He scored more than 11,000 points in 868 NBA regular season games, averaging 12.8 points, 6.7 rebounds, and 2.6 assists over his career. Following retirement he and former roommate Brian Davis had a Durham-based commercial property development company called Blue Devil Ventures.

10 2001 National Championship

The story of the 2001 championship season began in the spring and summer of 1999. After losing in the 1999 National Championship, Duke lost four of its superstars to the NBA, which seemingly depleted the team. But after a successful 2000 campaign, which saw the Blue Devils win the ACC championship, the team returned in the fall of 2001 ready to go all the way.

The Blue Devils started off the season hot by winning the Preseason NIT. In the process Coach K picked up his 500th win at Duke by knocking off Villanova at home. After that game the Cameron Indoor Stadium floor was officially renamed Coach K Court. Throughout November and December, the team continued to roll. The three-point shot proved to be extremely valuable as on any given possession guards Jason Williams and Chris Duhon—or forwards Shane Battier, Mike Dunleavy, and Nate James—could knock down long-range jumpers. In the last game before Christmas break, Duke lined up against Stanford. After leading the whole game, however, the Blue Devils missed free throws in the final seconds. Stanford came down and banked in the winning shot.

After the break Duke rattled off nine straight wins, including victories over four ranked teams. In that stretch was one of the great games in Duke history. Playing against Maryland at College Park, the Blue Devils found themselves down 89–77 with 1:05 to go in the game. However, James and Williams outscored Maryland 13–1 to send the game to overtime. In the extra session, Battier took over, scoring Duke's last six points and blocking a game-tying shot at the buzzer.

Duke lost its first ACC game of the year against North Carolina but rebounded and rolled over the next three ACC opponents before losing at the buzzer in Virginia. Duke's victory against Georgia Tech on February 21 featured the retirement of Battier's No. 31 jersey. The next game at Wake Forest was special as well as Duhon came back from an injury in the first half to knock down the game-winning shot at the buzzer.

Duke's final home game of the year saw a perturbed Maryland team looking for a settling of scores after the Blue Devils' last-minute antics in College Park. Duke led 60–51 with 15:30 left in the second half, but with just under 10 minutes remaining, Carlos

Boozer fractured his right foot, and a stunned Duke team watched as Maryland posted a 91–80 win on Senior Day. In the season finale in Chapel Hill, the Blue Devils came out firing as their new offense surprised the Tar Heels. With Duhon and sophomore Casey Sanders now starting, the Devils ran North Carolina into the ground 95–85. In the ACC Tournament, Duke ran over N.C. State to set up a third meeting with Maryland. At the end of another intense game, James' tap-in at the buzzer gave Duke an 84–82 win. The Blue Devils headed to the finals to face North Carolina once again. In a repeat performance, Duke took a 50–30 halftime lead and ran away with a victory and the ACC championship.

The NCAA Tournament campaign started out well as the Blue Devils easily rolled over Monmouth and topped a Missouri team coached by former Blue Devils guard and assistant coach Quin Snyder. As Duke moved on to the Sweet 16 in Philadelphia to play UCLA, the whole team was back in action. A recovered Boozer came in during the first half and helped spark a 12–0 run. In the second half, Williams scored 19 straight points for the Blue Devils to propel the team to a tough 76–63 victory. Facing USC in the regional final game, Duhon's clutch three-point shooting in the second half proved to be the key as Duke moved on to the Final Four, beating the Trojans 79–69.

The stage was set in Minneapolis for Duke to battle the Terrapins for the fourth time in a little over two months. Duke trailed by as many as 22 points in the first half before shaking off an 11-point deficit at halftime to complete the biggest comeback in NCAA Tournament semifinal history. Duke took the lead on Williams' three-pointer to make it 73–72 with less than seven minutes to go in the game. The Blue Devils closed out the game 95–84 to advance to the Big Dance.

Only one game remained. Inside the Metrodome on April 2, Duke took on fifth-ranked Arizona. The game was a back-and-forth affair throughout with Duke riding the all-around play of

Battier and the three-point shooting of Dunleavy for an 82–72 victory. Battier played all 40 minutes, scoring 18 points, grabbing 11 rebounds, and handing out six assists. Dunleavy led Duke with 21 points, including a career-high five three-pointers, while Boozer registered a double-double with 12 points and 12 rebounds. With its 82–72 victory, Duke became the first No. 1-ranked team to win the national championship since UCLA in 1995.

11 Bobby Hurley

The NCAA's all-time assists leader was born in Jersey City, New Jersey, and he played his high school ball at St. Anthony High School in Jersey City for his father—legendary coach Bob Hurley Sr. During his prep career, Bobby Hurley led St. Anthony's to four consecutive Parochial B state titles and put together an overall record of 115–5. In his senior season, St. Anthony went 32–0 and was ranked No. 1 in the country as Hurley averaged 20 points, eight assists, and three steals per game.

At Duke, Hurley became the consummate teammate, passing the ball for easy baskets, hitting tough shots, and playing winning basketball. When he arrived on the Duke campus, he was given the reins of the Duke team as the point guard, playing in all 38 games and helping the Blue Devils advance to the 1990 Final Four. In his first year, he was named first team honorable mention All-American by *The Sporting News*.

In Hurley's sophomore season of 1990–91, the Blue Devils captured the ACC title and their first national championship. He was named All-Final Four, third team All-ACC, and Midwest Region MVP. During that season he hit what the coach called, "the biggest shot in Duke history" when he nailed a three-pointer against UNLV with 2:14 left in the Final Four semifinal. Hurley had struggled against UNLV in the previous year's Final Four, but he more than redeemed himself. He always put himself in position to make the big pass, big play, or big shot. He set school, ACC, and NCAA records during his career for assists.

In 1991–92, Hurley's junior year, Duke went 34–2 and once again won the national championship along with the ACC regular season title and the ACC Tournament. Hurley averaged 13.2 points and 7.6 assists as he was named MVP of the Final Four, third team All-American, second team All-ACC, first team All-ACC Tournament, and All-East Region.

Hurley was named consensus first team All-American, first team All-ACC, and was a finalist for the Wooden Award given to the National Player of the Year as a senior in 1992–93. He averaged 17.0 points and 8.2 assists and set the NCAA career assists record with 1,076. Hurley's 264 three-pointers set the school record and still rank fourth all-time at Duke. Hurley also set the school record for assists in a season with 289 as a sophomore and holds the top three single-season assist marks at Duke.

It was his senior season that he showed off his total ability to play the game of basketball as he dispatched double-double nights of scoring and assists nearly every game. Against UCLA, the day Duke retired his No. 11 jersey, he scored 19 points and dished out 15 assists to have a hand in 50 of the team's 78 points. In the next game, his last in Cameron Indoor Stadium, he scored 19 points and handed out 12 assists. In the final game of his career, he had a career-high 32 points against California in the NCAA Tournament, while playing every minute of the game, adding nine assists, and committing just one turnover.

Following Hurley's graduation the Sacramento Kings selected him with the No. 7 overall pick in the 1993 NBA Draft. But his career was cut short by a tragic car accident following a home game in Sacramento, when Hurley suffered life-threatening injuries. He returned to the NBA for the 1994–95 season and played four more years for Sacramento and the Vancouver Grizzlies, but he was never the same player he was prior to the car accident. When he retired from playing, he became a racehorse owner and was hired as a scout by the Philadelphia 76ers.

Hurley entered the family business in 2010 as an assistant coach for his younger brother Danny, the former Seton Hall point guard who became the head coach at Wagner College. In 2012 both the Hurleys took coaching positions at Rhode Island. In March of 2013, Bobby became the head coach at the University of Buffalo, where he led the Bulls to their first NCAA Tournament appearance in 2015 and nearly defeated West Virginia in their opening game. Hurley continues to quickly ascend the coaching ladder as Arizona State named him its head coach in April of 2015.

12 Danny Ferry

There are several reasons that the No. 35 of Danny Ferry hangs retired from the rafters of Cameron Indoor Stadium. He played four seasons at Duke from 1985 through 1989, was named a first team All-American as both a junior and a senior, and received the 1989 Naismith Award as the nation's top collegiate player after averaging 22.6 points, 7.4 rebounds, and 4.7 assists.

But much more than the numbers and honors, Ferry was just a very good basketball player. The son of former NBA player and general manager Bob Ferry, the younger Ferry arrived at Duke well-schooled in the fundamentals, having played his prep ball at DeMatha Catholic High for legendary coach Morgan Wootten. At

6'10" Ferry was one of the most versatile players in the history of the ACC—able to dribble, drive, post up, shoot inside and outside, rebound, and play defense.

As a freshman in 1985–86, Ferry was an integral part of the record-setting Blue Devils team that was 37–3 and made it to the national championship game as well as winning the ACC Tournament. By Ferry's sophomore season, he led Duke in scoring, rebounds, and assists, which earned him second team All-ACC honors. As a junior Ferry averaged 19.1 points per game and led the team in scoring, rebounding, minutes, free throw percentage, and blocked shots. His junior season he was a first team All-American, a National Player of the Year finalist, ACC Player of the Year, winner of the McKevlin Award for the ACC's top athlete, MVP of the ACC Tournament and the NCAA East Region, and was first team All-ACC.

In Ferry's senior year, he helped his team advance to the Final Four and led the ACC with a 22.6 scoring average. Among the numerous accolades he earned his senior year were: National Player of the Year, first team All-American, ACC Player of the Year, winner of the McKevlin Award, MVP of the East Region, and *USA TODAY* Collegiate Achiever of the Year. He was the first player in ACC history to compile 2,000 points, 1,000 rebounds, and 500 assists over his career.

The Los Angeles Clippers selected him with the second pick of the 1989 NBA Draft, but he had made it known he did not want to play for the Clippers so headed overseas to play in the Italian League's Il Messaggero. The Clippers traded Ferry's rights to the Cleveland Cavaliers for whom he began playing in 1990. Ferry's NBA career included playing for the San Antonio Spurs (2000–03) and the Cavaliers (1990–2000). In his 13-year NBA career, Ferry averaged seven points and 2.8 rebounds in 917 career games. Shortly after winning an NBA championship with San Antonio during his last season as a player in 2003, Ferry began his NBA front-office career. He became the Spurs' director of basketball operations, where he remained until 2005. He served as the Spurs' vice president of basketball operations from 2010–12. In this position he oversaw the team's player personnel, coaching, officiating, on-court policy, and procedures, as well as scheduling. Prior to the Spurs, Ferry held the role of general manager for the Cavaliers from 2005–2010, where the Cavaliers posted a 272–138 (.663) record, enjoyed the NBA's best regular season record in both 2008–09 and 2009–10, and advanced to the NBA Finals (in 2007) for the first time in franchise history.

Ferry joined the Atlanta Hawks in June of 2012, bringing 23 years of NBA experience as both a player and front office executive. Ferry oversees the basketball operations program for the Hawks, including coaching, player personnel, contract negotiations, and salary cap management.

With the goal of creating sustainable success and building a championship-caliber organization, Ferry made a series of deft moves to better position the franchise. He hired Mike Budenholzer as head coach of the team on May 28, 2013. He has also engineered a number of trades and free agent signings, which have netted key veterans Paul Millsap, Kyle Korver, and DeMarre Carroll. On June 22, 2015, Ferry stepped down as general manager of the Hawks. Ferry's departure ended a 10-month indefinite leave of absence that followed the release of a conference call with ownership, in which Ferry was heard repeating culturally insensitive comments from a scouting report about forward Luol Deng, who played at Duke.

13 2010 National Championship

The 2010 Duke basketball team was one of teamwork, hard work, and consistent growth. Despite returning four starters from an ACC championship team that won 30 games a year before, the Blue Devils were often overlooked and ignored as a title contender in 2010. A group of seniors (Jon Scheyer, Lance Thomas, and Brian Zoubek) that endured a 22–11 record as freshmen, along with junior standouts Kyle Singler and Nolan Smith, set out to do something special with a group that most considered good but not great.

The Blue Devils started strong with six straight wins, including a 68–59 victory against No. 13 Connecticut in the championship game of the NIT Season Tip-Off. Duke out-rebounded the Huskies 56–43 in the contest with Thomas and Zoubek each grabbing 11 boards. After losing 73–69 on the road to Wisconsin despite 28 points from Singler, the team won the next seven games with six of the victories coming by 20-plus points. Duke climbed to No. 5 in the AP poll, and Scheyer established himself as an All-American candidate along the way. Duke dropped an ACC road contest to No. 20 Georgia Tech despite 25 points and six assists from Scheyer before returning home to post wins against Boston College and Wake Forest. The skeptics reemerged following another road loss for the Blue Devils, this time at the hands of N.C. State. The Wolfpack shot 58.2 percent from the field in an 88–74 victory. Duke's road woes changed in a primetime contest at Clemson with ESPN's *College GameDay* on site. The Blue Devils avenged a 74–47 loss in 2009 at Littlejohn with a 60–47 win against the No. 17 Tigers. Smith paced the team with 22 points on 8-of-13 shooting.

Duke hit a stumbling block again in Washington, D.C., against Georgetown with President Barack Obama and Vice President Joe Biden on hand. The Hoyas dismantled the Blue Devils' defense, shooting an opponent-record 71.7 percent from the field. Duke returned home to Georgia Tech and added road wins against Boston College and North Carolina.

On February 13, in his 1,000[th] career game at Duke, Mike Krzyzewski moved Zoubek into the starting lineup, and the senior center responded with 16 points and a career-best 17 rebounds against the Terrapins. He followed that up with a 16-rebound effort two games later, and suddenly the Blue Devils had an interior toughness to go with the NCAA's highest-scoring trio in Scheyer, Singler, and Smith.

Duke entered March ranked fourth in the polls with a 25–4 record. On senior night at Maryland, it took a few unfortunate bounces and a clutch performance by Greivis Vasquez to snap the Blue Devils' four-game road win streak and an eight-game win streak overall. But the Blue Devils put everything together in their next game, an 82–50 dismantling of North Carolina. Scheyer, Singler, and Smith combined for 65 points, and Duke jumped out to a 53–26 halftime lead. The Tar Heels had 15 turnovers and made just 16 field goals in the contest.

In the ACC Tournament, Duke posted wins against Virginia and Miami to reach the championship game. Tournament MOP Singler went 14-of-16 from the foul line, and Scheyer hit a clutch three-point field goal in the final 30 seconds to secure a 65–61 victory against Georgia Tech and claim Duke's ninth ACC title in the last 12 years.

The Blue Devils grabbed a No. 1 seed in the NCAA Tournament for the 11th time in school history and advanced through Jacksonville, Florida, by handily defeating Arkansas-Pine Bluff and California. Duke then posted a hard-fought, 70–57 win over Purdue as Singler netted 24 points and the Blue Devils posted

The Plumlee Brothers

The Plumlee brothers—Miles, Mason, and Marshall—grew up in Fort Wayne, Indiana, before playing their high school ball at Christ School in Arden, North Carolina. It's not a surprise that the brothers are athletic and tall. Their father, Perky, played basketball at Tennessee Tech, and their mother, Leslie, played for Purdue, where she set a single-game rebounding record with 25.

Born on September 1, 1988, Miles is the oldest of the brothers. Perhaps the most athletic of the three, the springy 6'11", 255 pounder had originally committed to play at Stanford, but after Cardinal head coach Trent Johnson left for LSU, he chose to attend Duke, where his brother, Mason, already had committed. After serving a limited role his freshman season, Miles earned the starting center position over senior Brian Zoubek at the beginning of the 2009–10 season before returning to a bench role later in the season. Plumlee finished the championship-winning season averaging 16.4 minutes, 4.9 rebounds, and 5.2 points per game.

Miles had his best year as a senior, grabbing the second most rebounds per game for the team with 7.1, which was second to Mason, and led the team in field goal percentage at 61 percent. He set a single-game Duke record under Mike Krzyzewski by grabbing 22 boards. During his four years at Duke, he played 135 games with 654 rebounds and 650 points. Selected 26th overall in the first round of the 2012 NBA Draft by the Indiana Pacers, he also has played for the Phoenix Suns and Milwaukee Bucks.

The middle brother, Mason, was born March 5, 1990, and was a big-time prep player at Christ School, a 2009 McDonald's All-American, Jordan Brand All-American, and a third team *Parade* All-American honors. At Duke, the 6'10", 235-pounder was a prodigious dunker and a member of the 2010 National Championship team with Miles. Mason, the most skilled and talented basketball player of the three, earned consensus second team All-American and first team All-ACC selections in 2013 as he averaged 17.1 points and 10 rebounds. The Brooklyn Nets selected him 22nd overall in the first round of the 2013 NBA Draft.

The third Plumlee to play at Duke committed right after his brothers won the 2010 NCAA title. Marshall is the youngest and biggest of the brothers. The seven-footer earned Gatorade Player of the Year honors in North Carolina and played in the 2011 McDonald's All-American game. After redshirting his first year, Marshall has provided boundless energy off the bench, excellent defense against numerous positions, and rugged screens to free up his teammates. Like his brothers, he won a ring with his coming after the 2015 season. Marshall, who is in the school's ROTC program, has said he will enlist in the military after he finishes playing at Duke.

a plus-21 rebound margin for the game. Left standing in the way of the program's first Final Four appearance since 2004 was Baylor. Duke trailed at the half but used timely three-point shooting and 23 offensive rebounds to claim a 78–71 victory. Smith scored a career high 29 points, and Thomas came up with several hustle plays down the stretch to secure the win.

Duke returned to Indianapolis, the site of its first NCAA title, to face West Virginia in the Final Four. The big three combined for 63 points as the Blue Devils shot 52.7 percent from the field in a 78–57 dismantling of the Mountaineers. The title game pitted Duke against hometown Butler and its 25-game win streak. The seesaw battle came down to the final seconds. Zoubek made his first free throw and then intentionally missed the second. After which, Gordon Hayward's half-court shot caromed off the rim at the buzzer, giving the Blue Devils a 61–59 victory and the program's fourth NCAA title. Singler, the Final Four MVP, led the way with 19 points while Zoubek added 10 rebounds.

14 Shane Battier

Battier came to Duke from Detroit Country Day School in Michigan and he never disappointed, leading the Blue Devils to two Final Fours and a national title. In 2001, the year he led Duke to the title, Battier swept the major National Player of the Year awards. He subsequently had his No. 31 jersey retired by the Blue Devils. "Shane is the most complete player I've ever coached. He may not be the most talented player we've had here at Duke, but he's the most complete," Mike Krzyzewski said. "You hear so many good things about Shane and you think nobody could be like that. But he is. He's the real deal."

His incredible athletic ability, hustle, and defensive prowess could be encapsulated in one particular play at North Carolina when Tar Heels guard Joe Forte broke away for a dunk. But right before Forte got the ball to the rim, Battier blocked it from behind, having hustled back down the court. That was part of a five-point swing keyed by Battier, who had 25 points, 11 rebounds, and four steals. While most players' careers are remembered by key dunks, drive, or jumpers, Battier was identified with memorable defensive efforts like eight blocked shots in an NCAA Tournament win against Kansas or a block of a Juan Dixon jumper at Maryland to seal the Blue Devils' "Miracle Minute" victory or a baseline save against Arizona that Duke converted into a winning basket against for another national title.

Battier began his career at Duke as an ACC All-Freshman Team performer, averaging 7.6 points and 6.4 rebounds per game in 1997–98. By his sophomore year, Battier was proving to be an outstanding defensive player, earning the first of his three National Defensive Player of the Year awards. His defensive effort was particularly important in leading the Blue Devils to the 1999 National Championship Game against Connecticut.

As a junior his play on the defensive end of the floor was just part of his total game. He led the Blue Devils in scoring at 17.4 points per game, blocked 70 shots, and shot 44.4 percent from three-point range. He earned second team All-American, first team All-ACC, first team All-ACC Tournament, and first team Academic All-American honors.

Battier's outstanding career at Duke was capped with the national championship in 2001 along with the ACC regular season title and the ACC Tournament title. As a senior in 2000–01, he averaged 19.9 points, 7.3 rebounds, 2.3 blocks, 2.1 steals, and 1.8 assists. He was named the 2001 consensus National Player of the Year, Defensive Player of the Year, first team All-American, Final Four Most Outstanding Player, ACC Co-Player of the Year, ACC Tournament Most Valuable Player, and first team All-ACC.

Known for his defensive prowess, Shane Battier blocks Joe Forte's shot to spark a five-point swing during Duke's 2001 road win versus North Carolina.

Battier was the sixth pick of the 2001 NBA Draft by the Vancouver Grizzlies, who were in the process of moving the franchise to Memphis. He played for the Grizzlies from 2001 to 2006, earning NBA All-Rookie team honors in 2002. He played for the Houston Rockets from 2006 until 2011 and then played for the Miami Heat from 2011 until 2014, where he won NBA championships in 2012 and 2013 and went to the NBA Finals in 2014. In his NBA career, Battier scored

8,408 points, pulled down 4,082 rebounds, and dished out 1,717 assists. After retiring from the NBA, Battier became a television analyst for ESPN.

15 Grant Hill

Grant Hill was considered destined play his college basketball at the University of North Carolina. "I was always a Carolina fan," Hill told biographer Bill Brill. "As far back as I can remember, I rooted for Carolina. When they won the national championship in 1982, that's when I discovered basketball." Hill lived in the Washington, D.C., suburb of Reston, Virginia, and did not play in many summer All-Star Games and camps. College coaches watched him at South Lakes High School, where his regular attire was a "Carolina hat, T-shirt, shorts, anything. They were the dominant team then."

And North Carolina coach Dean Smith understandably coveted Hill, who was highly skilled but extremely unselfish and reared by a great family. His father, Calvin Hill, was a former NFL and Yale football star, and his mother, Janet, attended Wellesley College, where she was a suitemate of Hillary Rodham Clinton, and worked as a lobbyist on Capitol Hill.

Part of Smith's recruiting strategy was to make the last home visit and have a player come to campus after he had been to all the other schools he was considering. Mike Krzyzewski knew that and invited Hill for his official visit the weekend before Hill was going to Chapel Hill and Smith was scheduled at the Hill home. It was also the weekend of the Blue-White scrimmage, with Cameron Indoor Stadium packed and the crowd well aware of Hill's presence. Hill had grown to like and respect Krzyzewski, and Coach K's counter was to ask a player he really wanted for a commitment at the end of the weekend.

This was the fall of 1988, after Duke had been to two of the last three Final Fours but was a young powerhouse not nearly as established as Smith's program. The Dean Dome was still relatively new, and Michael Jordan had been gone only four years, having made an impact on Hill as an impressionable grade-schooler. While encouraging every recruit to finish all of his official campus visits, Smith figured he had the advantage by making the *last* impression. But he never got the chance with Hill.

When Krzyzewski extended his hand and asked him to come to Duke, Hill shook it like he meant it. "I came back from my recruiting trip and I just knew that was where I wanted to go," Hill told Brill. "It's not like I had a great time on my visit or anything. It was just that when I got on campus, it fit. Everything I wanted—type of school, campus, coaching staff, style of basketball, opportunity to play—was there. I think it shocked my parents, my teammates, my friends. To tell you the truth, I think I shocked Duke."

Hill called Krzyzewski and committed that week. Knowing it was still a month from the official fall signing period, Coach K said that after the media got wind of it Hill would be better off cancelling his trip to Chapel Hill along with Smith's home visit the following Wednesday night. However, the Hills decided to tell Smith when he came up for dinner, thinking that they owed it to the coach whom the family had admired for so long.

After dinner at the Hills' home, Smith and assistant coach Phil Ford adjourned to the living room for the final recruiting pitch. Only Grant excused himself and went to his room to do his homework. That's when his parents thanked Smith for recruiting their son and told him he had committed to Duke and wasn't going to Chapel Hill the following Friday. In today's world of Internet message boards and social media, Smith would have found out already, but he was flabbergasted that the Hill family made him travel to Washington, when a phone call would have sufficed. Smith was upset and reacted sarcastically, as he often did when angry. "We wish Grant great success at Duke," Smith said, "but I could have been home having dinner with *my* family."

It still ranks as perhaps Krzyzewski's greatest recruiting coup and completely blind-sided Smith.

Hill got off to a great start in his first season with the Blue Devils, earning ACC All-Freshman and second team All-ACC Tournament honors playing on the first national championship team in 1990–91. He famously threw down perhaps the best dunk in Duke history as he skied above the rim to corral an alley-oop from Bobby Hurley during the national championship victory against Kansas. Hill's sophomore season was once again marked by being a part of the national championship team that was the top-ranked squad in the country from start to finish. He averaged 14.0 points, 5.7 rebounds, and 3.7 assists. In his junior year, he averaged 18.0 points and 6.4 rebounds per game. His honors included: the Henry Iba Corinthian Award for the nation's top defender, third team All-American, and first team All-ACC. In 1994 as a senior, he led the Blue Devils back to the Final Four and averaged 17.4 points and 6.9 rebounds per game. He was first team All-American and a finalist for the Wooden and Naismith Awards. Hill also garnered ACC Player of the Year, Southeast Region MVP, and All-Final Four honors. He became the first player in ACC history to have more than 1,900 points, 700 rebounds, 400 assists, 200 steals, and 100 blocked shots.

But Hill is perhaps best known as the passer on one of the most remarkable plays in NCAA Tournament history. With Duke down 103–102 in overtime and 2.1 seconds remaining after Kentucky's Sean Woods hit a floater, an unguarded Hill, then a sophomore, heaved the in-bounds pass 75 feet across the court into the hands of Christian Laettner, who dribbled once and spun before pulling up to make the game-winning jumper from just outside the free throw line as time expired in the East Regional Final to send the Blue Devils to the Final Four and an eventual national championship.

Hill was drafted by the Detroit Pistons with the third pick in the NBA draft. In his first season, he averaged 19.9 points per game, 6.4 rebounds, and five assists and shared the NBA Rookie of the Year honor with Jason Kidd. In 1995 Hill became the first rookie to lead the NBA All-Star fan balloting. Though a series of ankle injuries derailed his NBA career, Hill still played 18 years in the NBA with the Pistons, Orlando Magic, Phoenix Suns, and Los Angeles Clippers. He was selected to the NBA All-Star Game seven times, named first team All-NBA in 1997, and received the NBA Sportsmanship Award three times.

Following his retirement from the NBA in 2013, Hill went to work with NBA TV and as an analyst with CBS. Alongside Bill Raftery and Jim Nantz, Hill called the 2015 Final Four won by the Blue Devils.

16 Jason Williams

From the day he stepped on the floor of Cameron Indoor Stadium, Jason Williams was a transcendent player. He led the Blue Devils to a national championship in 2001. During his three years, Williams was a starter in all 108 games he played in at Duke, and the 2002 Player of the Year saw his No. 22 retired to the rafters of Cameron.

Williams grew up in New Jersey and attended St. Joseph High School in Metuchen. On the basketball court, he was a first team All-State player, the New Jersey Player of the Year, a *Parade* All-American, a McDonald's All-American, and the winner of the Morgan Wootten Award as the top prep player in the country.

He was a starter from his very first game at Duke and ended his first year as *The Sporting News* Freshman of the Year in 2000. During that campaign Williams averaged 14.5 points, 4.2 rebounds, 6.5 assists, and 2.4 steals per game while collecting ACC Tournament Most Valuable Player and ACC All-Freshman team honors. As a sophomore in 2000–01, Williams helped lead the Blue Devils to their third national championship and had Duke's second highest season points total with 841. Part of the All-Final Four team, he was also unanimous first team All-ACC, first team ACC All-Tournament, and a first team All-American as well as a finalist for both the Wooden and Naismith Awards. Williams received the latter two awards as the accolades continued to mount for him during his junior season. He ended his collegiate career with 2,079 points, 644 assists, 313 three-point field goals, and 235 steals.

Following his junior season, Williams entered the NBA Draft and was the second overall pick in the 2002 NBA Draft by the Chicago Bulls. During his rookie season in 2002–03, he started 54 of the 75 games he played in and averaged 9.5 points and 4.7 assists. Bulls coaches and administrative people all felt very strong about Williams' first season and were looking forward to a solid future with the Blue Devils guard.

But that all changed on the night of June 19, 2003, when Williams, riding his Yamaha motorcycle, crashed at the intersection of Fletcher and Honore streets in Chicago's Lincoln Park. His injuries included a severed main nerve in his leg, a fractured pelvis, and three dislocated ligaments in his left knee. Doctors grafted a vein from another part of my body and used it as an artery in his left leg. He nearly had to have his leg amputated. He was riding without a helmet or a licensed motorcycle along with violating the terms of his contract with the Bulls.

When it became evident that he would not return to play for the Bulls, they waived him and still paid him $3 million despite violating his contract. After extensive rehabilitation he signed on with the New Jersey Nets in September of 2006 but was released less than a month later. He tried to play for the Austin Toros of the NBA Developmental League, but the leg just didn't have the same strength and quickness as prior to the accident. Williams now works for ESPN as an analyst for college basketball games.

17 J.J. Redick

At the age of seven after watching the Blue Devils capture the 1992 NCAA Championship, J.J. Redick decided he was coming to Duke to play for Mike Krzyzewski. Because of breaking both his wrists, he learned to shoot with both hands. A native of Roanoke, Virginia, Redick entered Duke as a McDonald's All-American with a reputation as one of the best pure shooters in the game. Boy, did he live up to that, becoming one of the most prolific scorers in school, ACC, and NCAA history.

He closed his career as the leading scorer in ACC history with 2,769 career points and as the NCAA record holder with 457 three-point field goals. As a freshman he showed off an array of dazzling scoring moves as he lit up Virginia for 34 points N.C. State for 30 in the ACC Tournament final. As a sophomore he earned third team All-America honors, averaging 15.9 points per game and helping lead Duke to a 31–6 record and a trip to the 2004 Final Four. He also proved to be one of the greatest free throw shooters in the NCAA as he led the ACC while hitting 95.3 percent, including an ACC record of 54 straight free throws.

Following his freshman season, Redick became quite the showman as he played to the crowd, throwing his arms in the air after drilling another long-range three pointer and smiling at the opposing student body. He became the focal point for opposing defenses and fans. As a junior he took his game and gamesmanship to a new level as he averaged an ACC-best 21.8 points while earning unanimous first team All-American and ACC Player of the Year honors. J.J. claimed the 2005 Rupp Award after reaching double figures in scoring 31 times, including 21 games with 20 or more points. Despite those accolades—or perhaps because of them—his name was uttered in unflattering ways in opponent arenas. Fans would spew vitriol and shout obscenities, even targeting Redick's sister.

As a senior Redick recorded the most prolific scoring season in school history and became the second Duke player and only the eighth overall in college basketball history to repeat as National Player of the Year. He also repeated as a first team All-American (unanimous selection) and as the ACC Player of the Year. He led the ACC and finished second in the NCAA in scoring at 26.8 points per game while shooting 47.0 percent (302-of-643) from the field and 42.1 percent (139-of-330) from three-point range. He scored in double figures in all 36 games, and also claimed the James E. Sullivan Award as the nation's top amateur athlete following his senior campaign.

On February 4, 2007, Redick's No. 4 was retired at Cameron Indoor Stadium. He was drafted 11th in the 2006 NBA Draft by the Orlando Magic and spent six-plus years before being sent to the Milwaukee Bucks, where he played for 28 games, at the NBA trade deadline. In July of 2013, Redick was acquired by the Los Angeles Clippers, where Doc Rivers—and the father of former Duke player and current Clippers teammate Austin Rivers—is the head coach. In his two years with the Clippers, Redick has been a starter for the playoff-bound team at shooting guard.

Duke's all-time leading scorer with 2,769 points, J.J. Redick, acknowledges the Cameron Indoor Stadium crowd.

The Shot Doctor

In most corners of the world of basketball he is known as "the Shot Doctor," but in Durham he is known as Chip Engelland, a terrific shooter. A native of Los Angeles, Engelland, has always been around the game. He served as a ball boy for coach John Wooden's NCAA champion UCLA Bruins in 1975 and began his basketball career at Pacific Palisades High School, leading Los Angeles in scoring as a senior in 1979.

He then came to Duke, where he played for both Bill Foster and Mike Krzyzewski and scored more than 1,000 points and was named the team's captain in his senior year. He played in 113 games as a Blue Devil and connected on almost 52 percent of his field goals with most of the 411 career field goals being the long-range jumper version. He shot an amazing 55 percent from behind the three-point line and 85 percent from the foul line.

He moved into the starting lineup in 1982 and averaged 15.2 points a game and had a high of 27 points in a win against Holy Cross in one of the first college basketball games played at the Meadowlands and was named the ESPN Player of the Week for his performance. As a senior Engelland played behind Johnny Dawkins and Tom Emma at the guard position but still averaged 12.2 points per game coming off the bench and had his career high of 30 points in his last home game against North Carolina.

After graduating from Duke in 1983, Engelland went on to play professionally for nine years. First he played in the Philippines, where he became a naturalized Filipino citizen and spent two seasons as a member of the Philippine national basketball team. He was once known by Filipino fans in PBA as Chip "the Machine Gun" Engelland for his superb shooting skills. In 1993 Engelland started his coaching career, introducing his basketball camps called "Chip Shots" with the aim of helping players of all ages improve their shooting skills. Two years later he founded the In-Net Corporation, strengthening his reputation as a clinician and advisor.

He got his first job in the NBA in the 1999–2000 season, serving as a shooting consultant for the Detroit Pistons. Three years later, he signed with the Denver Nuggets as the director of player development, holding the position for two seasons. Since the 2005–06 season, Engelland has been serving as an assistant coach for the San Antonio Spurs, where he has won two championships with the Spurs in 2007 and 2014.

18 Art Heyman

Until Art Heyman came to Duke, the Blue Devils had never been the home to the No. 1 high school recruit in the country. But in the fall of 1959, that changed, and the top prep player in the nation began wearing Duke blue and white. People in Durham knew they had a special player. What they didn't know was they were about to go on a roller coaster ride of incredible basketball and even more incredible antics both on and off the court. Heyman was one of the greatest players in Duke basketball history along with being one of the larger than life characters to ever attend the university.

Heyman was born in New York City and played his high school ball at Oceanside High School in Nassau County, New York. He immediately made a huge impact at Duke as a freshman in 1959–60, averaging more than 30 points per game and recording a single-game high of 47 points. As a co-captain his sophomore year, Heyman earned All-American honors and was the nation's No. 8 scorer with a 25.2 scoring average. He also averaged 10.9 rebounds per game and led Duke in nearly every statistical category in 1960–61. Once again an All-American selection as a junior in 1962, he averaged 25.3 points and 11.2 rebounds per game. After leading the Blue Devils in nearly every statistical category, Heyman was a near unanimous selection on the All-ACC first team.

As a senior in 1962–63, Heyman left his mark on Duke by helping the team earn its first trip to the Final Four. He was the 1963 ACC Player of the Year and ACC Tournament MVP as his team captured the ACC championship. For the third year in a row, Heyman earned All-American honors along with being named the National Player of the Year. He scored 29 points and pulled down 12 rebounds in the NCAA semifinals against Loyola and was named Most Outstanding Player at the Final Four.

And while Heyman's 25.1 career scoring average shows his ability to get the ball through the basket, that was not what he was all about on the basketball court. He didn't have the most picturesque jump shot, but he had the will and skill to get the ball in the basket whether it be a jump shot a drive to the basket. Always in position to tap a missed shot back in or a free throw, Heyman just knew how to score. And despite standing just 6'5", he averaged at least 10 rebounds a year every year and ended his college career with a 10.9 rebound average.

But his statistical value was only part of the story with Heyman. His toughness, presence, competitiveness, and combativeness made him the central figure in coach Vic Bubas's development of Duke basketball. Heyman was involved in many fights during his career at Duke and many off-court antics that caused Duke officials a few gray hairs, but in the end, he was just a truly great basketball player. He was the type of player that irritated fans of the opposing team and he loved to rile up fans of the University of North Carolina, where he had originally committed to attend college, more than any other team. (In particular, he and UNC's Larry Brown, another playmaking guard of the Jewish faith from Long Island, helped fuel the rivalry.) In his final home game, against the Tar Heels, he posted 40 points and 24 rebounds, as the Blue Devils crushed Carolina and capped a perfect 14–0 ACC record. At halftime he was honored by the Duke student body.

Heyman became the first Duke player to be selected No. 1 in the NBA Draft, going to the New York Knicks. He played six pro seasons for seven different teams, being named to the NBA All-Rookie team. His temper and frequent outbursts with the Knicks and other NBA teams decreased his playing time. He moved over to the ABA for three seasons, playing with the New Jersey Americans, Pittsburgh Pipers, Minnesota Pipers, and Miami

Floridians. He teamed up with Connie Hawkins, averaged more than 20 points a game, and led the Pittsburgh Pipers to an ABA title in 1968. He retired from professional basketball in 1970 with 4,030 combined points in the NBA and ABA. Heyman went on to be a restaurateur in New York. His No. 25 was retired at Duke in 1990, and he passed away on August 27, 2012, in Clermont, Florida, at the age of 71.

19 Go Camping at Krzyzewskiville

For years Duke students have lined up to obtain entrance to Cameron Indoor Stadium so that they can cheer on their beloved Blue Devils. There are no student tickets for undergrads at Duke. Admittance is determined on a first-come, first-serve basis until the lower bleacher area is full. In the 1980s students started lining up for games, and every now and then, a group would get out their sleeping bags and sleep in line the night before to ensure they got the best seats.

In 1986 Kimberly Reed, a resident of the Mirecourt selective living group, took the practice one step further, and she and some of her Mirecourt friends decided to line up even earlier for the UNC game and sleep in tents. Showing up on Thursday for the Saturday tip-off, the 15 friends set up four tents and prepared to sleep outside of Cameron Indoor. They were quickly noticed by the rest of the student body, and by game time, there were 75 tents in line to see Duke battle their longstanding rival UNC. NBC put them on the evening news, and they made the front page of *USA TODAY*. Their dedication was rewarded with an 82–74 Duke victory, and tenting quickly became a Duke tradition.

The man for whom tent city is named, Blue Devils head coach Mike Krzyzewski, has been known to buy pizza for the Krzyzewskiville residents from time to time and has held open forum meetings with the Cameron Crazies before games against Carolina.

Krzyzewskiville is located at the northeast corner of Cameron Indoor Stadium and alongside Card Gymnasium. Graduate and professional students do not participate in Krzyzewskiville, as Duke's graduate and professional student council operates a separate weekend-long campout each September followed by a lottery for a small number of graduate and professional student season tickets.

The Line Monitor Committee of the Duke student government determines the number of tenting games in a single season. The game with North Carolina is always a tenting game, but sometimes there may be a second game where tent order determines seating. Months before the actual game, students begin putting up and living in tents outside Cameron Indoor Stadium. As many as 12 people can occupy a specific tent group, and that tent group may contain up to two physical tents. As regulated by the Duke student government, there must be a certain number of students in the tent at regular, periodic checks.

For the first two weeks, which start in early January, tents of 12 must have two people in the tent during the day and 10 people each night. For the next two weeks, tents must have one person in the tent during the day and six people each night. For the final two weeks before the game, tents still must have one person during the day but only two people each night. The two weekend nights prior to the game are personal check nights, and each of the 12 tent members must be at the tent for three of the five checks spread over the two nights. If a tent misses a tent check twice, it gets moved to the end of the line. If Krzyzewskiville is at full capacity of 100

Setting up tents in Krzyzewskiville in order to secure tickets to home basketball games has become a tradition at Duke.

tents and a waitlist exists at the time of the second miss, the tent gets removed completely.

Tenters who lose their spot or non-tenters can, however, take their chances at the walk-up line, which forms 48 hours before tip-off. The walk-up line consists of couples, and one member of each couple must be in line at all times. People in the walk-up line are not guaranteed to get into the game; people who have waited more than 24 hours sometimes do not get in.

Tents must register with the line monitors (students in charge of overseeing and enforcing Krzyzewskiville rules and regulations) prior to setting up. There are three types: Black registration is the longest and most intense option. All 12 tenters used to sleep in Krzyzewskiville during black tenting. Today, however, only 10 people must sleep in the tent during Black registration.

Blue registration is the next period in which a tent can register at any time before approximately two weeks prior to the game. After that period White registration goes into effect, which is significantly more complicated. For Blue registration a tent group need only give their names to the line monitors and start tenting. However, for White registration students must meet the line monitors at a location on campus that is disclosed on a website at a specified time. This results in a hectic dash to the location once it is made public. Most tenting groups station members around campus, one of whom is called when the location is disclosed online. Hundreds of tent representatives usually appear at the White registration location for the 30 remaining spots not taken by Black and Blue tenters, and the spots fill up in a matter of minutes.

Krzyzewskiville also serves as social function at Duke, as many students participate at least once. Duke has installed Wi-Fi service and Ethernet ports, so that students can participate in tenting without falling behind in their schoolwork, though the Internet is known to be very unreliable. Students complain that the cold weather also prevents them from getting any real work done. Heaters are not permitted in K-ville; students must keep warm by simply using sleeping bags and dressing appropriately. They, however, will be plenty warm once they enter Cameron Indoor Stadium.

20 Jeff Mullins

When asked about the play of Jeff Mullins, legendary North Carolina State coach Everett Case said, "There's nothing you can do to slow him down. He'll shoot your eyes out and when he goes on the fast breaks he shoots from 30 and 40 feet and makes them." His own teammate, Art Heyman, called him the greatest player and the nicest person he ever played with.

Mullins was all that and more. He was an offensive machine on a Duke team full of scorers. And because of his personality, he was able to get along with everyone on a loaded team and win a lot of basketball games. A native of Lexington, Kentucky, the talented 6'4" forward would be rewarded greatly over his career with All-American honors in college, a gold medal in the Olympics, and an NBA championship ring with the Golden State Warriors.

Mullins began putting up big numbers for the Blue Devils as a freshman, averaging a team-high 24.6 points per game in 1960–61. Mullins' sophomore season culminated with All-ACC and All-Tournament team honors after he averaged 21.0 points and 10.4 rebounds per game while shooting 51.4 percent from the floor. In his junior year of 1962–63, Mullins, along with Heyman, led the Blue Devils to Duke's first Final Four. Mullins was an All-American honoree and was selected to both the All-ACC and All-Tournament teams. He averaged 20.3 points on 54.9 percent field goal shooting and pulled down 8.0 rebounds per game. He was once again an All-American selection as a senior in 1964 after leading Duke to the Final Four for the second straight year. He averaged 24.2 points and 8.9 rebounds per game and earned ACC Player of the Year as well as ACC Tournament MVP accolades. He received the McKevlin Award, given to the

ACC Athlete of the Year, in 1964 and finished his Blue Devils career with 1,884 points. In the summer of 1964, Mullins became the first Blue Devil to be selected to the United States Olympic basketball team. The U.S. went on to win the gold medal at the 1964 Olympics in Tokyo.

Mullins scored in double figures in all 86 of his college basketball games, and his most memorable game occurred when he scored a career-high 43 points against Villanova in the NCAA Tournament in Reynolds Coliseum. He scored 28 points in the first half, including a buzzer-beating, half-court shot at the end of the half. The Blue Devils ended up winning the game 87–73 with Mullins hitting 19-of-28 from the field and 5-of-6 from the free throw line

After graduation Mullins was the fifth pick in the 1964 NBA Draft by the St. Louis Hawks. He ended up playing 12 seasons in the league and scored more than 13,000 points. After spending two years in St. Louis, he moved on to the Warriors, where he played for a decade. He averaged 16.2 points per game for his career and scored more than 20 points a game for four straight years, making the All-Star Game three times and winning the 1975 NBA title.

In 1985 he was hired as the head coach and athletic director at UNC-Charlotte. In his 11 seasons he won 182 games, a school record that stood until Bobby Lutz, a former Mullins assistant, surpassed that total in 2008. In 1994 his No. 44 jersey was retired at Duke.

21 Bill Foster

When Bill Foster took over the Duke basketball program, the Blue Devils had just gone through four years of double-digit losses, two consecutive losing seasons, and had lost its last eight meetings with archrival North Carolina. In less than four years, Foster returned the Blue Devil basketball program to the glory years of the '60s as they returned to their lofty ranking as the No. 1 team in the nation, won ACC titles, and played for the 1978 NCAA National Championship.

Foster was a multitasker with boundless energy, often banging out notes, plans, and to-do lists on a portable typewriter while sitting in the bleachers before practice as his players shot around. He soon recognized that, besides Duke being mired in the shadow of UNC and N.C. State, the university was in a debate over just how much athletics added to its growing academic reputation. Cameron Indoor Stadium, which had yet to become the mecca of college basketball because it often hosted half-empty home games, was in serious need of upgrades or even total demolition. Foster, the marketer, got busy promoting his new program and selling tickets and, while leaving his wife and three daughters home during long road trips, went looking for players who could change all this. He always carried a notepad so he could write down thoughts as they popped into his head about building Duke basketball.

His first collegiate coaching job came in 1960 when he was hired as the head coach at Bloomsburg State College, where he compiled a 45–11 record in three years. He also became friends with Harry Litwack, the longtime coach at Temple. The two ended up as business partners and operated the Five-Star All-Star Basketball Camp in the Pocono Mountains for 25 years. He moved to the Scarlet

Knights of Rutgers as their head coach in 1963, where he led them to a 120–75 record in eight seasons, taking them to their first post-season in 1967 as they finished the season with a 22–7 record and an invite to the NIT. That team included Jim Valvano, who went on to a Hall of Fame coaching career at N.C. State. Following the 1971 season, Foster moved to Utah to become the head coach at the University of Utah and in one of his trademark marketing deals renamed the basketball team the "Running Utes." He only stayed three years at Utah but led Utah to a 43–39 record and the 1974 NIT Championship game where it lost to Purdue.

In 1974 Foster would return to the East Coast and become the head coach of the Duke Blue Devils, a program he remembered well as a consistent winner under Vic Bubas in the '60s but now was suffering. In Foster's first season, his enthusiasm seemed to rub off on the players, whose four seniors were getting pep talks from their fourth coach in four years. Hubie Brown had been their freshman coach and then Bucky Waters as sophomores, Neill McGeachy as juniors, and now Foster. Brown left after their freshman season in 1972 and began a long career coaching pro basketball.

Kevin Billerman, Tate Armstrong, Pete Kramer, Bob Fleischer, and Willie Hodge were not a bad starting lineup—just one that had become accustomed to losing. Foster emphasized the running game, and Duke ran off to a 5–1 start, beating Princeton and Pittsburgh while losing only to LSU, going into the Big Four Tournament, a December event that paired Duke, UNC, N.C. State, and Wake Forest on a rotating basis and often resulted in three Duke-Carolina games during the regular season until the Big Four ended a 10-year run in 1980. In Foster's first Big Four, Duke's opponent on opening night was UNC, which was also 5–1 with freshman Phil Ford at point guard. Foster broke the Blue Devils' eight-game losing streak to UNC with a 99–96 overtime victory at a stunned Greensboro Coliseum. He joked after the game to his staff, "What was so hard about that?"

It would take him time, but by the 1977–78 season he was able to put together a talented squad with All-Americans like Jim Spanarkel, Mike Gminski, and Gene Banks around solid players like Kenny Dennard, Bob Bender, and John Harrell. They captured the ACC Tournament and went on a Cinderella-like run through the NCAA Tournament falling in the national championship game to Kentucky 94–88.

The next two seasons the Blue Devils spent the majority of the year as the No. 1 team in the nation, though they never made it back to a Final Four under Foster. He ended up leaving following the 1980 season to take the head coaching job at South Carolina. He guided the Blue Devils from 1975–80 to a 113–64 record, was ACC Coach of the Year in 1978, and won two ACC championships, and an ACC regular season title. Foster would finish his coaching career at the University of South Carolina and Northwestern University, where he also served as interim athletic director. After leaving Northwestern, Foster became associate commissioner and director of basketball operations for the Southwest Conference. He later worked as a consultant with the Western Athletic Conference and the Big 12 Conference.

22 Duke Chapel

Located in the center of campus, Duke University Chapel is the focal point of the university. An ecumenical Christian chapel and the center of religion at Duke, the chapel has connections to the United Methodist Church, and the Divinity School is located adjacent to the chapel. Constructed from 1930 to 1932, the chapel seats about 1,800 people and stands 210 feet tall. It is built in the

Collegiate Gothic style, characterized by its large stones, pointed arches, and ribbed vaults. It also has a 50-bell carillon and three pipe organs, one with 5,033 pipes and another with 6,900 pipes. Besides regular church services, the Duke Chapel is the sight of numerous weddings throughout the year.

A conscious decision was made to place the chapel at the center of the university and on the highest ridge of Duke University's West Campus. Although plans for a chapel were first made in April 1925, the cornerstone was not laid until October 22, 1930. In fact, when it was completed in 1935 at a cost of $2.3 million, the chapel was the last of the original buildings to be built on West Campus. It was first used during commencement in 1932 and was formally dedicated on June 2, 1935. Stained glass windows and other details were installed at a later date. The chapel was designed by Julian Abele, chief designer for the Philadelphia firm of Horace Trumbauer.

Duke Chapel is an example of neo-Gothic architecture in the English style. Gothic architecture is characterized by large stone piers, pointed arches, ribbed vaults, and flying buttresses, which allow the creation of vast open spaces uninterrupted by columns for support. The result is an imposing structure and vast interior space that invite visitors to marvel at the wonders of faith and creation. The chapel is constructed of a volcanic stone from a quarry in Hillsborough, North Carolina, which was purchased by the university for the construction of West Campus. Known as Hillsborough bluestone, the beautiful and distinctive stone actually ranges in color through 17 shades from rust orange to slate gray.

As you enter the chapel, carved on the ornate entrance are 10 figures important to Methodism, Protestantism, and the American South. On the outer arch above the portal are carved three figures pivotal to the American Methodist movement: Bishop Francis Ashbury stands in the center while Bishop Thomas Coke and George Whitefield stand on the left and right, respectively. On the

Built in Collegiate Gothic style, the Duke Chapel is one of the university's most distinctive landmarks.

left wall within the entrance portal are carved (from left to right) Girolamo Savonarola, Martin Luther, and John Wycliffe. On the right wall (from left to right) are Thomas Jefferson, statesman of the South; Robert E. Lee, soldier of the South; and Sidney Lanier, poet of the South. John Wesley, founder of Methodism, stands atop the inner arch within the portal, directly above the chapel doors. On Lee's carving, the Italian sculptors inscribed "US" on the belt buckle; it was partially chiseled away (since Lee was a Confederate general) but is still visible.

The bell tower of Duke Chapel is modeled after the Bell Harry Tower of Canterbury Cathedral. It is 210 feet tall and 38 feet square at its base. Like the rest of the edifice, its main body is constructed of stone from the Duke Quarry, while its upper trimmings are of limestone from Bedford, Indiana. Housed in the tower is a 50-bell carillon, a gift from the Duke Endowment. The heaviest bell, G-natural, weighs 11,200 pounds, while the lightest bell weighs just 10.5 pounds.

The 77 chapel windows were designed and constructed over a three-year period by 15 artists and craftsmen, including S. Charles Jaekle of G. Owen Bonawit, Inc. They are constructed from over one million pieces of glass, imported from England, France, and Belgium and varying in thickness between ⅛ and 3⁄16 inch. The large, upper clerestory windows along the nave and chancel depict scenes from the Old Testament, while the smaller medallion windows along the walls of the nave aisles represent scenes from the New Testament.

Duke Chapel houses three large pipe organs, each constructed in a different style, which are used for religious services, ceremonies, recitals, and the study of organ performance. Additionally, a portable "box" organ belongs to the chapel and accompanies small groups and organizations.

The Crypt is located in the basement. Several important people of Duke University are interred in the crypt directly beneath the

Memorial Chapel, including three presidents of the university: William Preston Few (1924–40), Julian Deryl Hart (1960–63) with his wife Mary Johnson Hart, and Terry Sanford (1969–85) with his wife Margaret Rose Sanford. The wife of James B. Duke, Nanaline Holt Duke, is also buried in the crypt; along with James A. Thomas, chairman of the Duke Memorial Association; and James T. Cleland, former Dean of Duke Chapel, with his wife, Alice Mead Cleland.

23 How the Blue Devils Got Their Name

Following the end of World War I, then-Trinity College ended its 25-year ban on football. During the first year, the team was known either as the Blue and White or the Methodists; neighboring Wake Forest was the Baptists.

The student newspaper, *The Chronicle*, campaigned at the start of the 1921 season for the school to adopt "a catchy name, one of our own possession that would be instantly recognizable nationwide in songs, yells, and publicity."

Among the nominations were Blue Devils, named after the Chasseurs Alpins of the wartime French army. They had become well known for their unique training and alpine knowledge and for their distinctive blue uniform with flowing cape and beret. Irving Berlin even captured them in song as "strong and active, most attractive...those Devils, the Blue Devils of France."

The Chronicle then campaigned that a name choice be made from among Blue Titans, Blue Eagles, Polar Bears, Blue Devils, Royal Blues, or Blue Warriors, each using the school's blue and white colors. None of the nominations produced a decision. There was some criticism that the term "Devils" might elicit some opposition on the Methodist campus. As a result, the football season passed without any selection of a name.

At the start of the '22–23 school year, the editors of *The Archive* and *The Chanticleer* (yearbook) agreed that *The Chronicle* newspaper staff should choose a name. So editor in chief William B. Lander and managing editor Mike Bradshaw began calling the athletic teams the Blue Devils. They acknowledged that it was somewhat unpopular, but they thought it the best of the names nominated.

Neither the press nor the cheerleaders used the name at first. *The Chanticleer* even made fun of it. But, much to the surprise of Lander and Bradshaw, no opposition materialized, even from the administration. So *The Chronicle* staff continued to call the various teams the Blue Devils, and the name eventually caught on.

24 Eddie Cameron

Edmund McCullough "Eddie" Cameron is one of the most important people in the success of basketball at Duke University. So significant was he to the program that the university chose to rename Duke Indoor Stadium in honor of Cameron in 1972. Cameron did everything in the world of athletics as a player, coach, and administrator.

Cameron attended Culver Military Academy in Culver, Indiana, before he became a fullback at Washington and Lee University, where he served as captain of both the football and basketball teams. As a basketball coach, he served one year at Washington and Lee (1924–25) and then at Duke from 1928–42, compiling a career record of 234–104. Under Cameron the basketball team surged to a new level of success. His teams at Duke ran up a 226–99 overall record and a 119–56 record in conference play. In his 14 seasons as head coach at Duke, the Blue Devils won Southern Conference Championships in 1938, 1941, and 1942. He also served as football coach at Duke from 1942–45, putting together a 25–11–1 mark and a Sugar Bowl title, and served as athletic director from 1951–72.

While Cameron's teams played most of their games in Card Gymnasium, Duke Indoor Stadium, later to be named Cameron, was actually financed because of his success in football, as Duke used money earned in the school's first Rose Bowl appearance in 1939 and from the 1945 Sugar Bowl victory against Alabama to partially pay for construction of the dramatic new stadium. Cameron coached the dedicatory game at Duke Indoor and the first victory in the stadium on January 6, 1940, when Duke defeated Princeton University 36–27.

Cameron changed the face of Duke athletics. He was excited at opening new facilities such as the move from Hanes Football Field on East Campus to the new 35,000-seat stadium on West or the move to Duke Indoor. But he was equally pleased with the planning and opening of a long-awaited 18-hole golf course, expanded baseball and track facilities, and the construction of a new indoor swimming pool.

In 1946 Cameron became permanent director of physical education and athletics when legendary coach Wallace Wade returned to coach football. Cameron's active participation in Duke athletics spanned 46 years, from 1926 to 1972—the second longest tenure in the school's history. However, according to stories in the Duke archives, his unofficial contribution continued 16 more years after retirement until his death in 1988 at age 86. He held more different positions and exercised greater responsibility in athletics, on and off campus, than any other Duke administrator. He was a founder of the Atlantic Coast Conference. He chaired the basketball committee of the Southern and ACC conferences for decades, where he steadfastly supported the crowning of a champion. He also served on the selection committee for the National Football Hall of Fame and the governing committee of the Olympics.

25 Smell the Flowers at the Sarah P. Duke Gardens

Many a romance has bloomed in the Duke Gardens, located on the Duke main campus, just steps away from classrooms, administrative offices, and the chapel. Those romances that began in the Gardens have many times reached fruition with weddings in the very same locale. A place for special occasions or just a casual walk in the park, the Gardens offer solitude in the middle of the Duke campus, where many a Duke student has relaxed and dreamed about whatever brings a smile to their faces.

The idea of a public garden arose in the early 1930s due to the vision and enthusiasm of Dr. Frederic M. Hanes, an early member of the original faculty of Duke Medical School. Dr. Hanes possessed a special love for gardening and was determined to convert the debris-filled ravine, by which he walked daily, into a garden of his favorite flower, the iris. In the previous decade, the land had been under consideration for creation of a lake. But funds were short, and that project was abandoned. So the idea for a garden took root.

Dr. Hanes persuaded his friend, Sarah P. Duke, widow of one of the university's founders, Benjamin N. Duke, to give $20,000 to finance a garden that would bear her name. In 1935 more than 100 flower beds were in glorious bloom in the area that is now the

South Lawn. They included 40,000 irises, 25,000 daffodils, 10,000 small bulbs, and assorted annuals.

But by the time Sarah P. Duke died in 1936, the original gardens were in decline. Dr. Hanes convinced his daughter, Mary Duke Biddle, to construct a new garden on higher ground, as a fitting memorial to her mother. Ellen Biddle Shipman (1869–1950), a pioneer in American landscape design, was selected to design the plans for both the construction and the plantings for the new gardens. Sarah P. Duke Gardens was dedicated in April 1939.

Duke Gardens is considered Shipman's greatest work and a national architectural treasure. Most of the approximately 650 other gardens she designed have long since disappeared. Since that time Sarah P. Duke Gardens has developed dramatically and beautifully. There are five miles of allées, walks, and pathways throughout the gardens. It now features four distinct areas: the original terraces and their immediate surroundings, known as the Historic Gardens, including the Mary Duke Biddle Rose Garden and historic Roney Fountain; the H.L. Blomquist Garden of Native Plants, a representation of the flora of the southeastern United States; the W.L. Culberson Asiatic Arboretum, devoted to plants of eastern Asia; and the Doris Duke Center Gardens, including the new Charlotte Brody Discovery Garden.

26 Dick Groat

The first person to ever have their number retired at Duke in basketball—or any sport—was Richard Morrow Groat, better known as Dick Groat. At 5'11", 185 pounds, the Swissvale, Pennsylvania, native was truly a gifted athlete. A talented baseball and basketball player, he could do it all. "Baseball was always like work for me," Groat said. "Basketball was the sport that I loved."

His tireless work at baseball paid off very well for Groat. He was the 1960 National League MVP when he won the batting title with a .325 average and led the Pittsburgh Pirates to the 1960 World Series title from his shortstop position. In his 14-year major league career, he was named an All-Star five times and was on the 1964 World Series champion St. Louis Cardinals as well.

While Groat loved basketball, he knew baseball was where he would make his living under the eyes of one of baseball's greatest general managers, Branch Rickey. "I made a deal with Mr. Rickey. I was a junior at Duke. I went home and worked out for the Pirates in the summer before I went back to Duke," Groat explained. "After I had worked out, he invited my mother and father to come to a game at Forbes Field where the Pirates played. I was sitting in his booth and he turned to me—remember I am only 20, I'm still a minor—he says to me, 'young man, if you will sign a contract tonight, I'm going to start you against the Cincinnati Reds tomorrow night.' I said, 'Mr. Rickey that's not even fair, you know I want to play major league baseball, but I owe my senior year to Duke and I am going back to play basketball and baseball. But I promise you, you make the same offer to me next spring, and I will sign with the Pittsburgh Pirates.'

"He shook hands with me and said we had a deal," Groat continued. "He lived by that handshake. I never heard from him again that winter, actually saw him for a moment at the Teague Award dinner, but he really didn't say anything. We had a great year in baseball at Duke that year, winning the Southern Conference championship and then playing in the College World Series at Johnny Rosenblatt Stadium in Omaha. I got home on Sunday night, Mr. Rickey contacted me on Monday, I signed Monday night, showed up at the Pirates on Tuesday, watched the game

Tuesday night, pinch hit on Wednesday, and was in the lineup the rest of the season."

But Groat did have a stint in professional basketball as the No. 3 pick in the NBA draft of the Fort Wayne Pistons. "After that first summer with the Pirates, I went back to finish my degree at Duke," he explained. "I was taking classes on Monday, Wednesday, and Friday. I had an AAU basketball team that played all over the state of North Carolina in the evenings so I was pretty busy. The Fort Wayne Pistons drafted me pretty high, said they would fly me in commercially for games, so I signed a contract and played two or three weekends. I got grounded one Sunday night in Detroit and couldn't make class on Monday. So when I got back to Durham, I called the Pistons and told them I loved playing for them, but I couldn't afford to cut myself out of school and not graduate. I had worked too hard and my father would kill me if I didn't graduate from Duke. They told me they understood, and I figured my pro basketball career was over. A week later they called me back and said they needed me and they had it all worked out. They had a private plane that would get me back to Durham on Sunday night after our game so I could make my 8:15 Monday morning class. They upped my salary to where I was making twice what I was making in baseball. I had a ball playing for them and had some of the scariest trips in my life. I never had to practice—just play on the weekend, averaged 12 points per game, and had a ball. After that season, I served two years in the military, and when I got out, the Pirates doubled my salary, and I never went back to the NBA."

But even with all the accolades of the NBA and Major League Baseball, the finest memory for Groat is his final game in Duke Indoor Stadium against North Carolina, though it got off to a terrible start. "My father fell on the way to the game, my mother and sisters were with him, and they delayed the start of the game until they returned from the hospital," he explained.

Groat pumped in 17 points in the first half as Duke opened up a huge halftime lead. When Carolina rallied to bring it back to eight points at 58–50 in the second half, Groat promptly hit eight straight shots to gain control of the game. He finished with 48 points, then a school and Southern Conference record, hitting 19-of-37 field goal attempts and 10-of-11 from the free throw line. The 48 points by Groat still stands as the most points ever scored by a Duke player against North Carolina. "When Carolina made a run at us, I started shooting, and it seemed like everything I shot went in the basket," he explained, sitting in the lobby of a hotel in Raleigh prior to working as color analyst for the University of Pittsburgh Radio Network. "Shooters know when they get that hot hand. It's so strange. As a senior in high school, I had the most points I ever scored in my last game at home. At Duke it was the most I had ever scored in my final game at Duke. Once you get going, it seems like everything would go down. It's a wonderful feeling."

He was removed from the game with 15 seconds left to a prolonged standing ovation. When the teams left the floor, his Duke teammates carried him off on their shoulders. Groat broke down in tears in the locker room as he accepted congratulations from his teammates for his scoring performance. He returned to the court and spoke to the fans about their marvellous support. After he left the court with his uniform still wet with sweat, he sat in the Duke locker room, physically and emotionally worn out, and the Carolina team came into the locker room and shook his hand. Each Tar Heel congratulated him on an incredible performance. "I was sobbing in the locker room," he said, "and I didn't even know my dad was standing beside me, and he said to me, 'Christ Richard, you didn't even want to come down here and now you don't want to leave.'"

27 Dukies on TV

It is difficult to turn on a television during the college basketball season and not see either the Duke Blue Devils playing, one of their former players announcing a game, or analyzing it from the studio. They are everywhere.

Beginning with ESPN the Blue Devils not only are on television, but also are in very prominent roles as Jay Bilas has ascended to the top announcing team, while also doing a great deal of work in the studio. And in the ESPN studio, in Bristol, Connecticut, Jay Williams talks about the game every evening. He and Bilas also work together on ESPN's *College GameDay* each Saturday, and Shane Battier was added to the ESPN stable of analysts for college basketball in 2014–15.

After retiring from the NBA, Grant Hill went to work for NBA TV as an analyst and host of *Inside Stuff* along with working with CBS on the NCAA Final Four. During the season you can catch Mike Gminski doing analyst work for the ACC Network and Fox Sports South. Also during the season and NCAA Tournament, you can see Duke alumnus Seth Davis working in the CBS studio and breaking news and announcer Jim Spanarkel doing games. Along with working NCAA Tournament games, the former Duke star handles TV analyst jobs for the Brooklyn Nets of the NBA and works with NBA TV.

Gminski began his career working for the Charlotte Hornets doing both radio and television work prior to broadcasting college games. "As a player here, you deal with the national media. That's not to say that guys at Carolina or Kentucky or a lot of national programs don't," Gminski said. "But I think that's part of it. It taught me on the other side of the microphone how to deal with the media and how to deal with different mediums—print and radio and TV. I think that exposure helped me. If you take the time as a player to have an understanding of what the other side needs and have an appreciation for what they do, I think it helps."

And the players also spent time talking with each other and learning from each other. "Jason, when he was first getting in, talked to me a little bit," Gminski said. "The best advice I can give is to work and prepare as hard as you can for every game—overprepare. I think where guys fall short in making that transition is that they forget how hard you have to work to be good at anything. Guys who work as hard with their broadcasting as they did as a player are usually successful. The ones who walk in and strap the mic on and think they can do a good job—that's not usually how it works. It's also important to be yourself. The people who get into trouble are the ones who try to affect a persona—whether it's speech or enthusiasm—that they're not. That's the thing that's most readily apparent to the viewer. You have to go in and be your personality. Let that come through."

Williams said his broadcasting career is a whole new world. "At first it was very difficult addressing the camera," Williams said. "You have four other cameras around you. You have your earpiece, and your producer telling you, 'You have camera two. Turn around and face camera four.' And they're saying it while you're in the middle of a statement. You can't break concentration or lose sight of what you're saying. It was very difficult at first."

Alaa Abdelnaby has been working with the CBS Sports Network and Westwood One Radio for the past several years, following his start with NBA-TV. The former Duke big man believes the Duke experience makes them better players and announcers. "Even when we were playing before we were broadcasters, there were always these commonalities we had between each other," he said. "Jay [Bilas] was always well-spoken. I remember as I was coming in, he was leaving. I remember the quote he had: 'Wherever

I will go, I will always have that No. 21 jersey emblazoned on my heart.' "I remember thinking to myself, *That is really, really well said.*

"I wondered if I could ever get to that level—not just on the court, but the fact that he carried himself so well," he added. "Coming here, that's one of the side effects of being a Duke basketball player. Everyone speaks well. Not that it's a competition thing, it's that everybody is very, very positively nurtured. You're encouraged to do it. I'm comfortable talking [to the press] or on the air because of what I went through here."

Even the boss at CBS Sports, which has the rights to the NCAA Tournament and Final Four, is a Duke graduate. Sean McManus, the CBS Sports president, has an easy explanation for why so many Blue Devils are on the air. "Their performance—whether it's Jay Bilas or Grant Hill or Mike Gminski—speaks for itself," McManus said.

28 The Legend of Fred Lind

March 2, 1968 was just another day in Duke basketball lore that let you know there are magical powers within the rock walls of Duke Indoor Stadium.

Following four consecutive ACC regular season titles, three ACC Tournament championships, and three Final Four appearances from 1963–66, the Blue Devils had fallen back to an NIT appearance in 1967 but had moved back into the top 10 rankings in the country in 1968 behind the play of 6'8" senior All-American center Mike Lewis.

Senior Night in Duke Indoor Stadium would find Lewis facing a North Carolina team with one of the country's best big men in Rusty Clark. The third-ranked Tar Heels also were loaded with great players like Charlie Scott, Larry Miller, and Bill Bunting and would end the year losing to UCLA 78–55 for the national championship.

But this day would end up belonging to a seldom-used reserve junior member of the team by the name of Fred Lind. "I remember Coach Bubas telling me on Friday that he might need me in the game tomorrow, so be ready, and I thought, *Yeah, sure*," Lind said. "I knew it would take something big happening, like Mike fouling out for me to get in the game."

The Blue Devils figured they would play some man-to-man defense, and there was a possibility of foul trouble. "We figured we needed height to match the Tar Heels on the boards and we figured we might need Fred in case Mike Lewis got in foul trouble,"

Evocative Game Story

Bruce Phillips of *The* (Raleigh) *News&Observer* provided an evocative description of this epic Duke-Carolina game, which made a surprising star of Lind.

While mindful that about all the two teams were playing for on this particular day was pride, the Blue Devils and Tar Heels couldn't have been more dogged in their determination if an all-expense paid trip to the French Riviera was in the offing.

It was a swirling, mad, nose-to-nose struggle of closely matched gladiators who said to hell with style and grace and went at each other with cudgels. It was a test of nerves, gut, and stamina.

And it was an affray with an unlikely hero, moments of uncivilized savagery, and considering the factors and implausible winner.

So intense and furious was the battle, no one was left out of it. Players on the floor, players on the bench, coaches, 8,800 lucky ones inside Duke Indoor Stadium, and thousands by the telly were drawn into the fight, whether they wanted to be or not. You just can't be oblivious to a war like this.

Vic Bubas explained. "So in our practice sessions during the week, we kept telling Fred to be ready. As it turned out, the young man more than met the challenge. We couldn't have won without his fine contributions."

And Lewis did indeed foul out. "As a veteran player, I should have never gotten myself in foul trouble. I got myself in foul trouble somehow. Fred was given the opportunity and he just maximized it," Lewis said. "It was difficult to watch, and who knew it was going to go three overtimes? And I ended up sitting there for basically another half of the game, and I was going crazy."

Lind had scored just 12 points for the season coming into the regular-season finale against the Tar Heels. He hadn't played a minute against Carolina since scoring 20 points against the Tar Heels junior varsity his freshman year. He would end up playing 31 minutes, scoring 16 points, and pulling down nine rebounds.

When Lewis fouled out with 3:54 to go, Lind went the rest of the way. He hit a pair of foul shots at the end of regulation to force overtime and knocked down an 18-footer with seven seconds left in the first overtime to force the second one. He came up with several key rebounds in the second overtime. In the final five minutes, he nailed a hook shot, blocked a couple of shots, and grabbed a critical rebound—all to the delight of his fellow students, who carried him on their shoulders when he was the last to emerge from the locker room.

Lind's biggest moment came in the final overtime when he, in a space of seconds, blocked Rusty Clark's layup from behind, looped a left-handed shot to give Duke an 83–82 lead, and then blocked a shot by Dick Grubar. "I just saw an opening," he said of the clinching basket. "I'm right-handed, but the shot called for a left-handed shot. I didn't hesitate."

But Lind didn't do it all alone. He had some great help from two unsung heroes, Steve Vandenberg and Joe Kennedy. Vandenberg had been held to three points in the first half and seven for the game. He exploded in the overtime, scoring all four of the Blue Devils baskets in the second overtime and hitting the game winning shot. Kennedy held Larry Miller to 15 points, and the All-American did not score a field goal in the last 25 minutes of play. "Joe Kennedy wanted the challenge of guarding Larry Miller and he did a fine job," Bubas said. "The fact that Kennedy welcomed that challenge tells you something about this ballclub."

While Bubas was getting tossed into the shower and Lind was basking in the glow of being the hero, the Tar Heels trudged down the long tunnel from Duke Indoor Stadium to their locker room in the basement of Card Gymnasium.

Smith came out of the locker room, leaned against the wall, and took a drag on his cigarette. "Lind was great," Smith said. "Coach Bubas must feel very good to have someone like Lind to come in and do such a tremendous job. I'd say they must have hit a fantastic percentage of their shots in the overtime. They have wonderful depth."

29 The Dominating 1999 Team

The signing of William Avery, Shane Battier, Elton Brand, and Chris Burgess led to one of the strongest teams in Duke history, especially when they joined forces with co-captains Chris Carrawell and Trajan Langdon. In 1999 the Blue Devils completed the coveted Triple Crown, winning three games against North Carolina, and those three contests were won by an average of 18.3 points. Even the ACC Championship Game in Charlotte wasn't that close with Duke winning 96–73. Duke spent basically the entire season ranked as either the No. 1 or No. 2 team in the nation and went 16–0 in the ACC. "I don't remember a team dominating the league the way they have," said North Carolina head coach Bill Guthridge.

The Blue Devils then rolled through the regional portion of the NCAA Tournament, winning by an incredible average of 29.5 points in their first four games. The Final Four was set for sunny St. Petersburg, Florida, where Duke stayed at the posh Don CeSar hotel. It is not your run-of-the-mill hotel. It's not even your run-of-the-mill luxury hotel. This hotel is a destination, a landmark. Opened in 1928 it became renowned as the playground on the Gulf Coast for America's pampered rich at the height of the Jazz Age and it still serves as a popular retreat for the rich and famous of today. The long elevated entrance lined with tall palm trees, the pool overlooking the Gulf of Mexico, luxurious rooms, and on-site restaurants made it one of the finest hotels any Duke team had ever stayed in.

Add in the richness of the Final Four—with all the big-time givers and stars checking in at the hotel—and this Final Four had a feel like no other. The team went through walk-through in the spacious, immaculate ballroom, which had been laid out to resemble a basketball court, and parties at the hotel included the likes of movie stars like Kevin Costner.

In the semifinals the Blue Devils faced their first real test of the season since they lost their only game 77–75 to Cincinnati in the Great Alaska Shootout in November. Thirty-one consecutive wins later, the top-ranked Blue Devils faced the No. 2-ranked Michigan State Spartans and crafty coach Tom Izzo. After taking a 32–20 halftime lead, the Blue Devils were puzzled by the Spartans' zone defense and the fact that Brand picked up his fourth foul early in the second half, but Duke still ended up winning the game 68–62. Though it was a win, it was the Blue Devils' lowest scoring output of the season and put questions into everyone's minds as they headed into Monday night's national championship game.

In typical Duke fashion, Battier refuted any talk of offensive woes with a comment on the Blue Devils' total play. "I don't think it was a bad game for us," he said. "We had a heck of a game defensively and on the boards. We're never going to judge ourselves on whether or not our shots go down."

Two nights later in the national championship game against No. 3 Connecticut, Mike Krzyzewski would judge one shot not going down and the way it was taken as a determining factor in the game. In the middle of the second half, Corey Maggette took a turnaround, fadeaway jumper from the middle of the lane that missed badly. It wasn't the miss that bothered Krzyzewski so much as it was the type of shot taken. Wild shots weren't part of the Blue Devils' motion offense.

Maggette was immediately replaced, and after the freshman sat on the bench several minutes, assistant coach Quin Snyder figured it was time to remind Krzyzewski to get the best athlete on either team, a guy who can jump out of the gym, back in the game. A few minutes later, Maggette reappeared in the game, which came down to a couple of missed opportunities by the Blue Devils at the end of the game. Langdon, who led Duke with 25 points, had the ball with a chance to tie the game, but he traveled as he spun in the lane with 5.4 seconds left, and the Blue Devils fell to Connecticut 77–74.

Following the game Krzyzewski's hip was in such bad shape that he had to be helped into a golf cart to take him to the postgame press conference. When he returned to Durham, he had the hip operation and then came the defections to the NBA. First there was Brand, who was expected to leave. Then, without Krzyzewski's blessing, Avery and Maggette departed. In fact Avery decided to leave after Krzyzewski told him he should stay.

For the first time Duke was facing defections—players leaving early for the NBA and changing the face of the program. A program that wrapped itself around four-year players like Johnny Dawkins,

Danny Ferry, Christian Laettner, and Grant Hill had amassed an incredible 69–6 record over the last two seasons with this current group. The basketball world was changing, and this was the first time Duke had felt the sting of the NBA reaching down and taking away its most talented players. It really bothered Krzyzewski, who was a relationship coach and loved developing players over a four-year period. "When they all decided to leave, it hurt my feelings a little bit," he explained. "I was sorry to see them go because you can't establish as strong a relationship in one or two years as you can in four. I could understand Elton's situation. He had missed a lot of time as a freshman with a broken foot, and the risk of something like that happening again was hanging over him."

30 Coach K and USA Basketball

Mike Krzyzewski's leadership abilities haven't been limited to the college ranks. He has been a part of 14 medal-winning USA Basketball teams, beginning with a gold medal as an assistant coach at the 1979 Pan American Games. He has been a part of 10 gold medal-winning teams as well as two silver medal and two bronze medal programs over the past 33 years. After becoming the head coach of the men's senior national team in 2005, Krzyzewski has led the program to a 75–1 record in international competitions, including an active streak of 63 consecutive wins. "He's successful because he understands his audience and he understands how to adapt—he's a great communicator," said Los Angeles Lakers star Kobe Bryant, who played for Krzyzewski on two U.S. national teams in the Olympic Games. "He's very passionate about his message, very passionate about the game."

After winning the gold medal at the 2008 Olympics in Beijing, the Team USA players, including Carlos Boozer (behind Coach K), place their medals on the neck of their coach, Mike Krzyzewski. (Getty Images)

90

Krzyzewski's involvement with the USA men's senior national team began after USA basketball had suffered a tailspin following a sixth-place finish at the 2002 World Championships and bronze medal showing at the 2004 Olympics. USA Basketball chairman Jerry Colangelo tabbed Mike Krzyzewski to lead the resurrection of the program on October 26, 2005.

Over the next six international events, spanning eight years, Coach K and Team USA won gold medals at the 2007 FIBA Americas Championship, 2008 Olympics in Beijing, 2010 FIBA World Championship, 2012 Olympics in London, and the 2014 FIBA World Cup as well as a bronze medal at the 2006 FIBA World Championship. Krzyzewski and Team USA suffered their only loss together in the 2006 FIBA World Championship in the semifinals against Greece. The program has responded by winning the next 63 games to re-establish the U.S. as the preeminent basketball power in the world.

Krzyzewski helped USA Basketball regain its position in international basketball by instilling the same team-first principles he utilizes as the foundation for success at Duke. He helped build a program that achieved its ultimate goal by claiming the 2008 Olympic gold medal with a 118–107 win against Spain. In the process Team USA also restored a tarnished image by winning over fans and fellow athletes. While earning praise for its unselfish play on the court, members of Team USA were equally admired for their patriotic support of fellow Americans in their quests for medals.

On July 21, 2009, it was announced that Krzyzewski would return as the head coach of the USA Basketball national team, and in the 2012 Olympics, he became the first U.S. coach of multiple Olympic teams since the legendary Henry Iba, who won gold in 1964 and 1968 and coached the team that lost the controversial 1972 gold medal game to the Soviet Union.

Team USA once again claimed gold in 2012 with a 107–100 win against Spain. Although some experts speculated that outside shooting could be the downfall of the 2012 squad, Coach K and his staff gave the players the confidence to take their open shots against the international teams' zone defenses. The group, led by Kevin Durant and Carmelo Anthony, responded by setting an Olympic record with 129 three-point field goals and shooting

Other Duke Figures and the Olympics

Duke has a long history of success in international basketball competition dating back to 1964 when Jeff Mullins became the first Blue Devil to play for and win a gold medal with the U.S. Olympic basketball team.

Since that initial appearance, Duke players and coaches have competed on the international stage nearly 150 times, winning 74 medals along the way. Blue Devils players and coaches have accounted for 54 gold medals in international competition through the years, including five from Mike Krzyzewski as a national team head coach. Mullins, Tate Armstrong in 1976, Christian Laettner in 1992, Grant Hill in 1996, and Carlos Boozer in 2008 each have Olympic gold medals. Former Blue Devils standout and assistant coach Johnny Dawkins was an alternate on the 1986 Olympic team and was also a part of the staff for 2008 Olympic team.

Five Blue Devils have played in the Olympic Games for countries other than the United States—Cameron Hall in 1976, Dan Meagher in 1984, and Greg Newton in 2000 for Canada. In the 2000 Olympic Games in Sydney, Crawford Palmer captured a silver medal for France. Luol Deng played for the host Great Britain team in 2012.

Duke's consistent presence on the international scene is evident by the program having at least one current or former Blue Devil compete on a USA Basketball team every year since 1988. "Duke players have been pretty well schooled fundamentally," said USA Basketball chairman Jerry Colangelo. "They have been well coached and really understand what it takes to be successful and what it necessitates in the way of work. So it is really good bloodlines."

44 percent from three-point range during the tournament. Team USA's finest shooting performance came in a 156–73 win against Nigeria in pool play. Krzyzewski's group set Olympic records for three-pointers (29, including 10 from Anthony), three-point percentage (.630), and points scored (156) in the win.

Krzyzewski announced after the 2012 Olympics he would not be returning to Team USA, but in May of 2013, he said that he had changed his mind and would return as head coach from 2013–16, including the 2016 Olympic games in Rio.

31 Gman

Growing up in Monroe, Connecticut, Mike Gminski had always been big and a good athlete for a kid his size. At age 11 he was 6'1" and won the national punt, pass, and kick competition. Very intelligent and in control of his life, the gentle giant had a plan. The summer before his sophomore year, he decided he would graduate in three years and took 14 classes between September and June. That summer he began visiting colleges, hoping to find one where he could continue his education and also play basketball.

Monroe High School coach Bob Baroni was very protective of Gminski, whom both Baroni and the 16-year-old's parents knew could be a valuable asset to the right college program. Because Gminski was also an honor student, they figured a long list of schools would be after the kid who was still growing. Gminski's first campus visit was to Duke, and that's all he needed. He was in Durham on a gorgeous October weekend with the fall foliage in its colorful glory, and the soaring Gothic campus almost calling his name. Gminski returned to Monroe, graduated early, and arrived at Duke as a peach-faced jolly giant in late August of 1976. His blond bushy hair made him seem even taller than 6'11". "The big kid is here," Blue Devils head coach Bill Foster said whimsically.

Gminski got off to a huge start as a freshman, averaging 15.3 points and 10.7 rebounds per game and subsequently being named ACC Co-Rookie of the Year in 1977. During his sophomore year, Gminski led Duke to the ACC championship and the NCAA championship title game. Gminski averaged 20 points and 10 rebounds per game on his way to earning first team All-ACC, All-NCAA Final Four, and All-East Region honors. In Gminski's junior season, he was named ACC Player of the Year and team Co-MVP along with Jim Spanarkel. Gminski averaged 18.8 points per game and 9.2 rebounds as the Blue Devils claimed a first-place tie in the ACC. In Gminski's senior year, he was a first team All-American selection and averaged 21.3 points and 10.9 rebounds per game. For the third time, Gminski was All-ACC and was named to the All-ACC Tournament first team. At the time of graduation, he was Duke's career leader in points (2,323), rebounds (1,242), and blocked shots (345). His No. 43 jersey was just the second jersey to be retired at Duke.

Gminski was drafted in the first round as the No. 7 overall pick by the New Jersey Nets in the 1980 NBA Draft. He played for the Nets from 1981 to 1988 and went on to play with the Philadelphia 76ers, as well as the Charlotte Hornets, before finishing his career with the Milwaukee Bucks, where he finally got to wear No. 43 after wearing No. 42 for the 76ers and Hornets. His best season in the NBA came with the 76ers in 1988–89 when he averaged 17.2 points and 9.4 rebounds per game. During his 1989–90 season with the 76ers, he and former Blue Devil Johnny Dawkins led the Sixers to the Atlantic Division title and the East Conference semifinals. Following his retirement from the NBA, Gminski became a radio and television analyst for the Charlotte

Hornets and has continued his television work with Fox Sports, ACC Network, and CBS. For the latter he also covers NCAA Tournament games.

32 The Fight

Many consider "the Fight" between Duke and North Carolina players in Duke Indoor Stadium (later renamed Cameron Indoor Stadium) in 1961 as one of the worst ever in the game of basketball. The fight, which came at the end of the February 4, 1961 game, had no significance on the outcome but did show that the Duke-Carolina rivalry had reached a new level of intensity.

This was the first time that Duke and Carolina had played with each being ranked among the top five programs in the country. Duke (15–1) was ranked fourth while North Carolina (14–2) was ranked fifth. Both teams were 7–0 in ACC play, and the Blue Devils' only loss (76–71) had come at the hands of the Tar Heels in the finals of the Dixie Classic when Doug Moe had shut down Blue Devils sophomore star Art Heyman.

The brawl in the February 4 game began with only seconds left in the game and Duke leading 81–75. Heyman, who had scored 36 points on 11 field goals and 14 free throws, had just hit two of those free throws with 15 seconds left in the game to clinch the win for the Blue Devils. Trying to score in a hurry, Larry Brown of Carolina dribbled the length of the court as time was running out and Duke head coach Vic Bubas yelled down to his defense not to foul. Brown and Heyman were both of the Jewish faith and playmaking guards from Long Island, New York.

In those days the benches at Duke were on the baselines under the baskets, and spitting at each other was a part of the game in the 1950s. As Brown drove along the baseline, Heyman spit at him and grabbed him for what would be an obvious foul. Brown threw the ball at Heyman and began swinging. The UNC players, led by Moe, came off their bench and jumped Heyman, forcing him to the floor before he fought his way out of the pile and started swinging wildly at anyone who came near him. By that time players from both teams, along with dozens of fans, were on the court, and the 10 Durham policemen in attendance were powerless to stop the isolated skirmishes popping up everywhere. "Larry and Art started it," UNC alum Charlie Schaffer said, "but then everyone got involved, and the fight lasted a good 10 minutes before they could break it up."

Referee Charlie Eckman ejected Heyman from the game for the hard foul, and suddenly Heyman and Brown were swinging at each other. The fight started right in front of the Carolina bench, and a free-for-all developed with Heyman being stormed by eight Tar Heels. "When Heyman went to the floor from the weight of the wave of Tar Heels descending upon him, he was punched and kicked from all directions. How he ever climbed to his feet where he could fight back was miraculous," wrote Jack Horner of the *Durham Morning Herald*. "There must have been 40 or 50 individuals on the floor, swinging wildly in all directions at the height of the minute or so of fisticuffs. It was a sad commentary to what had been a brilliantly played contest by two of the nation's top ranked teams."

ACC commissioner James Weaver suspended Heyman and Carolina's Brown and Donnie Walsh from playing for the remainder of the ACC season. Heyman's suspension was appealed by Duke, and Weaver traveled from Greensboro, North Carolina, to Durham to view the film of the game to make a decision on the suspensions. "We're sitting in the Duke locker room with the commissioner of the ACC," explained Duke assistant coach Bucky Waters. "He must have run over the film of the game 10 times. All of a sudden, the commissioner chuckles, he says, 'Never mind the altercation, watch Charlie Eckman.'"

Eckman was a very well-known and colorful referee of the era. In his career he served as an NBA basketball coach, minor league baseball player, broadcaster, author, and NCAA and NBA basketball referee. He officiated more than 3,500 games in 29 years. "As we watched we saw Eckman jump right into the eye of the storm trying to separate everyone, and suddenly he popped out when the melee expanded and headed for the netting behind the basket stanchion," Waters said. "Charlie doesn't come out from behind the basket until the fight is over and he comes out strutting in charge of everything. It was hilarious; everyone in the room was laughing."

After Weaver saw the film, he rescinded much of the blame from Heyman but kept the suspension in place. "After viewing the film, I realize Heyman did not start the fight," Weaver told the media. "The first two punches were thrown by Larry Brown. Heyman was merely defending himself."

Weaver, though, didn't waver on his suspension, and the Blue Devils, who had moved to No. 3 in the country after the win against Carolina, were never the same. They ended the year losing to a Wake Forest team with Billy Packer and Len Chappell in the ACC Tournament final and falling to a 22–6 overall record.

33 The War of 1989

Hosting its last ACC Tournament, The Omni in Atlanta, Georgia, was a tight arena by today's standards with funky angles and narrow aisles between the seating sections. Knowing how the Duke-Carolina rivalry was festering since the first game in Durham, the ACC foolishly assigned fans from the schools to adjacent sections separated by one of those thin aisles. It was a mild March 12 afternoon, and the body heat in the building was stifling and almost unbearable for some. The action on the court began aggressively and escalated from there.

Duke's Danny Ferry, a consensus All-American, was playing for the last time against the school he once loved and he was now loathed by its fans, who chanted "Fer-ry! Fer-ry!" every time he touched the ball. Some eye-popping statistics helped Duke overcome a dismal shooting day of 39 percent from the floor and only 3-of-23 from the three-point line. In all there were 59 free throws attempted on 49 total fouls called by officials John Moreau, Dick Paparo, and Lenny Wirtz. The Tar Heels shot just under 50 percent, but they turned the ball over eight more times than Duke, which also had 14 steals compared to Carolina's eight. The play under the basket and hand-to-hand combat on the perimeter were so aggressive that both coaches wound up yelling at opposing players to take it easy.

Less than two and a half minutes into the second half, Scott Williams challenged an inside shot by Duke freshman Christian Laettner and was charged with a foul that sent Laettner to the free throw line. UNC coach Dean Smith called Williams to come over to the Carolina bench to talk with him, and, as Williams walked past the Duke bench, Mike Krzyzewski gave Williams an earful, telling him he thought it was a dirty play. "I thought it was a fla-grant foul and I don't care for that," Krzyzewski said. "That's when somebody gets hurt."

Smith, in turn, yelled at Krzyzewski. "Hey, don't talk to my players," Smith yelled in his Kansas twang to Krzyzewski just 30 feet away.

"Hey, Dean, fuck you!" Krzyzewski yelled back, and his words traveled on a light rail along the scorer's table between the benches. Almost everyone sitting there heard the exchange.

Six minutes later things escalated further as Duke's Phil Henderson and Carolina's King Rice and Kevin Madden would be involved in yet another confrontation. "I was cutting through the lane, and Phil caught me in the throat with an elbow," King Rice explained.

The ball went out of bounds, and timeout was called. The two then headed for their respective benches and as they did they bumped shoulders. To Henderson it looked like Rice threw his shoulder into him on purpose. Henderson then headed into the Tar Heels huddle and pushed Madden, causing both benches to erupt and Henderson to earn a technical. "There were cheap shots out there all day. I just got caught," said Henderson following the game. "It was a retaliation thing, but I shouldn't have done it."

During the intense, physical contest, Ferry received a long fingernail scratch from left cheek to ear, and J.R. Reid had a large bump under his right eye. "I went up for a shot on the wing, and J.R. tried to put a hand in my face on the way up and scratched me," Ferry said.

The two big men also spent a great deal of the game talking trash to each other. With 4:20 left in the game, Reid hit a jumper from the lane as Ferry crashed to the floor. Reid looked down and shouted at Ferry. The Duke senior walked off the court with a bloody face after missing all seven of his three-pointers, including the last, a 75-foot heave that would have tied the score. "The ball did all it could to go in there," Reid said. "It was close. If it had gone in, I think it would have been their game. But it was our day in the sun."

Carolina hung on to win 77–74 and cut down the ACC nets for the first time since 1982. The game is still remembered by those in attendance as among the most intense sporting events they ever witnessed in person. Though Duke lost the battle, fans can take some solace in the fact that the Blue Devils won the war, reaching the Final Four for the second consecutive season—and what would become the second of five straight trips—while UNC lost in the regional semifinal to Michigan.

34 Dennard and Banks— So Long and Thanks

Walking up to Cameron Indoor Stadium in the afternoon sun, you could see a number of young people dressed in white T-shirts with two sketched out faces and a saying on the shirts—"Dennard and Banks—So Long and Thanks." It was Senior Day 1981 at Duke for two of the greatest characters to ever don a Duke uniform.

The first three years of their careers had been an almost Cinderella-like journey at Duke, playing for a national championship, being ranked No. 1 in the nation, being on covers of magazines, and being on national television. Things changed in their final year. Their senior year had not been what these seniors had hoped for. They had watched as the coach they came to play for walked away from the program.

In stepped a one-time Captain in the U.S. Army as their head coach, a guy who not only coached at the Military Academy, but also played there as well. He was coming from a job where discipline both on and off the court was a fact.

Discipline was not in the vocabulary of Banks and Dennard. Nicknamed "Tinkerbell," Banks had missed several practices over the years traveling back to Philadelphia to take care of family and had even been investigated for involvement with drugs at one point in his career. Dennard appeared on the cover of *Tobacco Road* publication nude with a basketball in the most appropriate of spots. He once left after the end of the season and drove with his head out the sun roof down to Florida for "his" spring break. Reverse dunks, windmill dunks, and over-the-head passes were much more the language of these two than any words used by members of the U.S. Army.

But the young head coach from Army liked that they knew how to win and that they played the game at one speed—full. So Krzyzewski knew he needed them and vowed he would make it through their senior season. "One year," he would say on several occasions. The 34-year-old had just one season to make it with them.

Banks was the Mr. All-Everything from Philadelphia, the big city of Brotherly Love. Dennard hailed from King, North Carolina. Unless you are from the state of North Carolina, there is no way you know where King is located. But the two struck up a relationship as soon as they arrived on campus in the summer prior to their freshman year. "We were both in Durham that summer," Dennard explained. "Gene was in a pre-college, summer school program, and I was working odd jobs around town. We played every night in the intramural building because they were tearing up the original floor in Cameron Indoor Stadium that summer."

The IM Building was just a basic gymnasium with a rubber floor and metal girders sticking out of the pre-fabricated building. "Some of the greatest pickup games I every played in were played in that old building," he continued. "Gene and I would light each other up, playing incredibly hard against each other, having a ball just playing basketball and gaining a great deal of respect for each other's game. We battled as competitors and became blood brothers, dark blue brothers to this day."

Four years later it was Senior Day in a packed Cameron Indoor Stadium with the Blue Devils, 14–11, playing their regular season finale against the No. 11 Tar Heels. Being the charismatic person that he was, Banks could say no to no one, and basically half the city of Durham was told by Banks that there would be tickets waiting for them at the door for this game. Most of them found a way to get in the building.

In those days the seniors were introduced and ran off the bench in a darkened gym with just a spotlight shining on midcourt. As the assistant sports information director, it was my job to make sure the senior introductions went off without any problems. I was sitting on the bench right beside the team where I could communicate with Dr. Art Chandler, the stadium public address announcer.

As the first senior, Jim Suddath, was announced, I looked around behind the bench in the bleachers to see where Banks had placed the box of roses he brought with him to the game and I had seen early in the day in his locker.

No roses.

I grabbed Banks by the shoulder and said, "Where are the roses?"

"You really think I should do it?" he asked.

"If you want to, Tink, it's your Senior Day," I said.

"They're back in my locker."

I grabbed a manager and sent him back to the locker room and decided Suddath had a much better college career than people thought and needed more time in the spotlight.

Dennard was next and spent what seemed like an eternity in the spotlight before the manager scurried around the back of the players on the bench and laid the white box with red roses behind Banks.

I nodded at him, saw Krzyzewski give me a look with a furrowed forehead, and I just grinned at him. As Banks was introduced to a thunderous applause, he tossed roses to all four corners of the building and then went to midcourt, where he grabbed his teammate Dennard and gave him a big hug.

Dennard, grinning the whole time, reminded Banks that he was full of shit and returned the hug. So it was no surprise that the two would hook up on one of the most coveted shots in Duke basketball history. "Two seconds to go—tie game at 56," Dennard explained. "Sam Perkins at the line—we have only one timeout. No matter what happened with the free throws, whether Sam made them or missed them, Coach Krzyzewski told us we were to call timeout. He made both of them, and before I could call timeout, Dean Smith called timeout for Carolina, which gave us an extra timeout, which proved to be a tactical error. We go into the huddle, and Coach Krzyzewski says to just get the ball to halfcourt and call timeout. We would not have had that opportunity if Dean hadn't called timeout to set up his defense. I threw it to Tommy Emma at midcourt, and he quickly called timeout."

Over the years the two have laughed about what ensued in the huddle. "K called the play for Chip Engelland because everyone would think I would be going to Gene, so we would use Gene as a decoy," Dennard explained. "Chip was a great shooter, but he was a sophomore, and this was our senior night, so Coach drew the play up, and Gene was supposed to set a pick down the baseline, and Chip came over to the sideline and hit the corner jumper. When we broke the huddle, I looked at Gene, he looked at me, and we really never had to talk. I did say, 'You know what to do, come to the top.'...I led him to where he had to turn; it wasn't something I did consciously. If I had thrown it directly to him, he wouldn't have time to catch, turn, and shoot. By leading him to the open spot he was able to catch it and shoot. The ball went in, and the place went crazy. It was the loudest I've ever heard the building for over a minute."

Dennard and Banks had a certain synchronicity. "Kenny and I never discussed what we were going to do; we just knew," Banks said. "I would never have a chance to make the shot if it weren't for the pass to set me up in the right spot. I was able to catch it moving and shoot it. I knew Perkins was following me so when I turned I figured he would be there but just arched it over his hand."

When the ball swished through the net, Cameron Indoor Stadium erupted. The shot by Banks had tied the game, and in his first season as the Duke head coach, Coach K was looking at the chance to win his third game of the season over a nationally ranked team and first over North Carolina.

But the shot had only tied the game, and there was still an overtime period to be played. Banks wasn't about to let the Blue Devils lose and have Carolina spoil his Senior Day. He did what Banks could do with his Adonis-like body. He rebounded, scored, and took over the game. Strapping the Blue Devils to his back, he scored six of the eight shots in the extra session, the final two coming with 12 seconds left to seal the win 66–65.

For Duke students and fans, February 28, 1981, may well have been the perfect day. A win against Carolina on Senior Day in Cameron Indoor Stadium to spoil Dean Smith's 50th birthday combined with a one-hour drive to Greensboro to the Greensboro Coliseum and the Bruce Springsteen concert.

35 Wojo's Senior Day

It would be only fitting that Mike Krzyzewski would call Steve Wojciechowski's senior game at Duke, "one of the greatest one-point games in the history of basketball."

Krzyzewski loved Wojo. They were kindred spirits. Krzyzewski grew up on the tough streets of South Side Chicago while Wojo grew up in Baltimore; his father was a worker on the docks.

Wojo was the epitome of what Krzyzewski wanted in a player. He was tough, hard-nosed, and intense. He wasn't blessed with natural talent; he was a player who had to work his way to being a great basketball player. He played each and every play like it was his last. Wojo was the essence of Krzyzewski on the court. He loved Wojo—still does.

It had been a long journey for Wojo, and his four years in college must have seemed like a lifetime. He began his Blue Devils career during the tumultuous 1994–95 season. A season that began with him starting in the fourth game of his career then tumbled through the death of his high school coach and mentor at Christmas, losing the coach he came to play for at Duke two weeks later, and then being benched as a starter and losing games.

"It was a nightmare," he explained heading into his final game in Cameron. "That's the best way that I can describe it. It seemed like everything that could possibly go wrong for me went wrong. I didn't handle it as well as I could or as well as I would if it would happen to me now. But that was all part of the maturation process that I had to go through to get to where I am now."

That maturation process was being a major part of a rebuild that included an ACC regular season championship team in 1997, but as he headed into his senior game against the Tar Heels, he had been on the winning side of this rivalry just once.

Earlier in the 1998 season, ranked as the No. 1 and No. 2 teams in the nation, respectively, Duke and Carolina met in Chapel Hill. It was only the second time in the history of the rivalry that the two met as the top teams in the nation. The Blue Devils came in with a 20–1 record with the lone loss at Michigan back in December.

The game pulled incredible numbers on both ESPN2 and the Raycom broadcast with the game being seen in more than 1.6 million households. The power of the Duke-Carolina game even reached into the NBA with this contest. On Thursday evening, the Charlotte Hornets' home game with the Vancouver Grizzlies, they announced 21,984 tickets had been sold, but only about 14,000 to 15,000 showed up for the game. That was the smallest attendance at that time in the history of the franchise. Hornets coach Dave Cowens' postgame press conference lasted just two minutes, and he ended it by saying, "Alright guys, let's go watch the game."

What the fans in the arena and on television watched was the *Antawn Jamison Show*. The No. 2-ranked Tar Heels didn't need much else as Jamison exploded for 35 points and 11 rebounds as they routed the Blue Devils 97–73. As the final second ticked off the clock, the Carolina student body stormed the court and celebrated once again beating their rival, this time the No. 1 team in the nation. "They are the real deal, they are a heck of a team," said Krzyzewski after the game. "It's obvious in their celebration how much they wanted to beat us and how happy they were. The game meant a lot to them, which it should."

I walked out of the Smith Center with Chris Carrawell, who said, "I'm going to remember this night, and my teammates will also. We're going to play them again and we'll be ready this time. They were ready for us tonight, and we'll be ready for them the next time we meet."

The next time would come on February 28. With the ACC regular season title up for grabs, it was the regular season finale and Senior Night. For the first 29 minutes of the game, it looked like the Tar Heels were well on their way to capturing their 10th win in the last 11 with their archrivals.

But it was the last 11 minutes that the Blue Devils shined with Wojciechowski setting the tone with his intensity, Elton Brand with his strong inside play, and Roshown McLeod with some timely buckets.

The Blue Devils fell behind 18–4 at the start of the game, and it looked like the seniors on this Duke team would be losing their final game in Cameron Indoor Stadium to their dreaded rivals. At the half, in an incredibly hot Cameron Indoor Stadium, the Blue Devils trailed 42–30. Krzyzewski had already sweat through his white dress shirt. When he returned to the floor for the second half, he had on a Nike polo-style shirt with his dark jacket. "It was all wet," he explained. "I was so mad that we were playing so poorly and working to try and get us back in the game. It was just all wet, so I decided to go with my cool look—as cool as you can look at 51."

The new look didn't seem to help much, and with 11:39 left in the game, the Blue Devils trailed by 17 points.

Suddenly the Blue Devils came alive. Senior McLeod and freshman Brand began to pound the Tar Heels inside. The Blue Devils scored 10 of their last 13 field goals in the paint and held Jamison to just one tip-in and one free throw over the last 11 minutes. All in all the Blue Devils scored on 15 of their last 18 possessions while holding Carolina to just two field goals in the last 11:39 of the game.

The comeback began when William Avery drove inside for a bucket and made two free throws. Brand, who came off the bench, playing in just his third game since having a cast removed from his foot, scored eight points in three minutes to make it a seven-point game. Avery made it 70–64 with a three just inside the six-minute mark, and McLeod finished off a 23-point performance with six points in the last three minutes, including a game-winning drive over Jamison with 59 seconds left. McLeod also made two big defensive plays at the end by stealing a lob pass and tying up Vince Carter for a jump ball with 45 seconds left to give Duke possession.

The key to the win, though, was the play of Wojciechowski, who with the help of assistant coach Johnny Dawkins from the bench, began to feed the ball to Brand on the low post where he could power inside and score. Each time the Blue Devils would bring the ball down to the offensive end late in the second half, Brand would set up, and Dawkins would scream, "Now," when he wanted Wojo to feed the ball to Brand. It worked to perfection.

Wojciechowski scored just one point, but his 11 assists and leadership on the court were the largest contributors to the 77–75 win and their second straight ACC regular season title.

As the game ended, the emotions of four years at Duke and what Wojo had learned from his head coach swelled over, and instead of hugging his teammates or any fans, Wojo made a beeline running straight to Krzyzewski, pushing players out of the way and giving his coach a huge hug. "Wojo has played well here," Krzyzewski said. "With all of it on the table—everything at stake today and Senior Day and all that kind of stuff—for him to get 11 assists and one turnover and play great D, it is one of the great performances here."

36 Washington Duke

George Washington Duke said that he considered himself very poor twice in his life—first, when he began making a living with nothing but "willing hands and a stout heart" and secondly upon returning to his home after the Civil War. In the first instance, he made a modest living farming and in the second he grew wealthy through manufacturing tobacco products.

With the assistance of his two sons, Benjamin Newton and James Buchanan, and his daughter, Mary Elizabeth, Washington Duke's early manufacturing business consisted of beating cured tobacco by hand with sticks, sifting it through a fine wire sieve, and packing it in small bags for sale. Selling the finished product took the Dukes through as many as 32 states, after which they would return and work the farm. By 1880 James B. Duke turned the firm of W. Duke Sons & Co. toward the mass manufacture and marketing of a new product—cigarettes. He emerged as president of the American Tobacco Company, which quickly became a multinational corporation.

Thus, at the age of 60, Washington Duke retired from the business and devoted himself to his family, his church, and the Republican Party. In 1901 Duke and his sons established Durham's first hospital for African Americans, Lincoln Hospital on Proctor Street. His civic-mindedness and love of the Methodist Church coalesced in 1890 with the successful campaign to persuade the Methodist-related Trinity College to relocate to the bustling city of Durham. Duke's offer of $85,000 and later donations totaling $300,000 for the college's endowment began a family philanthropic pattern that was continued by his sons and daughters and their children. In 1896 he offered Trinity an endowment of

$100,000 on the condition that women be admitted as residential students "placing them in the future on an equal footing" with the male students. This act attracted widespread attention. The National Suffrage Association offered Duke its vice presidency (which he declined). Duke later withdrew the condition since he did not want to interfere in any way in the administration of the college and felt that then-President Kilgo knew where he stood.

At first quietly, but consistently by Benjamin, and later spectacularly by James B., the family's contributions strengthened Trinity College and prepared it for its dramatic growth into a university. At the urging of president William P. Few, James B. Duke in 1924 agreed to rename the institution in honor of his father.

In the mid-1880s, Washington Duke built an impressive Victorian style mansion near the factory of W. Duke and Sons on Durham's Main Street. Known as "Fairview," the house was surrounded by handsome grounds, which included an impressive glass greenhouse. Duke's deceased wife's maiden sister, Miss Ann Roney, was housekeeper, and, after the death of his daughter, Mary Duke Lyon, in 1893, her children resided at Fairview. Washington Duke died in 1905, and his statue at the entrance of Duke's East Campus was dedicated in 1908. After the completion of Duke University's chapel in 1932, Washington Duke was interred in its Memorial Chapel along with his sons, Benjamin and James.

37 The Duke Brothers

James B. Duke
James Buchanan Duke was born near Durham, North Carolina, on December 23, 1856, to Washington Duke and his second

wife, Artelia Roney Duke. He briefly attended the New Garden School in Greensboro, North Carolina, (now Guilford College) and the Eastman Business College in Poughkeepsie, New York. His primary education, however, was in the family's business—first farming, then the hand manufacture and "drumming" (marketing) of tobacco products, and finally, the mass production and marketing of cigarettes.

At the age of 28, Buck, as he was called, opened a branch of the family's factory in New York City, which within five years was furnishing half the country's total production of cigarettes. Duke emerged as the president of the American Tobacco Company, which became a multinational corporation within a decade. Through numerous foreign and domestic combinations, Duke controlled the manufacture of a variety of tobacco products until the United States Supreme Court in 1911 ordered the dissolution of the tobacco trust.

Duke's older brother, Benjamin Newton, had launched the family into the textile business as early as 1892. As their textile interests developed, the need for economical water power led the Dukes into the hydroelectric generating business. In 1905 they founded the Southern Power Company, now known as Duke Power, one of the companies making up Duke Energy, Inc. Within two decades this company was supplying electricity to more than 300 cotton mills and various other factories, electric lines, cities, and towns primarily throughout North and South Carolina.

Lifelong Methodists, the two brothers practiced the kind of financial stewardship encouraged by their church and instilled in them by their father. Ardent Republicans and sympathetic to the downtrodden, the Dukes, individually and collectively, gave to a number of causes. In December of 1924, James B., who was by far the wealthiest member of the family, established the Duke Endowment as a permanent trust fund with designated beneficiaries. In 1892 Washington Duke had helped a Methodist-related institution, Trinity College, relocate to Durham, and since 1887 Ben had been a member of the school's board of trustees. A new university built around Trinity was to be the prime beneficiary of the Duke Endowment, and at the insistence of Trinity president William Preston Few, the college was re-chartered as Duke University in honor of Washington Duke and his family.

In addition to Duke University, he designated annual income to be distributed to non-profit hospitals and childcare institutions, to rural Methodist churches and retired Methodist preachers in North Carolina, and to three other institutions of higher education: Furman University, Johnson C. Smith University, and Davidson College. One of the largest foundations in the United States, the Duke Endowment, with offices in Charlotte, North Carolina, has now distributed more than $1 billion to its beneficiaries. James B. Duke died in New York City on October 10, 1925, and is interred with his father and brother in the Memorial Chapel on the campus of Duke University.

Benjamin N. Duke

Benjamin Newton Duke was the primary benefactor of Trinity College after it relocated to Durham in 1892. He also was the principal link between the Duke family and the college and university until his death in 1929. While his father and brother received extensive publicity for vital, substantial donations, "Mr. Ben," as he was affectionately known, quietly supported the growing institution in innumerable ways.

His support was so crucial that administrators acknowledged that, without his generosity, Duke never could have become a major university. President William P. Few always said that "Mr. Ben's" benefactions built Trinity College. He not only contributed money for construction, but he also donated funds for equipment, salaries, remodeling, landscaping, and simply for current expenses.

For all of Ben Duke's support, there is only a single sign identifying his gifts on campus. The stone column to the right at the main entrance to East Campus has a plaque dated July 12, 1915, acknowledging that the granite wall circling the campus is a gift of B.N. Duke. To the average visitor, Benjamin N. Duke remained unknown since he had no public statue dominating the campus like that of his father or brother.

At various times Ben Duke is credited with donations totaling $182,000 to the general fund, $156,500 to current expenses, and $443,696 to endowment. Specific dollar amounts adding up to $438,500 are identified for a gymnasium, Alspaugh and Southgate dormitories, athletic fields, new buildings, improvements to the campus, and scientific apparatus. For three years beginning in 1893, he donated $50 per year for tuition for 60 students from North Carolina. This $9,000 total in scholarships was critical in attracting students to the school during a national economic depression. Such aid may be seen as a precursor to the scholarship and loan fund set up in 1925 in memory of his son, Angier B. Duke.

No dollar figures are given, but "Mr. Ben" is credited with donating the following buildings and improvements: Asbury and Lanier in 1898; Branson in 1899; Bivins in 1905; West Duke and East Duke in 1911 and 1912; the erection of the granite wall in 1915; and the remodeling of Crowell. But Ben Duke's contributions to Trinity College simply cannot be calculated. In fact, perhaps his most far-reaching assistance is not even mentioned except in private correspondence. In 1896 Edwin Mims, the only professor of English, took a year's leave of absence. His temporary replacement was a young Harvard-educated professor named William P. Few. He was so well-liked that, when Mims returned, president John C. Kilgo asked Ben Duke to pick up Few's salary so he could continue at Trinity. Few in turn became the first dean of the college and Kilgo's successor as president.

During his 30-year tenure as president from 1910 to 1940, Few persuaded James B. Duke to assume the family's philanthropic role toward the college. This Duke did in a spectacular way, endowing a university to be named, at Few's insistence, "Duke University." According to James B. Duke, the university is named in large measure in honor of his father, Washington Duke, and his brother, Benjamin Newton Duke.

After the announcement of the Duke Endowment in 1924 and James B. Duke's premature death in 1925, Ben Duke was besieged with requests for money. Though confined to his home in New York due to illness, he continued his quiet philanthropy. Between 1926 and 1929, he donated approximately $3,000,000 to 27 different southern institutions of higher education. Other buildings named for B.N. Duke on private college campuses include Elon College and Lincoln Memorial University in Harrogate, Tennessee.

Today the Duke University community pays homage to Benjamin Duke through the B.N. Duke Memorial Organ in the Duke Chapel and through the prestigious B.N. Duke Scholars program. On October 2, 1999, a statue of Benjamin Duke was unveiled on the University's East Campus.

Brodie Duke

Brodie Duke is the least known of the Duke brothers. The eldest of Washington Duke's children, he was the first of the Duke clan to recognize the potential of Durham in expanding tobacco production and transport.

Brodie was born in 1846, the second child of Washington Duke and Mary Caroline Clinton. His mother died when he was one. Washington Duke remarried—to Artelia Roney—and had three children, Mary, Ben, and James. In 1858 both the eldest child, Sidney, and Artelia died. Brodie thus became the oldest surviving child and the only surviving child of his mother. At the end of the Civil War, he tried farming shares with his uncle William

Duke, as Washington Duke and his remaining children began to create their own small manufacturing venture.

Brodie was much more of a farmer than an industrialist like the rest of the family so he struck out on his own from his father's business. Brodie was the first of the Duke family to move to Durham. In 1874 the Dukes saw the opportunity and moved to Durham, building a frame tobacco manufacturing building on West Main Street. Around this same time, he joined with his father and the other sons to form W. Duke and Sons Tobacco Co.

Perhaps by virtue of being first on the Durham scene, but perhaps because he didn't remain as completely engaged in building a tobacco empire as his father and two half-brothers—Ben and Buck—Brodie accumulated a great deal of land on the west side of Durham, including most of what would become Trinity Park. He built his own estate on a 15-acre plot of land sometime prior to 1883, just one block west of his tobacco factory. The street we now know as "Duke Street" is so named because it initially led to and ended at his house and land.

In 1891–92 he traveled to Illinois to treat alcoholism and returned ostensibly sober. By 1893 he had declared bankruptcy, his mills were taken over by his brother Ben, and Brodie fell back into a hedonistic and destructive pattern. However, this did not stem his contributions to the development of Durham.

Brodie was divorced from his second wife by 1904 and, while on a multi-day bender in New York City during his younger brother Buck Duke's wedding, ended up married to his third wife (to whom he had also given several promissory notes and various prenuptial promises). The Duke family lawyers obtained a warrant for Brodie's commitment to a sanatorium, pleading temporary insanity due to intoxication. He managed to successfully sue for divorce on the grounds that he had no recollection of the series of events.

Despite his wayward ways, he seemed to evince some of the same streak of civic and educational generosity that possessed the remainder of his family. In 1886, he donated the land for the Main Street Methodist Church. He also donated the land that became (Brodie) Duke Park. Brodie died on February 2, 1919, and remained estranged from his half-brothers. Neither attended his funeral, a ceremony held in his home.

38 Dedication Day

January 22, 1972 is the day Duke Indoor Stadium was dedicated and renamed Cameron Indoor Stadium to honor retiring athletic director and former basketball coach Eddie Cameron. It was also the date of the annual Duke-Carolina game in Durham, and the Blue Devils were just 7–6 coming into the game against the nation's No. 3 team.

With the score tied at 74 and with eight seconds remaining, Duke called a timeout and set up a play for either Gary Melchionni or Rob West to shoot the ball to win the game. "There were two options," West explained, "Gary driving to the basket or passing it to me. Gary passed the ball to me, and I dribbled to the top of the key and took the shot."

The ball ripped through the nets, and, when the last gasp jumper by Carolina bounded off the rim, Duke owned a home-court win over its biggest rival for the fifth straight season.

Even though West was from New Jersey, he had a great understanding about exactly what the Duke-Carolina rivalry meant. "The Duke-Carolina games were important for a couple of reasons," he explained. "You always recognized the impact of the game because it was a meeting of two of the best basketball programs in the country. Most all of the guys on both teams were recruited by Duke and Carolina so you wanted to make sure and show your coach he should have recruited you and make the other coach wish he had gotten you. The Duke-Carolina games were always the dartboard on the schedule; you knew when they were coming up.

"I can still remember sitting in the locker room after the game with the net around my neck," recalled West some 30 years after the play. "What a great way to win the Duke-Carolina game."

And to this day, the guy who passed him the ball, Melchionni, whose son, Lee, played for the Blue Devils from 2002–06, is one of West's best friends.

39 The 7–0 Game

In the second meeting of 1979 between Duke and Carolina, the two teams entered the game in the familiar position of being ranked No. 6 and No. 4 in the nation. February 24, 1979, was Senior Day at Duke as the Blue Devils got ready to face the University of North Carolina, and that meant it was captain Jim Spanarkel's final game in Cameron Indoor Stadium.

On this cold, rainy evening, Cameron Indoor Stadium was very warm and very much alive, jammed to the rafters. While the fans cheered loudly for the four other seniors—Steve Gray, Scott Goetsch, Harold Morrison, and Rob Hardy—when No. 34 was introduced for the final time, the roar was deafening.

Spanarkel was a one-man fraternity. The 6'5", pigeon-toed, knocked-kneed guard from New Jersey was serving his second year as captain of the Cinderella Duke basketball team that spent the first month of this season as the nation's No. 1 team and had played for the NCAA title the year before. The crowd not only cheered for his records and accomplishments, but also for the fact that he had placed his heart and soul into this program to turn it around.

North Carolina coach Dean Smith knew this might happen and decided to take that emotion and enthusiasm out of the building. After Vince Taylor scored to take a 2–0 lead, Carolina opted to hold the ball and force the Blue Devils out of their 2-3 zone. While the Blue Devils sat back in their customary zone defense, the Tar Heels played keep away for 11 straight minutes before attempting a shot.

The first shot was attempted by center Rich Yonakor. It didn't come close to touching the rim and prompted the now-famous "Air Ball" chant by the Duke student body.

Over on the Duke bench, Bill Foster wasn't about to give in to Smith. He had seen enough of this stall tactic and with a lead was going to sit in his zone defense. "A 2–0 win is as good as winning, scoring 90 points," he said after the game.

His assistants kept asking him what to do, but Foster was going to sit in his zone and make Smith play him. "We jumped around on the court doing jumping jacks anything to stay active while Carolina held the ball," Kenny Dennard said. "They had to advance the ball forward every few seconds to retain possession so we had to stay ready. It was the weirdest half of basketball I have ever played."

In fact the Tar Heels committed a couple of turnovers and air balled another shot as Duke took a 7–0 lead. "It didn't get weird until the last five minutes of the first half," Gene Banks said. "We didn't think they were afraid of us early on, but then we realized they were afraid of going against us the way we wanted to play them, and I felt a lot of pride. We suddenly knew we had a chance of shutting them out for a half and we had gained their respect."

The Duke fans cheer one of their favorites, Jim Spanarkel, on Senior Day in 1979, following the famous stall game, which featured a 7–0 halftime score.

Following the game Foster was asked to reflect on the first half. "[I] thought we played pretty well," he said in his usual sarcastic tone. "We had a chance to score eight points and scored seven and were very effective on the defensive end."

Banks explained the locker room atmosphere at halftime. "It was quiet in the locker room," he said. "It was hard to figure out what was going on. We were concerned we were going through it another half, so we prepared for Carolina to hold the ball for another half. We knew what to do if they came out and wanted to play. Fortunately, they came out and played us toe-to-toe, and we really enjoyed playing them."

The Tar Heels abandoned their stall strategy in the second half, which was played at a normal pace. In fact, it was an even 40–40 over the last 20 minutes. Duke's seven first half points made the difference and enabled their beloved captain and his classmates to go home happy on Senior Day. Spanarkel scored 17 points on his night, 15 of them coming in the second half as he hit on 8-of-9 shots from the field. The students carried Spanarkel off the court on their shoulders, setting him down so he could run off the court with his index finger extended above his head.

While most people have a recollection of the 7–0 halftime lead and that Spanarkel did not lose his Senior Day, the incident that actually poured gas on the flames of the Duke-Carolina rivalry happened late in the game with 30 seconds left when Mike Gminski was fouled on a rebound by the Tar Heels' Al Wood. When Gminski tried to dislodge the Carolina blue player from his body, he elbowed Wood, who ended up in a heap on the floor, and players from both teams squared off.

Spanarkel's high school buddy and a friend of Gminski's, Mike O'Koren of Carolina, headed right for Gminski with his arms spread out asking, almost pleading, "Why, Mike? Why, Mike?" There looked to be another fight about to happen with Gminski holding his ground, standing there like a statue with the ball still clutched in his hands.

Smith headed out to check on his injured player on the floor, who actually was just stunned and wanted to get up. He was pointing at Gminski and telling Woods to "Stay down, stay down." Smith wanted to use the extra few minutes of his player lying on the court to give the officials an ear full about certain calls that had been made in the game.

O'Koren and Spanarkel met at midcourt, and Spanarkel reminded his high school teammate that Gminski couldn't have meant to do it on purpose. He wasn't that kind of player. In fact, Gminski never fouled out of a college game, but he was escorted from this one by referee Gerald Donaghy.

After the game Foster reminded everyone, "Well, you've gotta come down with the rebound. They said the elbow was flagrant. We had a freaky thing like that happen with Dave Colescott over at Carolina this year." In the earlier meeting at Carmichael Auditorium, Colescott ran into Gminski's elbow with his eye, causing Colescott to wear goggles for the next few weeks.

During the recruitment of Gminski, Carolina assistant coach Bill Guthridge said Gminski wouldn't be successful because he was a non-aggressor. Well, the non-aggressor had just knocked a Tar Heel on his butt, led his Duke squad to another victory over Carolina, and brought the rivalry right back where it belonged— where both factions not only respected each other, but also hated each other.

40 Duke vs. Shaq's LSU Tigers

On February 8, 1992, Duke took its No. 1 ranking to Baton Rouge to face LSU and its mammoth center Shaquille O'Neal, who had been outplayed at Cameron Indoor Stadium just a year before by Blue Devils center Christian Laettner. And the Blue Devils were without point guard Bobby Hurley, who had broken his foot in Duke's first loss, a 75–73 defeat, in the previous game at Chapel Hill against Carolina. That had snapped a 23-game winning streak.

While O'Neal, 7'1" and 295 pounds, had marked the game against Duke on his calendar, the Blue Devils needed a new guard. Mike Krzyzewski selected 6'8" sophomore Grant Hill. "I was a little nervous coming in here, not after the game started, but at the hotel and on the bus coming over here," said Hill after the game. "I played point guard before when Bobby was out against Boston U and Canisius. I played in high school. It was just a matter of starting."

Against No. 22 LSU and its hulking big man, Hill wound up with 16 points, nine rebounds, six assists, and only three turnovers. "We slowed things down and were very patient in the halfcourt," said Hurley, who tried to watch the game with a coach's eye. "Grant's so tall, he can see over things. I told him once he should shoot the open 17-footer, but mostly I just encouraged him. He was on his own."

Duke led 34–28 at halftime, thanks to a balanced scoring effort, which held off O'Neal and his 16 points. But after another Shaq attack, the home team took a 54–49 lead midway in the second half. That was when Laettner, Duke's All-American, took over. The 6'11" senior scored 12 of his 22 points in the final 9:06

as Duke closed on a 28–13 run to win going away 77–67. "For him to step up then, that was the turning point," Krzyzewski said.

The biggest shots were a pair of three pointers that he made after the Tigers had grabbed a 60–59 lead. Because LSU couldn't expect O'Neal to guard Laettner on the outside, the Tigers went into a zone. "We were in a 2-3 matchup, and when he shot those two, I was like 'Man, who's got him?' That's how the game goes," O'Neal said.

Meanwhile, LSU helped Duke's cause by missing 10-of-13 free throws down the stretch. "It's a mental game more than it is execution," said LSU coach Dale Brown. "That's why they are No. 1, and we're striving to get there."

O'Neal outscored Laettner with 25 points and had 12 rebounds to Christian's 10, plus seven blocked shots to none. "But we got what we wanted," Laettner said. Added Duke senior Brian Davis of his best friend and roommate: "He knows when we have to have it. We never worry about Christian. His shot is going to come."

Winning on the road without its star point against a team led by a once-in-a-generation big man represented a statement victory for Duke. "I was proud of the way we came together with Bobby out," Krzyzewski said. "I never saw a head down in the last two days. We really got together to play a terrific game."

41 Black Sunday

March 11, 1979, will live in infamy in Duke basketball history. It was the day the unthinkable happened.

The Blue Devils and North Carolina Tar Heels, both ranked among the top six teams in the nation and each with a good chance to win a national title, lost in back-to-back games on the same afternoon in the familiar—if usually hostile—confines of Reynolds Coliseum on the campus of N.C. State. It was a day that began with such nervous energy, hoping for a victory for their team and a defeat for the other but knowing the probability that both would advance to the Greensboro Coliseum and a possible fifth meeting in a season that was already filled with controversy and close games.

Duke began the new season still floating on cloud nine from the incredible 1978 run, losing to a Superman outing by Kentucky's Jack "Goose" Givens, who scored 41 points in the Wildcats' 94–88 win and made the cover of *Sports Illustrated* that called him the "Golden Goose." With all five starters returning, the Blue Devils were the unanimous choice in both preseason polls as the No. 1 team in the country. Heading into the 1979 season, the carry-over momentum made it seem like Duke, at long last, had found the magic bullet.

After a bitter season in which Duke and Carolina split four games and the programs picked at each other constantly, some civility seemed to return to the rivalry as both awaited the NCAA pairings on Selection Sunday, thinking, of course, they would be sent to different regions and had seen the last of each other except, possibly, at the Final Four. There were no rules about who could go where, or rhyme or reason (as if there is today), of what the NCAA selection committee would do. And with either diabolical glee or an inability to truly decide which team deserved it most, both were assigned to the East Region, given the top two seeds, and, after getting byes in the 40-team field, scheduled to play second-round games in Reynolds Coliseum on the following Sunday. The excitement and anxiety returned immediately, awaiting the unique circumstance.

Top-seeded Carolina would face the winner of Ivy League champion Penn and Iona College, ironically coached by Jim Valvano, who in two years would make his home in that building. Second-seeded Duke would await the winner of Temple and the same St. John's team that had beaten the Blue Devils in Madison Square Garden over Christmas. Few expected either to lose, and most anticipated both returning to the Greensboro Coliseum for the Sweet 16, two wins away from a fifth Duke-Carolina game of that season.

As Franklin Street and Chapel Hill bustled with the exhilaration of March Madness and the Tar Heels getting to play in their home state all the way through the regional, the Duke campus was more solemn over the physical condition of its basketball team, which that week began to look more like a M*A*S*H unit.

On Tuesday night Kenny Dennard severely sprained an ankle playing pick-up and horsing around with some inebriated buddies and Duke football players. Dennard was lying in room 204 at Duke Rehabilitation Center, his right ankle tender and sobbing, wanting to somehow be ready to play on Sunday but knowing it wasn't possible. Just down the road in room 4507 at the Duke Medical Center, guard Bob Bender was still convalescing from an appendectomy. While Dennard was in the bed with his swollen ankle elevated, Bender was allowed to leave the hospital for a few hours and wandered down to Cameron Indoor Stadium to shoot free throws and jogged lightly. "When I stop and go, my side starts to pull," he said, wincing in pain. "But I want to keep my wind up. I'm going to try to shoot free throws and jog constantly."

Dennard and Bender were released from the hospital Wednesday night, but neither was cleared to play. Foster made plans to be without them on Sunday and prepared freshman Vince Taylor to take Dennard's spot and John Harrell to start at point guard for the second straight game. Most of practice on Saturday was spent working with Taylor and Harrell and the other three starters. Bender and Dennard had been keys to the chemistry of this Duke team the past two years. Jim Spanarkel, Mike Gminski, Gene Banks, Bender, and Dennard were all stars in their own right who had sacrificed themselves for the sake of the team.

So practice in Reynolds Coliseum on Saturday afternoon was spent getting this new starting lineup to work together at the most crucial time of the year, when one loss ended the season. The team stayed at the Velvet Cloak Inn in Raleigh, and after an early team meal at the hotel, several of the players, including Gminski, headed to Brothers Pizza for a late-night snack.

Gminski's nickname was "Mikey" taken from the Life cereal commercial where Mikey ate the cereal that all the kids were scared to eat. Mikey Gminski was a big boy. Al McGuire called the 6'11", 250-pounder the "Aircraft Carrier" because of his wing span and the space he took up inside.

Meanwhile, the Tar Heels had stayed in Chapel Hill, as was Smith's policy for any game played within 90 minutes the campus. He wanted his players to go to class like normal students and sleep in their own beds the night before the game. But the night before this game was Saturday night, and some of the Tar Heels did what normal students do on Saturday night. That included juniors Mike O'Koren and Rich "Chickie" Yonakor hitting Franklin Street and a few of their favorite haunts.

No one got hurt, but not everybody made the soft curfew of midnight either. Smith reminded the team to get a good night's sleep at the end of Saturday's practice, but none of the Carolina coaches stopped by Granville Towers for bed check because they knew some players would not be in their rooms by midnight and they would have to report a violation of team policy to Smith. Besides, it was a mid-afternoon game in Raleigh, and any Tar Heels who did miss curfew had plenty of time to sleep it off before the 10:00 AM pre-game meal on Sunday morning. Party animals O'Koren and Yonakor were most likely to miss curfew, and a story that has lived forever in Chapel Hill was of one of them riding the back of the other as they left the Mad Hatter bar at 2:00 AM.

On Friday night, Bill Guthridge, Eddie Fogler, and first-year assistant coach Roy Williams had gone to Reynolds Coliseum to scout the first-round doubleheader. They watched Penn defeat Iona 73–69 and came away believing the Quakers were much better than a No. 9 seed. Their best player was Tony Price, who had 27 points and 12 rebounds against Valvano's team.

Did the Tar Heels take Penn too lightly and were they ready to play? Those questions would be asked throughout the off-season after Price scored 25 more points and pulled down nine more rebounds and Penn constantly held off Carolina comebacks. Finally, the Tar Heels inched ahead in the last minute, but a foul call that was hotly protested by the UNC bench sent Ken Hall to the free throw line, where he made both shots to seal the 72–71 upset. Penn proved its worth by going on to beat Syracuse and St. John's before falling to Magic Johnson and Michigan State in the Final Four.

The Duke players had watched the first half of the Carolina-Penn game from under the basket at Reynolds, which by now was packed with blue-clad fans of both schools. At halftime the Blue Devils went downstairs to get in uniform for St. John's. They could tell from the vibrations of the crowd above them that it was close and going down to the wire. They were ready to take the court for warm-ups as the game ended and came up the stairs as the Tar Heels were about to go down. Spanarkel and O'Koren, high school teammates, stopped to embrace. O'Koren was in tears; his junior season was over. In the stands the fans in light blue sat stunned. Some got up to leave; others stayed in their seats. Duke fans, who had cheered wildly for Penn in the second half, were giddy but also well aware that the same thing could happen to their depleted team.

By the time Duke and St. John's tipped off, the Tar Heels were on the bus back to Chapel Hill with their 23–6 record in the books. Williams was the most disconsolate, having experienced for the first time how suddenly the season ended with a loss in the NCAA Tournament. He got off the bus and walked home. "That was the first time, and every year since when the season ends with a loss, I am still affected by the swiftness and suddenness of it all," Williams has recounted through the years. "You play all season to get into the NCAA Tournament, and if you lose, there is no next game, no practice the next day. It's over just like that, and there is nothing you can do about it."

Almost as suddenly, things had gone from bad to worse for Duke. Dennard and Bender would be sitting on the bench in street clothes with a wrapped ankle and a stitched side, while Gminski, who said he could play, had placed a bucket under his chair to throw up in during timeouts or when he came out of the game. He had been upchucking most of the morning after apparently eating some bad pizza before going to bed and getting food poisoning.

Hard to believe that after all this team had been through, another shot at the national championship might be lost because of bad pizza, a pickup basketball game, and a nearly ruptured appendix all in the span of one week.

St. John's entered the game with a 19–10 record; its likable coach Lou Carnesecca and Foster were good friends from Foster's eight years at Rutgers. "We never played St. John's when I was at Rutgers, so maybe that's why Lou and I are friends now," Foster said, chuckling.

Carnesecca knew the sixth-ranked Blue Devils well, having defeated them in December. Duke had a big lead in the second half, only to fall to a furious comeback by the Redmen. "I'm quite aware of who we're playing and where we're playing," Carnesecca had said before the game. "But the crowd doesn't put the ball in the basket. I like my position at any time—and at my age—I like my position of just being alive."

Following their pregame warm-ups, the Blue Devils went back to their locker room and talked about this tournament now being their tournament with Carolina out. If they could win today through all their adversity, they would be on the way to playing again for the national title.

Things started well for Duke, which took an early 10-point lead with its makeshift lineup. St. John's strategy of using 6'8" sophomore Wayne McCoy to defend the G-man—who played 31 minutes sick to his stomach, scored 16 points, pulled down eight rebounds, and blocked two shots—didn't work. He also kept puking into the bucket behind the bench during several timeouts.

Again, St. John's rallied in the second half, and it was evident that Duke was just hanging on. With the game tied, Reggie Carter hit an eight-foot jumper, and the Redmen ended the Blue Devils' season 80–78. Now, the fans in royal blue had their chance to sit in stunned silence. How could it happen that both teams lost? A few Carolina fans had remained for the second game, and to them it was some consolation that at least their archrival would not be advancing either.

Duke actually played one of its best games of the turbulent season, shooting 55 percent from the floor and making 14-of-19 free throws. St. John's was just a little better, making 12-of-14 from the line and having the ball for the last shot. "When I go home, I'll go home proud," said Spanarkel, who as a senior had played in his final game in a Duke uniform, scoring 16 points in 38 minutes, several at point guard to spell Harrell.

Harrell and Taylor did well in their emergency action. Harrell played 27 minutes, hit all three of his field goal attempts, scored seven points, and had seven assists to only one turnover. Freshman Taylor played all but one minute, scoring six points and grabbing two rebounds in place of Dennard.

But sophomore Banks almost single-handedly kept Duke in the game with 24 points, 10 rebounds, and six assists in 38 minutes. It was perhaps his best performance of an otherwise checkered second season. After being named Duke's third straight ACC Rookie of the Year in 1978, his scoring average fell off by almost three points, and he was left off the All-ACC first team. "This season has been brutal—mentally and physically," he said after the loss to St. John's, sitting with his head down and jersey pulled halfway over his head.

Foster's staff followed him to the postgame press conference in the ROTC room in Reynolds Coliseum. Sports information director Tom Mickle said to make sure there were no weapons in the room that Foster could use to kill himself. Luckily there weren't because Foster looked like suicide was a viable option.

The usually quick-witted coach was anything but that after this loss. His face was ashen and drawn; the pressure of being No. 1 for the good part of an entire season and the disappointment of seeing it all fly away so quickly was etched in every corner of his face. The walk from the locker room on one side of the building to the ROTC room on the other side of the arena was agonizing. "Can you believe it ended like this?" He said as he shuffled down the long red and white concrete hallway. "After all we went through this year; it's hard to believe it ended like this."

42 Siler City—The Beginning of the Carolina Hatred

While Duke and Carolina competed fiercely on the hardwood in the shadow of king football, the rivalry began in earnest with basketball in the late 1950s when Duke hired an energetic young coach named Vic Bubas to compete against the legend in Chapel Hill, Frank McGuire, whose 1957 team had gone undefeated and won the national championship in storybook fashion—beating Michigan State and Kansas with Wilt Chamberlain, in Kansas City no less, on consecutive nights.

McGuire had an Underground Railroad pipeline to the high school stars of New York, and that looked like it was continuing in the spring of 1959 when the Irishman signed rivals from neighboring towns on Long Island. Larry Brown was considered the top lead guard in New York when he played for UNC alumnus Bob Gersten at Long Beach. Art Heyman, a 6'5" bull of a forward, was easily the best player in all of New York, putting up record numbers for nearby Oceanside. The two had even planned on rooming together at UNC.

Brown and Heyman would make up another juggernaut for the Tar Heels, who had lost to Maryland in the 1958 ACC Championship Game (denying their return to the NCAA Tournament) and were upset by Navy in a first-round game the following year after backing into the NCAAs due to a probation that kept ACC champion N.C. State out. Freshmen were not eligible in those days, so it would be the 1961 season before Brown and Heyman could play for the UNC varsity. Heyman never made it to Chapel Hill, creating the first of many controversies involving the two Jewish kids from the Island.

Upon moving from Everett Case's staff at State to take the Duke job, Bubas was aware that McGuire and Heyman's stepfather, Bill Heyman, were at odds. Heyman's birth father was Irving Sondak, who was a basketball player at NYU in 1929–30. Heyman lost his father when he was seven, and when his mother remarried, he took her name.

McGuire's nickname was the Godfather, and it was a given that when parents sent their sons to play for him there was no question they were in good hands. Bill Heyman was an engineer and asked questions that other parents did not, such as would his stepson take the classes he wanted and how much study time he would have.

McGuire was insulted, and on the Heymans' last trip to Chapel Hill as a UNC recruit in June of 1959, the coach and parent nearly came to blows at the old University Motel. Art, returning from the movies with a Carolina player, long claimed that he stopped the near fistfight before the first punch was thrown. The Heymans went back to New York, knowing that Art's recruitment was again open.

Bubas had been watching Heyman play summer league games on Long Island and took Heyman's parents to dinner to make his pitch on why Artie was better off at Duke. He would be the player around whom Bubas built the Blue Devils into a national power, and the coach answered all the academic questions cleanly. Since a national letter of intent was not binding in the eyes of the Atlantic Coast Conference until July 1, Heyman signed a second letter with Duke.

Long before they were coined the Cameron Crazies, Duke students could be entertaining and edgy with the visiting opponents. McGuire was a particular foil because of his stature, his impeccable dress, and his Irish brogue. The students who sat behind the UNC bench greased their hair with Brylcreem like McGuire and wore fashionable string ties around their necks. They taunted McGuire and the Tar Heels but usually went back to their dorms unhappy, as Carolina won 13 of the last 17 games McGuire would coach against their team. But they knew better days were ahead with the recruit Bubas had stolen from UNC.

As Duke fans delighted in the high-strung and immensely talented Heyman playing for the Duke freshmen, McGuire and Carolina seethed over the defection. It all came to a head on the night of December 9, 1959, in Siler City, North Carolina.

Each year the freshman basketball teams from the Big Four schools, Duke, North Carolina, N.C. State, and Wake Forest would play each other three times—once each at the home venue and then one on the road somewhere in the state of North Carolina. Duke had played Wake Forest in Hickory and N.C. State in Wilson. The game in Siler City would be the first against North Carolina with Heyman in a Duke uniform.

Bucky Waters, who played at N.C. State for Everett Case, was in his first season as an assistant coach at Duke and was the head coach for the freshman team. "We drove down in cars, and I had Art ride with me," Waters explained. "I told him I had no idea what was coming tonight from the Carolina team, but he needed to be prepared, knowing the feeling of hatred they had for him in walking away from their program…'It's going to challenge you, but you cannot knuckle under and let your emotions get the best of you.'"

Sure enough, in the first minute of the game, the taunting of Heyman began. "I'm sitting on the bench and I'm hearing, 'You Christ-killer, you monkey-Jew-boy,' from the Carolina guys at Art and I called timeout in the first minute," Waters said. "I looked at Art and said, 'I told you this was coming, I didn't think it would be this bad.' After having a few minutes to think about it, I called a second timeout and brought the guys back to the bench and looked at Art and the rest of them and said, 'Here's the answer to what they are doing: you just kick their ass, show them how good you really are, and don't get down on their level.'"

The game continued, and the Blue Devils and Heyman handled the insults and dealt out their own brand of abuse as they took a commanding lead. "I had promised Art I would get him out before I thought something was going to happen," Waters explained. "I was getting ready to take him out and remind him to not gloat when he came out. We had spread the floor, and Art came out of the corner to catch the ball, and Dieter [Krause] was two steps behind him and Dieter looked like he had a javelin in his hand as his fist nailed Art across the jaw, and Art goes down hard on the court."

Krause, a 6'5", 185 pounder from Norfolk, Virginia, had landed a haymaker on Heyman's face at midcourt, and both benches poured onto the floor. "I'm in my early 20s," Waters said. "I don't even try to hold my players back. I head right for the coach for Carolina, Ken Rosemond. I get him by the lapels of his jacket and throw him up on the scorer's table. His butt is hitting all sorts of toggle switches, and buttons and horns going off, and I told him exactly what I thought of a coaching staff that would stoop that low to do that to our players."

When things finally calmed down, Heyman had to be taken to the Siler City Hospital, where he received six stitches, five outside his mouth and one inside. Duke won the game 88–70, but it looked like they lost the war with Heyman's busted jaw. Heyman ended the game as the leading scorer with 34 points, while Krause led Carolina with 20 points. Larry Brown had 17 points, and the future mayor of Charlotte and North Carolina gubernatorial candidate, Richard Vinroot, scored two points.

Waters was very anxious upon meeting with Eddie Cameron as the Duke athletic director leaned back in his chair puffing on a pipe. "I knew I was going to get fired for the way I handled things," Waters said. "He asked me to tell him what happened. He stopped me and asked me to repeat what the players were saying to Art. He paused for a really long second after I finished talking, tapped his pipe out in the ashtray, and told me there was a lot about me that he liked and respected, and that was not the way we handled things here at Duke...and to not let it happen again."

43 Dine at Angus Barn

Located on the edge of the Raleigh-Durham Airport and right between the cities of Durham and Raleigh, the Angus Barn is recognized as one of the top steakhouses in the country and a must-see by all who either live in the Triangle area of the state of North Carolina or visit Duke.

The double doors of the now-fabled red barn swung wide on June 28, 1960 as the Angus Barn received the first guests of novice restaurateurs Thad Eure, Jr. and Charles Winston. *What was this mysterious red building perched atop a hill so far from civilization?* Well, the southern gentlemen with no previous restaurant experience established both a landmark and a legend right between Durham and Raleigh where nobody else dared conceive success.

More than 13 million guests later, generations continue to make the Angus Barn, affectionately nicknamed "Big Red" by Eure Jr., a cherished part of their lives. All guests experience what Eure Jr. and Winston originally envisioned: incomparable hospitality, excellent value, a meal of impeccable quality, and the rich, rustic Americana ambience for which the Barn is now known across the globe. Now owned and operated by Van Eure, daughter of the late Thad Eure Jr., and staffed by a loyal, hardworking team, many of whom have built their careers here, the double doors of the Barn open 363 evenings a year.

Although still famous as a "Beef-eaters Haven," the menu of the Barn has expanded to meet the dietary demands of even the most discerning, nutrition-conscious guests. In 1960, as Eure and Winston envisioned their restaurant, consensus suggested that a steak and potato-based menu was what the public wanted. And so began the Angus Barn's longstanding tradition of serving the best aged western beef available. Today the Barn serves an average of 22,000 steaks per month, but the menu also features poultry, seafood, and pasta.

A fire the morning of February 7, 1964, destroyed the building, but not the dream of the Eure and Winston families as they rebuilt the Angus Barn bigger and better. In 1989 *Wine Spectator* magazine bestowed its coveted Grand Award upon the Angus Barn for the first time. It would be an honor repeated each year for the next 20-plus years. It had been Thad Jr.'s vision to build a wine list to rival those of California restaurants. In May of 1991, the Barn made one of their boldest initiatives yet: the basement that once housed stacked boxes and cases of wine in a place called "the cages" was transformed into a spectacular, 28,000-bottle wine cellar and dining room for the ultimate dining experience.

The Angus Barn is now owned and operated by Van Eure, who continued to expand and build her parents' dream in 2008 as she and husband Steve Thanhauser opened The Pavilion at the Angus Barn. A spectacular lakeside oasis, The Pavilion was created for special events including weddings, receptions, corporate events, and banquets. The Pavilion seats 400 comfortably in rustic, wooded splendor.

44 The Missoula Mountain

One of the most beloved players to ever play at Duke was Mike Lewis from Missoula, Montana. At 6'8", 235 pounds, Mike was a big man who fit right into the Blue Devils offense of shooters like Bob Verga and Jack Marin.

Duke had never recruited a player from Montana. "I was flattered by their interest in me being from Podunk, Montana," Lewis said. "I had watched on television the 1964 championship game against UCLA and knew about Duke, and it was incredible they were talking to me. I came to Duke for my visit in the spring on Joe College weekend, and it was awesome. I was from Montana. What the hell was this all about? I saw Ike and Tina Turner in concert when they were young."

In three varsity seasons, 1966–68, the Montana native averaged double figures in points and rebounds every year, finishing with 1,417 points and 1,051 rebounds in 84 games. He was the first

136

Mike Lewis blocks the shot of North Carolina's Larry Miller in 1968, a year in which Lewis averaged 21.7 points and 14.4 rebounds.

player in Duke history to record at least 1,000 rebounds and the first to lead the ACC in rebounding.

In his senior season of 1968, he was the team's leading scorer, captain, and most valuable player. He ranked first in the ACC in rebounding for a second time, third in field-goal percentage, and fourth in scoring with a career high 21.7 points per game. His rebounding average of 14.4 that year was second in school history to Bernie Janicki's 15.9 in 1952. Lewis had eight games of 30 or more points with a career best of 35 versus Wake Forest. Against N.C. State he had 34 points and 22 rebounds.

It was in his first season that he made his first real impact on the Duke-Carolina rivalry. Lewis was the sophomore center on the No. 3-ranked team in the country. They rolled through the regular season with just three losses, beating Carolina 88–77 in Chapel Hill and 77–63 in Durham. In the semifinals of the ACC Tournament in Raleigh, Duke would face North Carolina again. The Blue Devils were averaging over 88 points a game, so Carolina's Smith thought it would be a good idea to hold the ball.

Tied at 20 with just seconds left in the game, the sophomore held the fate of the entire team in his hands at the foul line. "All I can remember is I made a move in the low post and got fouled," Lewis explained. "There wasn't a lot of time left, so I'm standing on the free throw line, and Verga comes by and says, 'No problem, do it just like in practice.' That's the last thing I needed to hear. I missed them in practice. So I missed the first free throw. I could have been blindfolded and have gotten it closer. But I took a deep breath, my knees are knocking, and I made the second one."

When Carolina inbounded the ball following the made free throw, Lewis stole the inbound pass. "Steal is probably the wrong word to use. They threw it right to me," Lewis explained. "It wasn't like I made some phenomenal defensive play. I just happened to turn around, and there was the ball."

What Lewis remembers most about his years at Duke is the discipline and care his coach Vic Bubas showed him. "After I graduated, that didn't end my relationship with him," he explained. "I can call him. I did and I have called him for advice in my career after basketball. He is just one of those people that I just value his advice and I valued the example that he set.

"Don't get me wrong; there were times when I could have killed him when I was playing. I thought I knew everything. I was a big hot shot. I didn't like some things he did. We got kicked off the team that one year for drinking. We got caught, we knew it was against the rules. He didn't give us another chance. He kicked our ass off the team for a game. It was in the paper, it was on the front page of the paper in Missoula for my parents to see, my hometown newspaper. That was sweet. The guy had rules, you want to be here, then you go by the rules. So later in life, when I thought about disciplining my kids, I thought about that. It made an indelible mark on me."

Lewis was chosen first team All-ACC and made several All-America teams. He was drafted by the Boston Celtics but opted to play professionally in the ABA for six seasons.

45 Bill Werber, the First All-American

Legendary Duke basketball coach and administrator and namesake of Cameron Indoor Stadium, Eddie Cameron always felt that the best player he ever coached was on his first team back in 1929. Bill Werber, a 5'10" guard from Berwyn, Maryland, directed Cameron's first two teams to Southern Conference championship games, and his athletic exploits have stood the test of time as one of the great athletes in school history and the first Duke basketball player to be named an All-American.

Werber starred in the backcourt for the 1928, 1929, and 1930 teams, along with his classmates and future Duke Hall of Famers Boley Farley and Chalky Councilor. Those three were joined by center Joe Croson in 1929 and 1930 to form a quartet that played almost every minute during the school's first two Southern Conference seasons. Werber was the No. 2 scorer behind Croson on both teams with 277 points overall and was named All-Southern both years. His reputation skyrocketed in 1929 when journalists at the conference tournament in Atlanta proclaimed him one of the best players in the history of the event. As a senior in 1930, he was even better for a team that posted a record of 18–2, enjoyed a 15-game winning streak, and upset national power Loyola of Chicago. He was named Duke's first All-American following that season.

Werber was also an exceptional baseball player, starring for the varsity at shortstop from 1928 to 1930 before launching an 11-year career in the major leagues with five teams, including the World Series champion Cincinnati Reds in 1940. In his book, *Memories of a Ballplayer: Bill Werber and Baseball in the 1930s*, Werber detailed his under-the-table signing with the New York Yankees after his freshman season at Duke. A handshake agreement between one of the team's scouts and Werber's father provided the funding for the last three years of Werber's college education with the stipulation that he would sign with the Yankees after graduation in 1930, which he did. He played in 1,295 major league games, most at third base, and batted .271.

46 Capel's Shot

The 1994–95 Duke basketball season was one of the strangest ever for the Blue Devils. After barely missing out on another national championship the previous April, the Blue Devils found themselves nine months later without their head basketball coach as Mike Krzyzewski was out of commission following back surgery. Even with all the turmoil surrounding the Blue Devils, they still found a way to play an incredible basketball game, one that lives on in the annals of Duke-Carolina, against their heavily favored archrival. And, perhaps, the ultimate proof that, regardless of the team records going in, anything can happen in this rivalry.

The Tar Heels were loaded with the forward tandem of Jerry Stackhouse and Rasheed Wallace and a three-guard lineup of Jeff McInnis, Donald Williams, and Dante Calabria. They were 16–1, having just beaten No. 16-ranked Wake Forest in Winston-Salem. By comparison, Duke had lost seven of its last eight but had played far better in the win at Notre Dame and the two-point loss at Maryland just five days earlier. Still, this did not set up as a regular Duke-Carolina game. Smith vs. Gaudet didn't have the same ring as Smith vs. Krzyzewski.

Strangely, this made the game even more appealing to many in the national media. They knew that when Duke and Carolina played basketball, it was bound to be a good show. And this highly unusual circumstance might make it even better. For the first time ever, there were two telecasts of a game from Cameron Indoor Stadium by the ACC Network and ESPN2, the second cable station for the so-called "World Wide Leader" that had been launched the year before on the strength of subscriptions sold to a nation that wanted to see the ballyhooed No. 1 vs. No. 2 matchup in Chapel Hill.

Krzyzewski's absence loomed for sure, but once the ball went up at 9:07 PM, it was just another Duke-Carolina game. And what a game it was with wild runs by both teams and numerous lead changes throughout both halves. Before the game Gaudet had joked about the prime-time 9:00 start and predicted "we'll still be in overtime by midnight." Early in the game with Cameron packed and the temperature sweltering, UNC's Dean Smith made the unconventional move of taking off his suit jacket and rolling up his shirt sleeves.

The attending media, a national TV and radio audience, and the 9,000-plus squeezed into Cameron Indoor Stadium witnessed an unforgettable basketball game with regulation ending in an 81–81 tie. A nearly half-court shot by Jeff Capel ripped through the nets to send the game to a second overtime. Cameron erupted, and it looked like the Devils would finally have their own miracle finish to talk about.

Most ironic about this game was that Duke rallied from eight points down with 17 seconds remaining in the first overtime. "Eight points and seventeen seconds" is a legendary phrase in the rivalry, referring back to Carolina's comeback in the 1974 game in Chapel Hill.

The Blue Devils trailed 94–86 in this one with 17 seconds showing on the clock. Freshman Trajan Langdon ignited the comeback by hitting a three-pointer from the right wing. UNC's McInnis hit a free throw at the other end for the Tar Heels, and Capel answered with a drive and a free throw to make the score 95–92 with five seconds to play. Capel then fouled Carolina reserve Serge Zwikker, who missed the first free throw, and Smith called a timeout with four seconds on the clock to calm his big Swedish center and, if he missed again, set up something to defend a three-point shot to tie. "In the timeout Coach Brey diagrammed a play,"

Capel said. "We had Trajan and Chris [Collins] in the corners. We felt like there was going to be pressure and we would kick the ball up, but there was no pressure. They were really concentrating on Trajan and Chris."

The actual pressure was on Zwikker. If he made the second free throw, the game would be over, but it rattled out, and Cherokee Parks grabbed the rebound, passed it quickly to Capel, who took two long dribbles as he crossed midcourt and let loose a 35-footer as Ed Geth raised his arms highs while running at him. The shot swished through the nets.

"What was it, four seconds on the clock?" Parks said. "That's a long time. People don't realize it. I was standing about 10 feet behind Jeff when he threw it up and I thought it had a great chance of hitting something. If there had been somebody pressuring, it could have taken a couple of seconds to find someone, but there was no one there, so I just gave it to him, and he was able to get as close to the bucket as he could."

"Fluke things happen to us all the time," Stackhouse said, "so it ain't like anything we haven't seen before. I felt like Capel's shot was going in as soon as it left his hand."

Duke coach Pete Gaudet was smiling in the huddle as the teams prepared for another extra period, perhaps remembering his offhand comment that the game would go to double overtime and last past midnight. Both predictions came to pass.

After Carolina survived by outscoring Duke 7–5 in the second overtime, which ended with a missed jumper from freshman guard Steve Wojciechowski, Tar Heels students rushed Franklin Street, set bonfires, and partied into early Thursday. All for beating a team that fell to .500 for the year and 0–8 in ACC play. "If you don't like that, you don't like college basketball," a still-sweating Smith said afterward. "That's the best team we have played based on that game."

Despite playing on a less talented Duke squad, Parks' eighth Duke-Carolina game was the biggest classic of them all. "I've always said it doesn't matter what the records are," Parks said. "Both teams could be 0–20; both teams 20–0. It doesn't matter. Everybody's always up for the game. It's always going to be a good game, regardless."

47 Austin Rivers' Game-Winner and the One-and-Dones

Prior to the start of the 2012 Duke-North Carolina game, deep in the recesses of the Dean E. Smith Center, Blue Devils head coach Mike Krzyzewski scribbled one word on the blackboard for his team to remember—"Courage." In the end, the night would come down to one courageous shot from a freshman playing in his first Duke-Carolina game, yet a player with a very strong basketball pedigree in his DNA. That player would be Austin Rivers, the son of a former NBA star and current NBA coach Doc Rivers.

It had been a very interesting season so far for the Blue Devils as they made the annual trip to Chapel Hill for the first meeting of the year. The Blue Devils were ranked No. 10 in the country coming off a 78–74 home loss to Miami just three days earlier and were facing a talent-laden Tar Heels team ranked No. 5 in the nation.

Duke played well early, but the Tar Heels exploded for a 14–4 run to start the second half and build a 13-point lead. It was time for the Blue Devils to claw their way back into the game. A Kendall Marshall errant pass led to a Mason Plumlee steal and a Seth Curry long-range three. Harrison Barnes, who had played so well all night for Carolina, charged into Ryan Kelly, and Tyler Zeller, who had been so dominant all evening for the Heels, missed key free throws and tipped in a Ryan Kelly shot into the Duke basket.

Part of a career-high 29 points, Austin Rivers, a one-and-done player, sinks a last-second shot over Tyler Zeller to defeat North Carolina in 2012. (AP Images)

Suddenly the game was a two-point contest in favor of the Tar Heels with the game clock running down with mere seconds remaining. Duke had the ball and as the seconds counted down, and Curry flipped the ball to an open Rivers in the right corner of the court. The last six seconds seemed to take forever as Rivers watched to see where Zeller, the Carolina big man, was going to position himself. With three seconds on the clock, Curry screamed at Rivers to shoot the ball. Rivers felt just enough room between himself and Zeller to finally take the jumper, and as the ball drifted

One-and-Dones

Starting in the 2006 NBA Draft, high school players were not eligible to enter the draft directly after graduating from high school. The rules now state that high school players will gain eligibility for draft selection one year after their high school graduation, and they must also be at least 19 years old as of the end of the calendar year of the draft. The rule is Article X in the NBA Players Agreement. Of late Duke has been led by several notable one-and-done players, including Austin Rivers, who will be forever remembered for his shot.

Corey Maggette attended Duke prior to the one-and-done rule. He played in 39 games as a freshman at Duke, averaging 10.6 points per game and 3.9 rebounds during the 1998–99 season. He was known for his breakaway dunks as he soared above the rim and put something a little extra on each and every one, almost hitting his head on the rim several times. (Against Florida, Maggette was T'd up after dunking, doing a pull-up on the rim, and high-fiving the backboard.) He had a total of 29 dunks and incredibly the same number of three pointers, showing that he was a true threat as an inside-outside player.

Maggette's career came with controversy as he opted to enter the NBA draft following his freshman season against the recommendation of Mike Krzyzewski. He was also the subject of an NCAA investigation when he left Duke. In 1997 prior to entering Duke he accepted $2,000 from Myron Piggie to play for his summer team, the Children's Mercy Hospital 76ers. The payments were made before he entered Duke, and university officials were unaware of the payment. The NCAA closed the investigation in 2003. In the 1999 NBA Draft, Maggette was the 13th overall pick by the Seattle Supersonics and was traded shortly after to the Orlando Magic, as part of a deal.

He played just one season for the Magic prior to being traded to the Los Angeles Clippers, for whom he averaged more than 17 points per game and become a consistent rebounder and driver. The Clippers' career leader from the free throw line, making 3,122 and attempting 3,791, he helped to lead them to their first playoff win in 13 years. The last five years of his career, he would end up playing for four NBA clubs: the Golden State Warriors, Milwaukee Bucks, Charlotte Bobcats, and Detroit Pistons. He tallied 13,198 points in the NBA with his best years coming with the Clippers in 2004–05 when he averaged 22.2 points and in 2007–08 when he averaged 22.1 points.

Luol Deng also attended Duke prior to the one-and-done rule, but he played just one season for the Blue Devils prior to jumping to the NBA. In that one season in 2003–04, he appeared in 37 games and made 32 starts. He averaged 31.1 minutes and scored 15.1 points per game en route to a berth in the 2004 Final Four. He is only the 10th freshman in ACC history to lead all rookies in scoring, rebounding, and field goal percentage. After his freshman season, the native of Wau, Sudan, declared for the 2004 NBA draft and was the seventh selection in the draft by the Phoenix Suns. He was immediately traded to the Chicago Bulls. Deng now starts for the Miami Heat.

Kyrie Irving came to Duke as one of the most highly sought-after guards in the country. He was a McDonald's All-American and part of the gold medal-winning team at the FIBA Americas Under-18 Championship. In the first eight games of his freshman season, the New Jersey native set the world on fire, scoring 17.4 points per game on 53.2 percent shooting while averaging 5.1 assists, 3.8 rebounds, and 1.5 steals. But an injury suffered in his home state at the IZOD Center in East Rutherford, New Jersey, sidelined him for the majority of the season. A severe ligament injury in his right toe kept Irving on the bench until March 17, the day before the Blue Devils' first-round game with Hampton in the NCAA Tournament. Irving's put-back against Michigan helped Duke advance to the Sweet 16, where it would fall to Arizona despite Irving's 28 points. Irving declared for the NBA draft after playing just 11 games for the Blue Devils. He was the No. 1 pick of the 2011 NBA Draft by the Cleveland Cavaliers and had an incredible rookie season, being selected the 2012 NBA Rookie of the Year. In his young career, Irving already has played in three All-Star Games.

Jabari Parker was a standout high school basketball player, helping his team win four straight state championships for Simeon Career Academy and was named the National High School Player of the Year by Gatorade. The Chicago native was assigned to wear No. 1 as a Blue Devil, the only other player to wear No. 1 at Duke—just like Irving had.

Parker's first game with the Blue Devils was a huge success as he poured in 22 points against Davidson. He continued to be impressive as a freshman with a 27-point outing back in Chicago at the United Center against Kansas and 23 points in January against N.C. State. Parker was looked at for the majority of the season as not only one of the top freshmen, but also one of the top college basketball players in the country. In his final game at Cameron Indoor Stadium, Parker poured in a career-high 30 points and winning an ACC record-tying ACC Rookie of the week award for a tenth time.

In the ACC Tournament, Parker had back-to-back 20 point performances in a semifinal win over N.C. State and a championship game loss to Virginia. Parker ended his lone season in heartbreaking fashion, losing to No. 14 seed Mercer in the first round of the NCAA Tournament. But the Associated Press first team All-American was selected second overall in the 2014 NBA Draft by the Milwaukee Bucks, for whom he averaged 12.3 points before tearing his ACL early in the season.

Jahlil Okafor, **Tyus Jones**, and **Justise Winslow** starred for the 2014–15 national championship squad. Like Parker, Okafor was a Chicago native, having played his prep ball at Whitney Young, where he played against Parker. Possessing mammoth but soft hands and deft footwork, Okafor, a first team All-American and the ACC Player of the Year, averaged 17.3 points and 8.5 rebounds while shooting 66.4 percent from the floor. Duke received a double coup when best friends Okafor and Tyus Jones declared their intention to play for the Blue Devils on the same day. Throughout the recruiting process, the big man and point guard repeated their plan to play together and they followed through. The 6'11", 270-pound Okafor was drafted third overall by the Philadelphia 76ers.

Okafor's friend Jones averaged 11.8 points and 5.6 assists, but his impact was so much more than that. Showing great poise while starting at point guard from Day One, he had an impressive 2.9:1 assist-to-turnover ratio and would raise his performance when it mattered most. His clutch baskets led to comeback victories against North Carolina and Virginia, but he saved his best for last when scored 23 points, including two three-pointers in the last five minutes, in the Blue Devils' win against Wisconsin in the national title game. For his efforts he was named Most Outstanding Player of the Final Four. Just the second Duke freshman with 400 points and 200 assists, Jones was drafted 24th overall by the Cleveland Cavaliers and then traded to the Minnesota Timberwolves, his hometown team.

The powerfully built 6'6" 225-pound Winslow excelled on the defensive and offensive end, and his athletic jams and blocks were *SportsCenter* highlight staples. A versatile player, he could guard smaller or bigger players, and Duke started him at the four position during the season's stretch run. He was perhaps at his best while playing in his hometown of Houston during the Sweet 16 and Elite Eight victories, which propelled Duke to the Final Four. Winslow had 21 points and 10 rebounds against Utah and 16 points and five rebounds against Gonzaga. Playing like a runaway freight train on the fast break, Winslow averaged 12.6 points to go along with 6.5 rebounds and 2.1 assists during the season. He was drafted 10th overall by the Miami Heat.

through the air, which seemed to take an eternity, you could see a slight smile on Rivers' face. He knew it was going in. *Swish*. The Blue Devils had beaten a very good Carolina team 85–84. "I swear the ball was in the air for like 10 minutes," Rivers said. "My heart dropped. I shot it with confidence, but when I was walking back, it looked good, and I was like, 'Please go in.' When it went in, my heart jumped. It was the best feeling I've ever had in my life."

For the night Rivers made six three-pointers (five more than the entire UNC team), scored a career-high 29 points—the most any Duke freshman has ever scored against North Carolina—and answered every question about his ability, his decision-making, his toughness, and his will. And he also had his name permanently etched in the annals of the Duke-Carolina rivalry. "It's amazing what can happen when you have courage," said Rivers following the game.

48 Cap Card

Wilbur Wade "Cap" Card is known as the "father of intercollegiate basketball in North Carolina" along with being the "father of Duke basketball." As the first basketball coach at the university from 1906–12 and the first athletic director from 1902–48, Card is credited with introducing college basketball to the state of North Carolina.

Card was born in Franklinton, North Carolina, on October 29, 1873, and attended Trinity College in Durham in 1895, becoming one of the school's best athletes as an outfielder and batter, breaking a number of baseball records, and eventually earning his nickname "Cap" as team captain in 1899. He graduated from college the following year.

In 1900 Card entered the School of Physical Education at Harvard University and later trained and worked at the Sargent Normal School every summer through 1913. After graduating from Harvard in 1901, Card worked as director at the YMCA in Mobile, Alabama. In 1902 he was invited by president John Carlisle Kilgo to return to Trinity College and become director of the new physical education program there.

He worked out of the university's first gym, the Angier B. Duke Gymnasium, and was the first to organize a basketball team at the school. Card put the first team together and trained them for three weeks, as none of the members had ever played a basketball game before. He also prepared the gym for its first game.

College basketball began in the state of North Carolina after coach Richard Crozier of Wake Forest College, now a university, approached Card in 1905 about holding a game. After recruiting a makeshift team and setting the gym up for basketball, he coached

Trinity College during its inaugural game played in 1906 as Duke lost to Wake Forest 24–10. The most intriguing part was that Card also umpired the game while Crozier refereed. Card would go on to coach the team for seven years and finish in 1912 with a 30–17 lifetime record as Trinity (and Duke's) first men's basketball coach.

He would remain at the school during the very formative years as the director of athletics until 1948. His replacement as basketball coach was one of his former players, Joseph E. Brinn.

Card continued to do groundbreaking work in the field of physical education, serving as the state chairman of the American Physical Education Association.

On September 3, 1948, Card died from a heart attack at age 74. He is buried at Maplewood Cemetery in Durham. In his honor the gymnasium at Duke University was renamed Card Gymnasium in 1958. The gym, which opened in 1930, is located adjacent to the Cameron Indoor Stadium and was the home for the Blue Devils until Duke Indoor Stadium, later renamed Cameron Indoor Stadium, was opened in 1940.

The cost of construction for Card Gym was listed at $345,557, and capacity was about 3,500, though there are reports of 5,000 reportedly jammed into the building for a game against North Carolina in 1933. The first game was played December 19, 1930, a 22–21 loss to Villanova in the final minute. Duke's George Rogers scored the first varsity basket in the gym, and the last game played in Card Gym was on December 16, 1939, a 59–28 victory against Hampden-Sydney.

49 The Architects of Cameron

The first drawings of historic Cameron Indoor Stadium allegedly were sketched out on the back of a matchbook. Whether that really happened or not, the official architectural plans for the stadium were drawn by the Philadelphia firm of Horace Trumbauer. Trumbauer was a self-made man, a poor boy who left school at 16 to apprentice himself as a draftsman to a local architect. In 1890, at the age of 21, he opened his own office and quickly rose to prominence in the Northeast. His designs for the mansions and estates of the wealthy northeastern magnates brought him to the attention of James B. Duke, who first commissioned Trumbauer to design his New York townhome during the early part of the century.

Over the years it has come to light that plans for campus, as well as designs for later buildings, including Cameron Indoor Stadium, were drawn up not by Trumbauer himself, but by his chief engineer, Julian Abele, one of the nation's first African American architects. Trumbauer instantly recognized the talent of Abele when he observed some of the student's award-winning drawings. Upon Abele's graduation in 1902 as the first black student in architecture at the University of Pennsylvania, Trumbauer financed further study for him at the Ecole Des Beaux Arts in Paris. Abele joined Trumbauer's firm in 1906, advancing to chief designer in 1909.

They forged a close relationship based on respect for talent and friendship. Trumbauer excelled as the front man dealing with major clients, but he avoided publicity and public appearances. Abele was the African American chief designer essential to the internal operation of the firm, a position too confining for his deserved reputation. Abele, himself, was not elected to membership in the Philadelphia AIA until 1941.

The original design for the Indoor Stadium at Duke was significantly less grand than the one from which the building was actually constructed. The first plans called for 5,000 basketball "sittings," and even that number was considered extravagant. The Palestra in Philadelphia sat 9,000 at that time and was considered the palace of all arenas. Duke president William Preston Few insisted on the 8,000-plus seat design, which Trumbauer's firm, under the expert architectural eye of Abele, was able to design.

50 C.B. Claiborne

Claudius Barone Claiborne, who enrolled at Duke in the fall of 1965 and played three varsity seasons of basketball for coach Vic Bubas, was Duke's first African American athlete. It was a very interesting time for Claiborne, who was admitted in just the third class of minority undergraduate students at a very white university. "I felt a lot like a pioneer," Claiborne said. "That's what that experience was like. It seemed like everything I did was new."

Claiborne came to Duke from Danville, Virginia, where he was an all-state player and the top-ranked student academically at his all-black high school. He was one of 225 winners of a four-year college scholarship from the National Achievement Scholarship Program and planned to attend North Carolina A&T. But a Duke supporter in the Danville area got the Blue Devils coaches interested, and Claiborne's high school coach encouraged him to go to Duke, partly to break the athletic color barrier.

Claiborne played on the freshman team in 1966 and appeared in 53 varsity games from 1966–67 through 1969, scoring 218 points with 100 rebounds. He scored 13 points during a start against Penn State during his sophomore season and had seven double-figure games in his senior season, including the first four. His career high of 15 was against Clemson.

Tom Carmody, coach of the freshman squad in those days of freshman ineligibility, spoke highly of Claiborne once practice began in the fall of 1965. In an interview with *The Duke Chronicle*, he called the wing "a swift, smooth ball player with a fine outside shot" and "one of the most unselfish players I've ever coached."

Claiborne finished sixth in scoring and third in rebounding on an 11–5 freshman squad led by guard Dave Golden and center Steve Vandenberg. There were racial incidents on the road, but typically they went unreported. Taunts and other forms of abuse would accompany Claiborne throughout his career, especially when Duke played at the University of South Carolina. But this, too, was accepted with scant comment, including by those in the Blue Devils contingent.

As a sophomore, Claiborne, limited early in the season by a torn ligament in his knee, appeared in a dozen games. Duke finished 18–9, losing to North Carolina in the finals of the ACC Tournament. Claiborne got his first start on January 3, 1967, in a five-point home win against Penn State for which Bubas suspended nine players, including four starters, for violating team rules.

Claiborne, often playing as a defensive stopper, participated more extensively in 1968 on a team that went 22–6, capping the regular season with a triple-overtime home victory against third-ranked North Carolina. Claiborne played a crucial role and his road roommate, reserve forward Fred Lind, was the unlikely hero.

Claiborne appeared in 22 games on a 1969 team that dropped to 15–13 in what proved Bubas' finale as a head coach. The senior enjoyed consecutive strong showings in the late-December Sugar

Bowl in New Orleans and contributed 6.5 points per game that year to double his scoring average from '68. Yet his playing time diminished as the season progressed.

Claiborne's arrival made Duke the second ACC institution to integrate its varsity roster. Maryland's Bill Jones was the first African American varsity player in 1966, Claiborne's year on the freshman team. North Carolina, N.C. State, and Wake Forest brought in black players during Claiborne's junior and senior seasons.

From a national perspective, Claiborne enrolled at Duke during the same academic year in which the all-black Texas Western team defeated the all-white Kentucky team for the NCAA title. Duke's varsity team was at the Final Four and lost to Kentucky in the semifinals by four in a battle of the No. 1 and No. 2 teams in the nation.

Claiborne once said that he could not recall any overt racism within his team but experienced plenty of it from fans at road games. Teammates said that he handled it well. "C.B. was a great guy, very proud and stood his ground," teammate Steve Vandenberg recalled. "He was like Jackie Robinson in that way. He just took it. He was very stoic, very scholarly about it."

Racial tensions on campus led to a sit-in at the Allen Building during Claiborne's final semester in 1969. Several members of the African American Society took over the building and threatened to destroy valuable records in the university's administrative headquarters if certain demands were not met, such as the creation of a black dorm, a black student union, and an African American Studies Department. Claiborne participated and missed a couple of days with the team, including a game at West Virginia. The other players unanimously supported his return to the team afterward. Claiborne was the only African American on the roster throughout his career, though Duke's first black athletic scholarship player, Don Blackman, was on the freshman team in Claiborne's senior season.

Claiborne earned an engineering degree from Duke. He had a postgraduate offer to join the Harlem Globetrotters, but with a wife and young child, he chose to enter the business world instead. Later he received two master's degrees (from Washington University and Dartmouth College) and a doctorate from Virginia Tech. His academic career, a cross-country journey that spans more than a quarter-century, led Claiborne to Texas Southern, where he is a professor in the business school.

51 Ferry Scores 58

Senior Danny Ferry entered the game at Miami on December 10, 1988, coming off one of the worst performances of his career as he fouled out in 12 minutes against Stetson. It did not look like this would be an incredibly memorable night for the team's leading scorer as the Blue Devils faced the University of Miami in the Hurricanes' new pro-style arena, which was half full with a crowd of 6,654, though that number still represented a school attendance record.

Things didn't get off to a great start as Ferry picked up two early fouls in less than nine minutes and headed to the bench. But the Blue Devils as a team weren't having a great night either. A few minutes later, they trailed 32–28 to the hot-shooting Hurricanes so Ferry was reinserted into the lineup. That's when he took over the game. By the end of the half, Ferry had made 15-of-17 shots for 34 points, and the Blue Devils were in charge. He just kept shooting, and it seemed like every shot was going in. Actually, he missed three of his 26 shots.

Danny Ferry, who scored a single-game, ACC-record 58 points in the contest, shoots against Miami in 1988. He missed only three of his 26 shots. (AP Images)

In the 117–102 Blue Devils win, Ferry scored a school and ACC-record 58 points. Dick Groat had held the Duke record of 48 points for more than 36 years. The ACC record of 57 was held by N.C. State's David Thompson against Buffalo State in 1974.

Ferry, who scored 13 points in succession in two and a half minutes at one point in the game, also set new Duke records for field goals in a game with 23. The previous record had been 19 by Jeff Mullins and Groat. "I was confident and the guys were yelling at me to shoot," Ferry said. Bob Ferry, Danny's father and general manager at that time of the Washington Bullets, saw the game in person. "He's very capable of a game like this," his dad said.

Quin Snyder, a senior guard on the team and Ferry's best friend, jokingly put it in perspective after the game. "As you can see, he didn't beat me and the rest of the team. We got 59; Dan can only get 58…He was in the groove. You could see it. We kept telling him to shoot. He was unbelievable."

Duke shot 75 percent for the first half and 67.2 percent overall in what was one of the highest scoring games in school history. "One of the most phenomenal I've ever seen," said Miami coach Bill Foster, who is not to be confused with the former Duke coach of the same name. "And he wasn't getting any gimmies. Hell, we hammered him, and he still made them. He amazed me."

52 Miracle Minute

During Duke's game at Cole Field House in College Park, Maryland, on January 27, 2001, Maryland had basically controlled the game the entire evening. Though the No. 2-ranked Blue Devils were riding an eight-game winning streak and an 18–1 record, the No. 8-ranked Terrapins looked to be in firm control.

With 1:15 left in the game, things looked bleak for the Blue Devils to as they trailed 89–77. Even with tough defense and hitting some big shots, they still trailed 90–80 with 61 seconds left in regulation as the Maryland student body began to chant "Overrated, Overrated" at the second-ranked Blue Devils.

It was at this point that the Blue Devils staged one of the greatest comebacks in college basketball history. With 54 seconds left, Jason Williams made a layup. Until that point in the game, Williams had not made a three-pointer, being very closely guarded and harassed by nemesis Steve Blake. The play of Blake forced Williams into 10 turnovers.

But Williams stole the inbounds pass after the layup and made a three and eight seconds later he hit another three. Suddenly, it was 90–88, and JWill had scored eight points in 14 seconds. Nate James then stole the ball from Maryland star Juan Dixon and was fouled when he tried to follow a Mike Dunleavy shot. The two free throws by James tied the game at 90, and the game went into a shocking overtime after Drew Nicholas missed a jumper for the Terps.

In the extra period, Shane Battier gave Duke the lead for good at 95–92 with a three-pointer, and the Blue Devils made five of their six foul shots to win 98–96. Maryland's last chance was a 10-foot jumper by Juan Dixon, but Battier blocked it.

Mike Krzyzewski said the key play was Williams' steal of the inbounds pass and subsequent three-pointer. "That was a monster shot," he said. "He shot it almost sitting on our bench." Williams wound up with 25 points after playing poorly for 39 minutes.

Maryland fans didn't take kindly to the collapse. Carlos Boozer's father stormed into the media room where the press was waiting for Krzyzewski and said that his wife had been hit in the head by a water bottle. Chris Duhon's mother said water bottles twice hit her.

Despite the vicious postgame reaction from Maryland, Duke had the victory. "That was an amazing win for us," said an elated but exhausted Krzyzewski. "Down 10 with a minute left, we just hung in there. Our kids made winning plays."

53 Red Auerbach

In the NBA register, he is listed as serving as an assistant coach at Duke in 1949–50. But in reality the famous NBA coach wasn't in Durham long enough to coach in a game for the Blue Devils.

Hired by Eddie Cameron in the summer of 1949, Auerbach was viewed as a potential successor to head coach Gerry Gerard, who had been diagnosed with cancer. Thinking that Gerard was recovering, Auerbach left for a pro job before the 1949–50 season got underway. But he made at least one valuable contribution to Duke basketball history during his brief tenure: he spent many a lunch hour working one-on-one at the Indoor Stadium with Dick Groat, helping to develop one of the top Blue Devils players of all time leading up to the player's sophomore season.

Auerbach's legacy after leaving Duke is well known. Voted the greatest coach in NBA history in 1980, he amassed 938 victories in 20 years, won nine NBA titles, and was inducted into the Hall of Fame in 1969. As a general manager and team president of the Celtics, he won an additional seven NBA titles for a grand total of 16 in a span of 29 years.

Auerbach is remembered as a pioneer of modern basketball, redefining basketball as a game dominated by team play and defense and for introducing the fast break as a potent offensive weapon. He groomed many players who went on to be inducted into the Basketball Hall of Fame. Additionally, Auerbach was vital in breaking down color barriers in the NBA. He made history by drafting the first African American NBA player, Chuck Cooper, in 1950, and played the first African American starting five in 1964.

54 Duke-Carolina Pranks

The student bodies at Duke and Carolina are both a major part of the best rivalry in college basketball. The Cameron Crazies are well known for their antics during games. Unlike most schools where students are relegated to seats in the upper deck and the big-check donors receive the prime real estate, the Duke students are right near the floor. Those students—dressed in all sorts of attire and painted up with blue faces and bodies—get all the publicity, while down the road in Chapel Hill, the crowd is known for how Florida State guard Sam Cassell dubbed them in 1991. "It's not a Duke kind of crowd," he said. "It's more like a cheese-and-wine crowd, kind of laid back."

But whether it is in the Dean E. Smith Center or Carmichael Auditorium, when Duke and Carolina play, the place is rocking. In 1978 when Phil Ford hit a long-range shot at the end of the first half for Carolina, the roar was so loud and raucous that the covers for the lights on the catwalk-like press box fell on the writers.

The student bodies have always pulled pranks on each other, but one of the best took place prior to the February 13, 2013, game. The head of Duke's Blue Devils mascot was stolen and placed on a pole—*Game of Thrones* style—above a University of North Carolina campus store prior to the showdown in Durham.

A few days earlier, the Blue Devil and the North Carolina Ram mascot had been in Durham to shoot a video promo for the game for ESPN. Following the shoot the Blue Devil mascot, showing professional courtesy, took the Rams mascot down to his secret room in the basement of Card Gymnasium to change clothes. In this room the Blue Devil stores his uniform and alternate head. He also has taped to the walls all the little catchy phrases he places on his forehead with athletic tape prior to the game. Things like "End of the Rhode" for a game against Rhode Island; "Smoke the Bruins," referencing a UCLA player accused of marijuana possession back in the '90s; and, of course, the infamous "Buckwheat" headband in 1988 referring to the hairstyle of Notre Dame guard David Rivers. The Blue Devil later apologized for that one.

In 2012 Duke students dressed Chapel Hill's famous Silent Sam statue in Duke clothing. Silent Sam is a statue of a Confederate soldier located on the North Carolina campus at McCorkle Place, the university's upper quad, facing Franklin Street, that was erected in 1913 as a monument to the 321 alumni of the university who died in the Civil War and all students who joined the Confederate Army.

Carolina fans have pulled some pretty good pranks themselves. Following the Blue Devils' national championship in 1991 and several months prior to the 1992 Duke-Carolina game in Chapel Hill, a ball and net from the 1991 Final Four went missing out of the trophy case in Cameron Indoor Stadium. The next day following Carolina's 75–73 victory, the ball and net showed up very neatly displayed at the Old Well on the Carolina campus.

But Duke fans believe that the greatest prank ever pulled off in this rivalry was in 1998 when four students stole Michael Jordan's retired jersey from the rafters of the Dean Dome and hung it inside of Cameron Indoor Stadium. How they got up there—and even in the Dean Dome—was never revealed.

55 Renovations to Cameron

For more than 35 years, Duke basketball teams played in the Indoor Stadium with very little being done to update the historic palace. But as the basketball program grew in proportion and prestige, there was more than one request for sprucing up of the facility. One of the most persuasive had come from head basketball coach Vic Bubas during the 1960s. In a memo to athletic director Eddie Cameron, Bubas listed the improvements being made by every neighboring college arena. He noted that Duke had the attendance and interest to merit renovations but said, "We don't need a new building. We can paint and clean the one we have." Evidently the $15,000-plus price tag for painting the stadium didn't fly. By the mid-1970s, however, it had become apparent that Cameron needed much more than a fresh coat of paint.

The main concern was the playing floor itself. Tom Butters, assistant to the chancellor at the time in early 1977, knew exactly what the problem was. "Our old floor was literally gone," he explained. "It had been sanded and refurbished to the tongue and groove each year. I remember eight times we had to fix the floor last season with patchwork just so it was playable."

Such a major undertaking had to be carefully planned. "I talked with the people who count—the players, coaches, doctors, and some fans. We wanted a floor with the most resiliency, one that was best for the players' legs, and one even on which the fans would enjoy hearing the ball bounce."

Through the spring and summer of 1977, the floor in Cameron Indoor Stadium was torn up, and 30,000 wooden slats were hand laid. Underneath, 1/16 of an inch of new cement covered by thick foam padding stabilized and cushioned the new floor. In addition the stadium was almost entirely redone on the ground floor. The face-lift included refurbishing both lobbies and adding a Hall of Fame Room, new student seating, and a new two-tiered football dressing room complex. New basketball goals were suspended from the ceiling. Duke was only the second major college to install suspended goals, which reduce the injuries resulting from collisions with the basket stanchions.

In February 1986 NBC sports commentator Dick Enberg told the world about the latest planned renovations for Cameron. "They're going to make a real sports antique out of it…complete with brass railings and stained glass windows." For Duke officials watching the Sunday afternoon broadcast of the Duke-Georgia Tech game, this was certainly news. Planned renovations did not, as some rumors indicated, include stained glass windows, but they did include new side walls, a new electronic scoreboard, and even brass railings.

Renovations began in 1987. The lobbies and concourse were remodeled during the summer of 1987. Then in 1988, work began on the interior of the arena. An updated electronic scoreboard, new sound system, and decorative wood paneling gave Cameron a more modern look while maintaining the original elegance. The addition of 750 new student seats increased the capacity to 9,314.

In the early 1990s, Mike Krzyzewski and athletic director Butters decided the time was right to give Cameron an addition with new locker rooms, coaches' offices, an academic center, and a new sports hall of fame. Several years later ground was broken for the new Schwartz-Butters Athletic Center after the end of the 1997–98 season. That complex now houses the men's and women's basketball programs, as well as Duke's athletic academic center.

The first part of that expansion and improvement project was the installation of a new floor in Cameron Indoor Stadium after the 1996–97 season. The latest advancements in floor technology were utilized to give the Blue Devils one of the finest playing surfaces in the entire country. Prior to the 1999–2000 season, a new press row was added. As a response to health and odor concerns for players and fans alike, air conditioning was added in 2001–02. For its 100th season in 2004–05, the concourse was enhanced to celebrate Duke's tradition in men's and women's basketball with the addition of poster displays, and all the banners were replaced in the rafters. Prior to the 2008–09 season, a new video scoreboard replaced the electronic board over center court. Before the 2009–10 season, additional changes were made, including installing LED ribbon boards to the front of the press table and painting the upper seats Duke blue.

Even with all its renovations, Cameron Indoor Stadium has maintained its integrity as one of the best places in the world to watch a sporting event.

56 Gerry Gerard

From 1943 to 1950, Gerry Gerard served as the head basketball coach for the Duke Blue Devils. Gerard was named the head coach when Eddie Cameron became the head football coach after Wallace Wade left to serve in the military during World War II.

A native of Indiana, Gerard played football at Illinois and backed up famed All-American Red Grange. When Gerard came to Duke in 1931, it was to run the intramural sports program. Four years later he started the soccer program and he coached the squad for the first 11 years. He officiated football and basketball games and was also known for his work as a local radio announcer in those sports. He became Cameron's assistant basketball coach in 1941 and served for two years prior to his promotion. Even after moving up, he continued to officiate football contests, occasionally missing an early-season basketball event to fulfill a football obligation.

While coaching the basketball team, Gerard led the Blue Devils to the Southern Conference championship game in six of his eight years and won two titles in 1944 and 1946. He was named the league's coach of the year in 1948 and 1950. His first team was one of his best. In 1943 he finished with a mark of 20–6 overall and 12–1 in the conference. It was stocked with Durham natives and won 16 of its last 17 games before falling to George Washington in the Southern final. Duke won the league tourney the next year in improbable fashion as it entered the event with a 10–13 record. The Blue Devils blew out William & Mary before defeating N.C. State and North Carolina for the crown and an even 13–13 record.

The 1946 team was another of Gerard's best, as it went 12–2 in the conference season and rode the scoring of Ed Koffenberger to the tourney crown. The Blue Devils finished the year with a record of 21–6. Koffenberger set Duke's career scoring record in the following year as Duke went 19–8, but the Blue Devils bowed out of the Southern Conference tourney in the first round, even though it was held on their home floor for the first time.

Gerard's health began to deteriorate at the end of the 1949 season. He was able to return in 1950, but in November 1950, he took a leave of absence because of illness. His two-year battle with cancer came to an end in January 1951 at the age of 47. In December of 1951, Duke and North Carolina met in a benefit game for Gerard's family, and in 1987 Gerard was inducted posthumously into the Duke Sports Hall of Fame.

57 Harold Bradley

Harold "Hal" Bradley became head basketball coach at Duke with less than a month left until the start of the 1951 season but guided the Blue Devils to a 20-win campaign. Bradley coached the Blue Devils from the 1950–51 season for nine consecutive seasons through the 1958–59 season. He had winning seasons each and every year, winning 68 percent of his games with a 165–78 record.

Bradley was the head coach at Duke for several of the school's biggest moments in basketball. He coached Dick Groat, the first athlete at Duke to have his jersey retired and first National Basketball Player of the Year, in his junior and senior seasons. He coached the Blue Devils' last Southern Conference team and its first ACC team and was the first coach to take Duke to the NCAA Tournament. He was the only Duke coach to win a Dixie Classic and the first to direct a team that finished in the national rankings. The only thing he never did was win a conference championship, though he played in three championships, losing all of them to N.C. State on the Wolfpack's home court.

A product of Hartwick College in upstate New York, Bradley was about to begin his career as his alma mater's head coach and athletic director when Eddie Cameron hired him away to Duke because cancer had forced coach Gerry Gerard to take a leave of absence. With Groat as the catalyst, Bradley guided the Blue Devils to records of 20–13 and 24–6 in his first two years and a pair of trips to the Southern Conference finals. The 1952 team—ranked No. 12—was the first in school history to be ranked in the final Associated Press poll. It won 15 straight games before losing the tournament finale. Bradley's 1954, 1956, and 1958 teams also were ranked, finishing 10th in 1958.

Bradley liked to play more of an up-tempo, fast-paced game and led Duke to their first 100-point game in 1952 and 12 more times during his tenure. Duke finished fourth in the country in scoring in 1953 and 1954 and set a school record with an 85.2 average in 1955.

Bradley coached Duke to first place in the first ACC race of 1954 and again in 1958. The Blue Devils never finished lower than third in his six seasons. His 94–37 record, a 71.8 percentage in conference games of both the Southern and ACC, was better than his overall percentage.

It was a Bradley-coached team at Duke that won its first game over a No. 1 team when it defeated top-ranked West Virginia and future Hall of Famer Jerry West in 1958. Bradley was successful against North Carolina, posting a 14–11 record, including an eight-game winning streak. But he was 8–16 against N.C. State. The Blue Devils lost three times to N.C. State in 1955 but made their first trip to the NCAA tourney replacing the ineligible Wolfpack.

Bradley coached four teams that won at least 20 games. He made his most notable coaching change in 1958 when he switched to an all-senior lineup with no one taller than 6'6" and went on an 11-game winning streak, which included the upset of West Virginia and two wins over nationally ranked N.C. State.

Bradley's worst record was his last, a 13–12 mark in 1959. Ironically, that was the only year he was selected ACC Coach of the Year while directing a youthful and lightly regarded contingent to third place. Most of those players helped Vic Bubas to win the ACC championship the next year. Bradley left Duke for Texas at the end of the 1959 season, where he coached the Longhorns to three Southwest Conference titles before retiring in 1967.

58 Visit the Nasher Art Museum

The Nasher Museum opened in 2005 as a major center for the arts on Duke University's campus and the surrounding Research Triangle area. The museum organizes and presents leading-edge exhibitions that travel to institutions worldwide, including *Archibald Motley: Jazz Age Modernist* (2014), *Wangechi Mutu: A Fantastic Journey* (2013), *The Vorticists: Rebel Artists in London and New York, 1914–1918* (2010), and *Barkley L. Hendricks: Birth of the Cool* (2008). The traveling exhibition *El Greco to Velázquez: Art during the Reign of Philip III* was named one of *Time* magazine's top 10 shows of 2008. The strengths of the museum's permanent collection are Medieval art, art of the Americas (largely pre-Columbian), Classical Antiquities, and modern and contemporary art.

In the summer of 2006, even Duke basketball became part of the museum with an exhibition titled *Something All Our Own: The Grant Hill Collection of African American Art* that featured works from the collection of Duke alumnus and NBA basketball star Grant Hill. The exhibition included 46 collages, paintings, prints, and mixed media works by such artists as Romare Bearden, Elizabeth Catlett, John Biggers, Hughie Lee-Smith, Malcolm Brown, Phoebe Beasley, and John Coleman, among others.

The museum's contemporary collection features a growing list of artists, including Barkley L. Hendricks, Christian Marclay, Wangechi Mutu, Ai Weiwei, Fred Wilson, and Lynette Yiadom-Boakye. More than 100,000 people visit the museum each year.

The 65,000-square-foot Nasher Museum was designed by architect Rafael Viñoly. The centerpiece of Viñoly's modernist design is a dramatic 13,000 square-foot glass and steel roof rising to a height of 45 feet above the great hall. Five concrete pavilions fan out from a central courtyard to house three large gallery spaces, an auditorium, two classrooms, a shop, and a café. The museum presents a dynamic schedule of programs, including free Family Days, performing arts events, lectures, film series, and social gatherings.

The Nasher Museum's growing permanent collection includes some of today's best contemporary art with a rare focus on work by artists of African descent. Other major strengths in the collection include European medieval art, European and American paintings, classical antiquities, African art, and ancient American (Pre-Columbian) art.

Formerly the Duke University Museum of Art, the museum was founded in 1969 with the acquisition of 200 medieval works from the Ernest Brummer Collection. The museum was housed in a former science building on the East Campus until the new building opened on Duke's central campus in 2005. The museum was renamed the Nasher Museum of Art at Duke University in honor of the late Raymond D. Nasher, a Duke alumnus, collector, and benefactor.

59 Visit East Campus

East Campus was the original location of Duke after it moved to Durham from Trinity, North Carolina, when a large philanthropic gift from James B. Duke in 1924 led to the changing of its name to Duke University. East Campus, located 1.5 miles from West Campus, currently functions as a freshman campus as well as the home of several academic departments.

The park-like East Campus encompasses 97 acres of open lawns and mature trees. The art history, history, literature, music, philosophy, and women's studies departments are housed in Georgian-style buildings on East. Programs such as dance, drama, education, film, and the university writing program also reside here. The self-sufficient East Campus contains the freshman residence halls, a dining hall, coffee shop, post office, Lilly Library, Baldwin Auditorium, a theater, Brodie Gym, and tennis courts. East Campus is surrounded by established residential neighborhoods and is a short walking distance to Ninth Street and the thriving downtown district.

The 100-acre campus became somewhat isolated when a site for campus expansion was chosen about a mile away. At that point East Campus became the Women's College and remained that way until 1972, when Duke became a coed institution. The landscape character of East Campus is very different from that of West Campus, which is known as the "university in the forest" and evokes the image of a university within a park with its open lawns and impressive stands of mature trees. This difference reflects the contrast that exists between the East Campus Georgian architecture and the Collegiate Gothic style of West Campus, which is one of the unique aspects of the Duke campus. Approximately 100 acres in size, East Campus is an important element in the fabric of the Durham community, surrounded by established residential neighborhoods, and is within walking distance to downtown.

East Campus is the site of two of the major statues on campus, the first being the statue of the father of Duke—Washington Duke—sitting in a chair, and the second is a statue of the Sower of Knowledge.

60 Stay at Washington Duke Inn & Golf Club

Located across the street from Cameron Indoor Stadium and the Duke athletics complex, the Washington Duke Inn & Golf Club first opened its doors in 1988. The hotel was named for Washington Duke, who emerged from his modest beginnings as an American Civil War soldier in 1865 went to become an industrialist and philanthropist.

Known for its beautifully manicured grounds, stately golf course views, and luxury accommodations, the Washington Duke Inn & Golf Club is an unrivaled destination among hotels in Durham. Recipient of the prestigious AAA Four Diamond award for 14 consecutive years, the storied hotel enjoys a prime setting on the Duke University campus and is the site of many a get-together for dinner or drinks before or after any and all basketball games.

Amid 300 acres of tall pines and rolling countryside, the Washington Duke Inn offers guests a serene retreat far removed from the hectic pace of everyday life. The luxurious hotel features 271 elegantly appointed guest rooms and suites, the Robert Trent Jones-designed 18-hole championship Duke University Golf Club, award-winning dining, exceptional meeting facilities, and a three-mile hiking trail through the Duke Forest.

The Duke family continues to uphold a long-standing tradition of community service, philanthropy, and loyalty to Duke University, which is evident throughout the Washington Duke Inn & Golf Club. Family artifacts and photographs have been donated for display in the hallways, and the family coat of arms has been incorporated in the Inn's logo.

Ambassador Angier Biddle Duke (1915–95), great-grandson of Washington Duke, followed family tradition and embraced public service at a young age. The Washington Duke Inn's exhibit of Ambassador Duke's memorabilia includes papers, artifacts, and gifts he received during his tenures as ambassador to El Salvador, Spain, Morocco, and Denmark, and the many decorations he received from presidents and royal families.

The Duke University golf course was first envisioned in the early 1930s when coach Wallace Wade, coach Eddie Cameron, and president William Preston Few inspected portions of the Duke Forest and discussed the desirability of a university course. By 1941 actual plans were drawn up by the renowned architect, Perry Maxwell, on a site that is now the location of the Duke Faculty Club. The original golf course construction was planned to begin prior to World War II, but when Japan bombed Pearl Harbor in 1941, the plans were put on hold by Wade, Duke's athletic director at that point.

At the conclusion of the war, the plans resurfaced, and the present site of 120 acres was selected. The property was carefully chosen for its unique blend of unusual changes in elevation throughout its mildly rolling terrain. It typified the Piedmont of North Carolina at its best, sprinkled with meandering streams and blessed with a variety of hardwoods, towering pines, and beautiful shrubbery. Duke sought out Robert Trent Jones, whose golf course design work was widely respected. "The routing of a course is the most important element of design," Jones said. "Designing a great golf course is like putting together the pieces of a jigsaw puzzle. In almost all cases, it is best to let the land suggest the course. Use the land; don't abuse it. Fit the holes into the terrain available, moving as little dirt as possible. The great architect should create the illusion that the golf holes were on the ground just lying there, waiting to be grassed over."

Finally, on September 26, 1957, Duke University Golf Club opened to the public. It was immediately labeled as one of the top university golf facilities in the nation. The attention was great enough to attract the 1962 NCAA Golf Championship. Twenty-six years later, in 1988, Tom Butters, Duke University vice president and director of athletics, recognized that the golf course desperately needed restoration. The passing years had been more than unkind to the once incomparable Duke layout. The compacted greens and fairways were struggling to grow grass, its tees were chewed up, and the bunkers were in need of repair. The board of trustees approved an endowment program to fund the restoration of the golf club. The five-year plan necessary to achieve this goal was put in place with the final major construction to begin in June 1993 and be complete by April 1994.

During the summer of 2000, the club was shut down for the month of July to put new sand in the bunkers and to install six new tee boxes to prepare for hosting the 2001 NCAA Men's Golf Championships, which was a huge success. In the fall of 2005, the Karcher-Ingram Golf Center was completed. Named after Jack, Lois, and John Karcher, as well as David and Sarah Lebrun Ingram, the $3 million, two-story 5,500-square foot building houses coaches' offices, men's and women's team locker rooms, a trophy room, lounge, a club repair room, a student-athlete study area, and an indoor training and practice facility. The Duke golf teams also have a new $1 million outdoor practice facility, which includes putting and chipping greens; a full-swing and short-game area, including sand and grass bunkers; a practice fairway bunker; and target greens.

61 Jay Bilas

Because of the incredible reach of television, especially a network like ESPN with its millions of viewers, Jay Bilas is known more for his broadcasting role than as a basketball player. He is one of the most recognizable Duke alumni in the world. Bilas receives more airtime than any Duke graduate and has become one of the most familiar faces in sports broadcasting.

But prior to becoming a TV star, Bilas was a basketball player. He played at Rolling Hill High School in Southern California, where he averaged 23.5 points per game and 13.5 rebounds his senior season. He came to Duke as part of Mike Krzyzewski's first big recruiting class in 1982 along with Johnny Dawkins, Mark Alarie, and David Henderson. Brought in as a forward, Bilas had to bulk up to become the Blue Devils' 6'8" center guarding the likes of David Robinson and Ralph Sampson in his career. During his four years, he played in 127 games, scored 1,062 points for an 8.4 average, and grabbed 692 rebounds. He shot 55.7 percent from the field, leading the team in that category for three seasons.

Two of his best games came against archrival North Carolina. He played solid defense and had a double-double with 10 points and 11 rebounds when the Blue Devils upset the No. 1–ranked Tar Heels in the semifinals of the 1984 ACC Tournament. He had a great performance against UNC when Duke won at Carmichael Auditorium in 1985, ending an 18-year drought of winning a game in Chapel Hill. For the game he had 17 points and 11 rebounds. In the 1986 NCAA East Regional Finals against Navy, his defense on Robinson and 10 rebounds were major factors that helped the Blue Devils advance to the Final Four.

Jay Bilas (far right), who works on ESPN's College GameDay *with former Duke star Jay Williams (second from left), has become one of the major voices of college basketball.*

Following his college career, Bilas was a fifth-round selection in the 1986 NBA Draft by the Dallas Mavericks. He never played in the NBA but played professionally overseas for teams in Italy and Spain. He returned to the United States and worked as an assistant at Duke for three seasons from 1990 to 1992 while also attending Duke Law School and received his J.D. degree in 1992. During that time period, he was part of two NCAA championship teams and coached teams in the Final Four all three years he was an assistant. At the same time, he appeared in the science fiction movie *I Come In Peace* with Dolph Lundgren and became a practicing attorney for a law firm in Charlotte.

Beginning with the 1993 season, Bilas began working on his broadcasting career as he served as color commentator for the Duke Radio Network as well as hosting features on the Duke television show *Inside Basketball with Duke's Coach K.* He also did early work on television for the Raycom/Jefferson Pilot Network. In 1995 he began working for ESPN and has been under contract to the network since 1998. He worked his way up the broadcasting ladder, working Mid-Continent Conference and Big Sky Tournament games in Montana as well as serving as an analyst for WNBA games in 1999 and studio analyst for the NCAA Women's Championship Tournament in 2000. He has since served as an ESPN studio and game analyst working on *College GameDay* along with working for CBS as a game analyst for their coverage of the NCAA Tournament. In 2007 and 2008, he was nominated for an Emmy for Outstanding Performance by a Studio Analyst. Even with that gaudy broadcasting resume, Bilas remains a counsel with Moore and Van Allen law firm.

62 Read *The Chronicle*

First published as *The Trinity Chronicle* on December 19, 1905, *The Chronicle* is the daily student newspaper at Duke. The paper's name was changed to *The Chronicle* when Trinity College was renamed Duke University. One of the most highly honored college newspapers in the United States, *The Chronicle* commands a budget of more than $1 million and employs a staff of 120. Its coverage gained national significance in light of the 2006 Duke lacrosse team scandal, and it has been widely lauded for having balanced coverage, even as most national publications jumped to conclusions.

The Chronicle has a print readership of roughly 30,000, and its website, The Chronicle Online, has an average of more than 70,000 hits each day. At the 2009 Associated Collegiate Press National College Media Convention in Austin, Texas, the paper won the Best in Show category for four-year daily tabloids. In 2007 *The Chronicle* took home four awards from the ACP, including online Story of the Year for its ongoing coverage of the Duke lacrosse scandal. In 2006 the paper took second place in the Best in Show category in St. Louis, Missouri. *Towerview*, a monthly newsmagazine distributed with the paper, won Best in Show in the Magazine Feature-Special Audience Category, while its editor, Alex Fanaroff, won first place in the "features story" category. The paper also won Best in Show in the tabloid division in 2005 in Kansas City, Missouri, and finished in second place in Editorials that year.

Former Chronicle writers who have stayed in the journalism business include *New York Magazine* founder Clay Felker along with *The Washington Post* sports reporter and noted author John Feinstein and *The Wall Street Journal* travel editor Scott McCartney.

The most publicized incident with the Duke basketball program and *The Chronicle* occurred late in Mike Krzyzewski's first decade as head coach, when the paper ran a report on the progress of the team. It was actually a report card with some tough grading, and Krzyzewski was very unhappy with how *The Chronicle* graded his basketball team and players. The coach summoned several members of the sports staff to the locker room and blasted them in front of the team, igniting a wave of negative reaction in the media.

63 Madison Square Garden and the Meadowlands

The world's most famous arena has been host to an incredible number of significant Duke basketball games since 1944. On November 15, 2011, the Blue Devils defeated Michigan State 74–69 to give head coach Mike Krzyzewski his 903rd win, making him the winningest coach in Division I men's basketball. Then on January 25, 2015, Krzyzewski became the first coach in the history of Division I men's basketball to win 1,000 games as Duke defeated St. John's 77–68.

Madison Square Garden in New York City has been the site of great triumphs and very tough losses over the years for the Blue Devils. The Garden, built in 1925 for $5 million at 8th Avenue and 50th Street, had an extensive college basketball tradition, beginning in 1934 with a doubleheader that attracted more than 16,000 fans. In 1938 the National Invitation Tournament began at the Garden, and soon college basketball became a mainstay at the facility.

The Blue Devils' first visit to the Garden occurred on January 1, 1944. They dropped an overtime game to Long Island University despite 27 points from Gordon Carver in front of 16,108. Following World War II, the Blue Devils returned to play New York University in January 1947 and January 1948 and lost both games before crowds of 18,034 and 17,931, respectively.

Several NCAA Tournament games in the 1940s and 1950s were held at Madison Square Garden, including Duke's first appearance. The Blue Devils lost to Villanova in a first-round NCAA tripleheader in 1955. Duke also played NYU again at the Garden twice in the 1950s, beating Princeton there in the opening round of the NCAAs in 1960 and made its first NIT trip to the Garden in 1967.

The Meadowlands

Located in East Rutherford, New Jersey, the Meadowlands sports complex has played host to some of the most significant moments in Duke basketball history. Duke's success in the building has led fans and foes alike to refer to the Meadowlands as Cameron North. The Blue Devils have compiled an overall record of 21–1 with their only loss at the Meadowlands coming in February of 1989 when they fell to Arizona 77–75.

The complex includes MetLife Stadium—home to the NFL's New York Giants and New York Jets—a horseracing track, and a basketball arena. The basketball arena, Brendan Byrne Arena, originally named for the sitting governor of New Jersey, opened July 2, 1981, with the first of six sold-out concerts by Bruce Springsteen. The arena was renamed for its corporate sponsor, Continental Airlines (now United Airlines), in early 1996 and again in 2007 for Izod.

Duke competed in five NCAA regionals hosted by the Meadowlands and won all five to earn trips to the Final Four. Duke's first under Mike Krzyzewski occurred in 1986 after the Blue Devils defeated David Robinson and Navy. Final Four appearances in 1988, 1989, and 1999 also followed triumphs at the Meadowlands. Duke upset higher-ranked Temple and Georgetown in the 1988 and 1989 regional finals and then rode a last-second shot called "Special" by Christian Laettner to upset Connecticut for a Final Four berth in 1990. Duke also won an NCAA regional title at the Meadowlands in 1999.

Duke's first Meadowlands experience was a victory over Holy Cross in 1982, a contest nationally telecast by ESPN. Duke has waged battles with Notre Dame (1985), Arizona (1989), Rutgers (1993), Texas (2006), and faced Kentucky twice there in the Jimmy V Classic (1999 and 2002).

A little-known fact is the Meadowlands was built by a Duke graduate. Francis Werneke, a native of Jersey City, New Jersey, received his civil engineering degree from Duke in 1941. He did the project after his retirement from the Port Authority of New York and New Jersey. While with the Port Authority, he directed the building of several landmarks, including the twin towers of the World Trade Center and the third tube of the Lincoln Tunnel.

The Meadowlands closed in 2015. Duke's final game at the site was on December 18, 2014, a 66–56 victory against Connecticut.

The Blue Devils dropped their NIT opener to Southern Illinois, which went on to win the event. The following season, on February 8, 1968, Duke and Southern Illinois met again in the facility's final college basketball doubleheader. Behind 28 points and 18 rebounds from center Mike Lewis, the Blue Devils gained a measure of revenge with a 24-point win against the Salukis before a crowd of 5,487. NYU then topped Manhattan in the nightcap to close out the old Garden's college card.

A new $43 million Madison Square Garden complex opened at 7th Avenue and 33rd Street atop Penn Station the following week, and Duke was back in March for another NIT visit. The Blue Devils also made NIT trips to the Garden in 1970 and 1971, twice appeared in the ECAC Holiday Festival, and made seven trips to the Garden for the Preseason NIT.

Duke first won the Preseason NIT in 1986 with big wins over St. John's and Kansas to get their Final Four season of 1986 off to a great start. David Henderson was named the MVP of the tournament. The 2001 Blue Devils, eventual NCAA champions, won the Preseason NIT at the Garden in a defensive duel with Temple. Jason Williams and Carlos Boozer combined for Duke's final 26 points in that game, including a 9–0 run over the final three minutes. Boozer finished with 26 points, earning MVP accolades. The title helped Williams forget about his Duke debut at the Garden the previous season when the Blue Devils dropped a pair of games in the Coaches vs. Cancer Classic.

Duke's 2006 season also began with a title at the Garden in the newly named NIT Season Tip-Off. J.J. Redick scrapped together a hard-fought 31 points in a semifinal win over Drexel, while Shelden Williams scored 30 to key a championship victory over Memphis 70–67. Williams' total included a tip-in with 32 seconds left to break a 67–67 tie, and he was named the event's MVP.

Home-and-home series with St. John's brought Duke to the Garden in 1999, 2001, 2003, and 2005. In 2009 the Blue Devils captured another Preseason NIT with a win against UConn and lost in the finals of same tournament in 2013 to Arizona 72–66.

With a large base of alumni in the northeast area of the country, the Blue Devils began to play nonconference games at the Garden in 2003 with the first in December against Texas before a packed house of 19,558. They have continued with games in the Garden against Oklahoma, Gonzaga, Pittsburgh, Washington, and UCLA.

64 Early All-Americans

After Bill Werber became the Blue Devils' first All-American in 1930, they had to wait 10 years for their next All-American.

Bill Mock

Mock, a 6'2" forward from Altoona, Pennsylvania, played on the 1940 and 1941 Duke basketball teams. He came off the bench for most of the 1940 season but was the leading scorer on the team, which finished the season as the Southern Conference runner-up. He was a unanimous All-Tournament selection and was selected third team All-American by the Newspaper Enterprise Association.

He did not repeat those honors in 1941 and was the fifth leading scorer on the conference championship team. Mock, however, hit the winning shot against North Carolina in 1941 with 2:09 left in the game, allowing the Blue Devils to freeze the ball for the remaining time.

Gordon Carver

Carver, a native of Durham, was one of the most versatile athletes to ever don a Duke uniform. Carver starred for the Duke basketball team in 1943, 1944, and 1945 and helped to lead them to the Southern Conference Tournament finals each year. Duke captured the title in 1944 as Carver scored 11 points in the title game. He made the All-Tournament second team in 1943 when he led the event in scoring with 40 points and the first team the next two years. Carver was one of the top scorers for the 1943 and 1944 teams, collecting 292 and 297 points, and he added 94 points in 1945 for a career total of 683. He finished as Duke's career scoring leader and held the mark until 1947.

Carver's 297 points in 1944 established the school's single-season scoring record, which lasted until Ed Koffenberger broke it in 1946. The 6'1" forward was also a back and punter on the football team. He once ripped off a 70-yard run, the fourth-longest in school history at the time, against Virginia.

Some of his best work came during the holiday season. On January 1, 1944, Duke made its first basketball appearance at Madison Square Garden in New York and lost an overtime game to Long Island University despite a career-high 27 points from Carver. The next year he spent New Year's in New Orleans as the captain of the football team, helping Duke beat Alabama in the Sugar Bowl. Carver's ankle-grabbing tackle on the last play of the game secured the win. Carver earned his undergraduate degree in 1944 and played his last year while in medical school. He was presented with the Robert E. Lee Award as the outstanding student on campus and the Teague Award as the top amateur athlete in the Carolinas.

65 Visit the Duke Basketball Museum

Sports fans have made Cameron Indoor Stadium one of the must-see stops on the Duke University campus for many years. The storied history of the five-time national championship Duke basketball program can be found at the Duke Basketball Museum, located adjacent to Cameron in the Schwartz/Butters Athletic Center.

The success of Duke basketball is archived with a multitude of trophy displays, including a ring of the five title trophies, interactive videos, and memorabilia, which are all on display. Inside the museum there are also great photo opportunities that put you in the middle of two iconic areas of Duke Basketball—the tent city known as Krzyzewskiville and the Cameron Crazies. "This is an appropriate tribute to the tremendous heritage of Duke athletics," Mike Krzyzewski said. "When you see the accomplishments of all of those who've represented this athletics department collected in one location, Duke's longstanding excellence becomes apparent."

The re-creation of the 6,600-square foot space took place over the summer and fall months of 2010 after the men's basketball and men's lacrosse programs captured NCAA championships, which led to a broader need to celebrate the extraordinary success of every sport at Duke. And residing next to the museum is the newly located Duke Athletics Hall of Fame, featuring portraits of its Hall of Fame members and celebrating all of Duke's 26 intercollegiate sports. They have combined to capture 16 national championships since 1986.

The Duke Basketball Museum and Duke Athletics Hall of Fame is open from 9:00 AM to 5:00 PM weekdays and is typically open three hours before a game and then closes at tip-off during the weekends. The area is free of charge for all visitors.

66 Attend Countdown to Craziness

Beginning in 2009, Countdown to Craziness has been an annual get-together in Cameron Indoor Stadium to kick off the basketball season. The event features a night of entertainment with live music, highlight videos, segments from Duke University Improv, and on-court contests all leading up to the introduction of the team, the unveiling of that year's team poster, the Blue-White scrimmage, and a dunk contest. It not only is a treat for fans, but also attended by many talented recruits who are considering playing for Duke.

The evening begins late afternoon in Krzyzewskiville, which is located adjacent to Cameron Indoor Stadium. Fans enjoy a live DJ, face painting, and inflatable games. Doors to Cameron Indoor Stadium usually open at 6:00 PM with several on-court presentations and contests leading up to when the Duke team is introduced at 8:00 PM with the Blue-White scrimmage following about 30 minutes later.

Countdown to Craziness kicks off with on-court activities that include performances by the Duke cheerleading squad, dance teams, vocal ensembles, and myriad other student groups. Cameron Indoor Stadium is transformed into a glittering stage for all the player introductions and games as the stage lighting gives the basketball floor almost a Las Vegas show atmosphere.

Each year, Countdown to Craziness provides fans in Cameron Indoor Stadium a glimpse of the upcoming season's Duke men's basketball team. The 2014 version did not disappoint, as freshman center Jahil Okafor looked right at home by leading all scorers with 27 points in the team's annual intrasquad scrimmage. The dunk contest serves as the culmination of the evening's Countdown to Craziness festivities. Marshall Plumlee was crowned the 2014 Duke Contest Champion. "Countdown to Craziness is great because we love our fans," Plumlee said. "We have a great fanbase with the Crazies. It's a chance to give back to them and give them something to get excited about. Hopefully with everyone getting to see us scrimmage and see the talent out there, they are even more excited for the season. We can really go into the season and hit the ground running."

67 Johnny Dawkins' Epic Weekend

February 15–16, 1986, may go down as two of the greatest days in the history of Duke basketball. Besides winning its five national titles and its great victories over archrival North Carolina, February 15–16 pop out as the two days that Duke re-established itself as one of the nation's truly elite basketball programs—and it did so in less than 24 hours. Following a victory at Stetson on Tuesday night, the No. 2-ranked Blue Devils faced No. 17 N.C. State in Raleigh at 7:30 PM on Saturday night and then returned to Durham for a 1:00 PM Sunday tilt with No. 14 Notre Dame.

The first game was on Saturday evening in a packed and very warm Reynolds Coliseum on the campus of N.C. State in Raleigh. Coached by Jim Valvano, N.C. State was desperate for a big win that would impress the NCAA Tournament committee. The Wolfpack led much of the game and, with the score tied at

70 in the closing seconds, worked the ball for a layup by Chris Washburn, but he shot too hard, and Duke rebounded.

As the clock wound down, Johnny Dawkins was in the deep left corner and took the shot, which he missed, but Nate McMillan was called for fouling Dawkins on the shot. McMillan protested vigorously. Dawkins was a left-handed shooter, and McMillan felt he had hit his right hand, which should not have been a foul, but the call stood. Dawkins, who may well have won his National Player of the Year award on this weekend, made both shots for the 72–70 victory.

Less than 16 hours after the game ended in Raleigh, the Blue Devils were back on the floor to face Notre Dame in Cameron Indoor Stadium in front of a national television audience on NBC. The exhausted Blue Devils stayed basically even with the Fighting Irish for the entire game and with six seconds left in the game held a 75–74 lead, but the Irish had the ball at mid-court.

Johnny Dawkins, Duke's first star under Coach K, was 1986's Naismith Player of Year in part because of his performance on February 15–16 of that year.

In the Duke huddle, the Blue Devils anticipated that David Rivers would take the final shot, so the first inclination from the coaching staff was to put defensive stalwart David Henderson on Rivers, but Dawkins spoke up and said he had Rivers.

The inbounds pass—as anticipated—did go to Rivers, who went up the side rather than try the middle, the play that coach Digger Phelps had designed. As the clock ticked down, Rivers went up for a shot, and Dawkins blocked it cleanly, after which the Duke students rushed the floor. "He's the premier player in our conference," Mike Krzyzewski said of Dawkins. "Whatever role we put him in, he came through."

With Tommy Amaker limited to 18 minutes because of foul trouble, Dawkins played the point for more than half the game. He scored 18 points in 37 minutes after collecting 24 points in Raleigh the night before. "Dawkins has been consistently excellent for four years here," Krzyzewski said. "I'm a better coach because of Johnny Dawkins."

One week and two more victories later, Duke was elevated to No. 1 for the first time in the Krzyzewski era.

68 Boozer's Injury

Senior Night for the Blue Devils in 2001 would come against Maryland, a team the Blue Devils had to defeat in overtime earlier in the year in what most will remember as the "Miracle Minute" when Jason Williams hit two three-pointers and a layup to force the game into overtime tied at 90. Duke went on to win the game 98–96. Senior Night was set to be the crowning glory for senior Shane Battier, who, just six days earlier, had his No. 31 retired.

But the coronation against Maryland didn't happen.

A 23–7 run to end the first half gave the Blue Devils a 50–43 advantage at halftime, and everything looked to be lining up correctly for another jubilant Senior Night in Cameron Indoor Stadium. Suddenly, with 14:32 left in the game, Boozer, the big man for the Blue Devils, came off the floor limping. Trainer Dave Engelhardt worked to try and get Boozer back in the game, but when he tried, it continued to hurt.

Without Boozer's strength inside, the Terrapins went to their big men Lonnie Baxter, Tahj Holden, and Terrence Morris. Boozer's replacement, Casey Sanders, quickly picked up four fouls, and the Blue Devils fell 91–80. While the loss was crushing, the prognosis of facing the Tar Heels and March Madness without Boozer was even more daunting to the coaches, fans, and players.

But the coaching staff quickly went to work. As soon as the press conferences and glad-handing with parents and recruits was over, Mike Krzyzewski and his staff rolled up their sleeves—actually putting on warm-ups—and went to work to devise a plan to not only defeat Carolina, but also to thrive in the NCAA Tournament without knowing when Boozer would or could return.

The 2001 Duke basketball team was one of the strongest in the history of the school. The starting lineup was made up of five future NBA players in Shane Battier, Mike Dunleavy, Carlos Boozer, Chris Duhon, and Jason Williams. Even with Boozer on the sideline, this team had talent, and Krzyzewski knew he just had to come up with the plan that would fit his team.

During the 2000–01 season, the Duke Radio Network carried a call-in show after each home game. Fans would ask questions of color analyst John Roth and associate head coach Johnny Dawkins. Each time, without fail, someone would call and ask why Sanders wasn't being used more in the lineup.

Sanders was a 6'11" McDonald's All-American from Tampa, Florida, who came to Duke after having recorded 26 double-doubles and being named Mr. Basketball in Florida. To that point in the season, though, Sanders had played in 26 games but was averaging a little over eight minutes per game, 1.5 rebounds, and 2.3 points per game.

The Maryland game took place on Tuesday night, so in order to have the time to prepare, Krzyzewski gave the Blue Devils Wednesday off, and he and his staff came up with a plan. When they walked into practice on Thursday, he told them, "If you do what I say, we'll win the national championship."

The plan was to move Chris Duhon to the point, bring in Sanders, and run, run, run. By inserting Duhon as the distributor, the Blue Devils became a very quick team, so they tried to move the ball up the court at a faster pace and pushed the tempo of play with each and every possession. It was a classic team effort by the Blue Devils. With Duhon running the point, Williams was free to create and shoot the ball. He knocked down seven three-pointers for a total of 33 points in the game. And the defense was led by Battier, of course, as they swarmed the ball and totally disrupted the Tar Heels' plan to go inside on Sanders.

The moment that set the tone for the outcome of the game occurred with 16:45 left in the game. Carolina's Joe Forte stole the ball from Dunleavy at the top of the key and took off down the floor for what looked like a sure two points. But that wasn't the way Battier saw things. Coming from behind he used all of his 6'8" frame to catch Forte in stride and force him to jam the ball into the front of the rim. Dunleavy grabbed the rebound and dished it out to Williams, who raced down court and nailed a three.

When Forte made the steal, the Blue Devils led by three points at 50–47. His miss, combined with Williams' three, was a five-point swing. "Forte had made a big defensive play, and I knew I had to try and get down the court and at least cause him some problems," explained Battier after the game with what looked to be a permanent smile on his face. "Not only was the block and miss by Forte big, but the three by Jason was exactly what we needed to top it off."

Williams led all scorers with 33 points, but Battier had a typical Battier night with 25 points, 11 rebounds, five blocked shots, and four steals. In the coaches' locker room following the game, Krzyzewski had a big smile on his face and just looked up and said, "Wow, how about the game Battier played?"

The 95–81 victory gave the Blue Devils a share of the ACC regular-season title for a record fifth straight time and started them on a roll of 10 consecutive victories and the 2001 National Championship.

69 K's First Win Over No. 1

After the Blue Devils played for the national championship in 1978 under Bill Foster and spent parts of the 1979 and 1980 seasons ranked as the No. 1 team in the nation, the early years of the Mike Krzyzewski era were rocky. A trip to the postseason NIT highlighted the 1981 season and then back-to-back 10–17 and 11–17 records left Duke basketball at its lowest point in many years.

That low point was erased March 10, 1984, in the semifinals of the ACC Tournament as the No. 16-ranked Blue Devils faced the No. 1-ranked Tar Heels. "The three games we played against Carolina in 1984 were a microcosm of the Duke basketball program at the time," Mark Alarie recalled. "We were continuously working to make our team better. We had won a lot of games but had not played well against ranked teams. In 1984 we played well in the first game against Carolina and then had them beat in Chapel Hill before letting it slip through our hands. We knew we could beat them if we got another shot in the ACC Tournament."

Alarie scored 21 points and held Sam Perkins to nine. Johnny Dawkins scored 16 points and twice, with the score tied in the final three minutes, hit crucial go-ahead baskets. David Henderson, the conference's most effective sixth man, had 14 points, hit four critical free throws in the final minute, and survived a defensive encounter with Michael Jordan during the Tar Heels' best chance to force the game into overtime.

But there was a lot more to this game.

For a team gunning for the national championship they felt entitled to win, the Tar Heels did not take the two close losses to Duke to heart. To them, the Blue Devils were still also-rans in the ACC compared to N.C. State, Maryland, Virginia, and Wake Forest. And truth be told, Carolina was not nearly the team that had started the season 21–0 after Kenny Smith missed eight games with a wrist he broke against LSU in early February.

Sometimes the biggest games turn on the little plays and the small moments. *The* play that defined this Duke-Carolina game and the renewed rivalry took place long before the climactic final seconds. With the score tied at 67, Henderson had just bounced the ball off his foot and out of bounds, followed by a TV timeout with 3:42 remaining in the game. Over in the UNC huddle, Dean Smith set up a play designed to get Jordan the ball in the lane close to the basket.

Jordan worked for position on Henderson down in the lane. When he finally secured his spot, placing Henderson in an apparent hopeless defensive position behind him, Matt Doherty fed Jordan the ball. Given that he was at a disadvantage, Henderson did what any good defensive player would do and reached over Jordan's shoulder and swatted the ball away. He got a pretty good piece of the ball and an even better chunk of Jordan's shoulder. Nine times out of 10, officials will call that a reaching foul, but they didn't this time. Play continued to the amazement of both Duke and Carolina players and fans. The whistles of Hank Nichols, Joe Forte, and John Clougherty, three of the best in the business, were silent. "Henderson fouled him and it wasn't called," Smith said, "and that's the way it goes."

"I leaned on him," Henderson explained, "and when the ball came in, I reached over and knocked it away. You never know how the officials are going to call that, especially an official behind you who may not have a good view of the play. That's the reason I jumped back and raised my arms—to show that there had been no contact…But I know they normally call the foul on a play like that."

The loose ball wound up with Alarie, who quickly moved down the court toward the basket. His shot missed, but Dawkins tipped the ball in to give Duke a 69–67 lead. The final minutes in the game would come down to a free throw contest for the Blue Devils. The first to be tested was the most logical from UNC's standpoint, brick-mason Danny Meagher, who had missed the critical free throw just a week earlier in Chapel Hill. "Dean was always going on about me being a flopper and a tough player," Meagher said. "I learned quickly to hate Carolina. I knew he was coming for me in the tournament and I wanted them to foul me. Krzyzewski leaving me in the game gave me a lot of confidence."

Meagher got just two chances at the foul line late in the game and hit both of them. When Henderson converted a one-and-one free throw opportunity with 17 seconds left, the Blue Devils led 77–73. A rebound basket by Jordan with five seconds left pulled the Tar Heels to within two points. Then Henderson opened the door by missing a one-and-one with four seconds remaining, and the Tar Heels had a shot to tie.

Carolina took a timeout with three seconds left. Doherty inbounded the ball in the backcourt in front of the Duke bench. After using most of the allotted five seconds looking for a play to develop, Doherty tried to hit Jordan in the left corner near the side-line, but the ball landed beyond Jordan's grasp near a water bucket at the Tar Heels bench.

Jordan, who scored 22 points in the game, had run from near midcourt from right to left behind several picks to the left corner; Henderson stayed with him. "There were so many seven-footers around the lane, it was tough guarding him," Henderson said. "We headed toward the basket, and someone slowed me up a little, and he got a step on me. If the pass had been there, he probably would have caught it because I wasn't going to foul him. But he couldn't reach it."

Carolina fouled immediately on the Duke inbounds play, and Dawkins went to the free throw line with a one-and-one opportunity. When he missed with two seconds left and with Carolina out of timeouts, Sam Perkins grabbed the rebound and heaved the ball down court toward the basket, missing by the wide margin that once separated these two basketball programs. "When Dawkins missed, I thought there was a chance Perkins was going to bank it in," Krzyzewski said. "It's never over until it's over, especially in this game."

Outside the jubilant locker room in the bowels of the Greensboro Coliseum, an exhausted Krzyzewski said, "It is the greatest win any of these players have realized."

70 Wallace Wade

One of the most influential men in the foundation of Duke basketball is legendary football coach and athletic director Wallace Wade. In addition to funding the facility through the success of his football team, he came up with the basic idea of Duke Indoor Stadium, later named Cameron Indoor Stadium, along with assistant football coach and basketball coach Eddie Cameron. Whether the story was true about them drawing the stadium up on the back of a matchbook, it was Wade's 1938 football team's trip to the Rose Bowl that served as the base financing for the Indoor Stadium.

Wade served as the head football coach at the University of Alabama from 1923 to 1930 and at Duke from 1931 to 1941 and again from 1946 to 1950, compiling a career college football record of 171–49–10. His tenure at Duke was interrupted by military service during World War II. Wade's Alabama Crimson Tide football teams of 1925, 1926, and 1930 have been recognized as national champions, while his 1938 Duke team was not scored upon during the regular season, giving up its only points in the final minute of the 1939 Rose Bowl. Wade won a total of 10 Southern Conference football titles, four with Alabama and six with the Blue Devils. He coached in five Rose Bowls, including the 1942 game, which was relocated from Pasadena, California, to Durham, North Carolina, after the attack on Pearl Harbor.

Wade served as the head basketball coach at Vanderbilt University for two seasons from 1921 to 1923, tallying a mark of 24–16 while he was an assistant football coach there. He was also the head baseball coach at Vanderbilt from 1922 to 1923 and at Alabama from 1924 to 1927, amassing a career college baseball record of 87–45–2. Wade played football at Brown University.

Following his third national championship, Wade shocked the college football world by moving to Duke University, which had less of a football tradition than Alabama. Though Wade refused to answer questions regarding his decision to leave Alabama for Duke until late in his life, he eventually told a sports historian he believed his philosophy regarding sports and athletics fit perfectly with the philosophy of the Duke administration and that he felt being at a private institution would allow him greater freedom.

Wade entered military service after the 1942 Rose Bowl loss, and Cameron filled in for him as head football coach from 1942 to 1945. Wade returned to coach the Blue Devils in 1946 and continued until his retirement in 1950. In 16 seasons Wade's Duke teams compiled a record of 110 wins, 36 losses, and seven ties.

From 1951 to 1960, Wade was the commissioner of the Southern Conference. He was inducted into the College Football Hall of Fame in 1955. In 1967 Duke's football stadium was renamed Wallace Wade Stadium in his honor. Wade died in 1986 in Durham at the age of 94 and was buried in Maplewood Cemetery in Durham. In 2006 a bronze statue of Wade was erected outside of Alabama's Bryant-Denny Stadium alongside the statues of Frank Thomas, Bear Bryant, Gene Stallings, (and recently added Nick Saban), the other head coaches who led Alabama to national championships.

71 Bucky Waters

Raymond C. "Bucky" Waters served as head basketball coach at Duke from 1970 to 1973. A former N.C. State basketball player, he worked as assistant coach at Duke under Vic Bubas prior to becoming head coach at West Virginia. He had been successful at West Virginia and had a new arena coming out of the ground and a big-time recruit in 6'1" guard Will Robinson, who would go on to earn All-American honors in 1972 and become the Mountaineers' third all-time leading scorer.

Fred Brown was the athletic director who had the guts to hire a young 29-year-old assistant from Duke, and West Virginia was a power in basketball thanks to its greatest former player, Jerry West, Zeke from Cabin Creek. Waters had beaten the Blue Devils two of the three times they had played and had a 1–0 record against North Carolina, so it was logical that his old boss would want to talk with him about the job. But not so soon. "It was a surprise when Vic called in the middle of the season and told me he had something important to discuss with me," Waters said. "He said he was tired of getting on another plane and chasing another high school kid. And because of our past relationship and what I had done against Duke at West Virginia, I was going to be in the bulls-eye. He wanted me to have a chance to think about what I wanted to do."

Waters thought about it and decided he had a better job at West Virginia and told his wife, Dottie, they were staying in Morgantown. He and Brown went to see West Virginia president Dr. James Harlow. "We were in Dr. Harlow's office working on the wording of the statement, the love of the school, the new arena, and the phone rings," Waters said. "The secretary says it's for me. It was Eddie Cameron and president Doug Knight. I had sent them a telegram and thanked them for the honor of being offered the Duke job. But for professional reasons, I was staying at West Virginia."

Dr. Harlow made everyone leave the room while Waters talked with Cameron and Knight. "They started telling me how they needed me to come back to Duke," Waters said. "No increase in money or anything, just that they really needed me to come back. I loved Duke; they knew I did in my heart. I told them I would get right back to them. When the West Virginia people came back in the room, they asked if I was ready to begin the press conference. I told them I had changed my mind and I was going to take the Duke job. Dr. Harlow could tell I was still confused. He asked me what was in my heart, and I told him going back to Duke. He looked right at me and asked if Sonny Moran, my assistant, could coach. I said he could, and he turned to Fred and told him to announce Moran as our new head coach."

Duke hired the crew cutted Waters to replace Bubas in the turbulent, demonstration-marred early '70s. Having served under Bubas for six years and with head coaching experience, Waters seemed like a logical successor. But the conservative Waters was precisely the wrong man at the wrong time, as protests and pot

Neill McGeachy

When Bucky Waters resigned as the head basketball coach at Duke in 1973, athletics director Carl James had barely a month to find a successor before preseason practice began. He reportedly tried to hire legendary Kentucky basketball coach Adolph Rupp, but when that didn't work, he turned to someone already on campus in assistant coach Neill McGeachy, naming him head coach three days after practice had already started.

A native of Statesville, North Carolina, McGeachy was coached in high school by Dave Odom, who went on to become the head coach at Wake Forest for players like Tim Duncan and Randolph Childress. McGeachy spent two years as an assistant coach to Terry Holland at Davidson, one year as the Duke freshman coach, and one as Waters' top assistant before being named head coach.

He did not step into a very promising situation as the Blue Devils head coach. He was given a one-year contract coming off the school's first losing season in more than three decades, and the schedule was one of the most demanding in the country, mainly because the Blue Devils played in a very tough ACC that year. The Blue Devils had nine games that year with teams that finished ranked among the top 10 teams in the nation, including defending national champion N.C. State, Maryland, North Carolina, and Notre Dame.

McGeachy became a cruel footnote to history when he coached Duke to a 10–16 record, ironically including the school's 1,000th victory, and two of the more memorable losses—both to North Carolina—in the school's history.

The first, on January 19, 1974, occurred with the game tied. Carolina All-American Bobby Jones then stole an inbounds pass at Cameron Indoor Stadium and laid it in to beat the final buzzer. "That was one of the finest college games I've ever seen or taken part in," McGeachy said. "But when Jones made that steal, my whole life flashed across my mind."

The other came a month later and remains the most famous comeback in the history of the storied rivalry when the Tar Heels rallied from eight points down with 17 seconds to play in Chapel Hill to send the game into overtime, where they won 96–92. "Sometimes I think at that time there was a disease hanging over Duke basketball," said Blue Devils guard Pete Kramer, who missed the free throw before the legendary long shot by UNC's Walter Davis tied the score at the end of regulation.

The bitter endings to both games obscured a great coaching job by the personable McGeachy, who got his last-place team (2–10) ready to upset its top 10 rival twice. Winning both games—or perhaps either—might have helped him get the job permanently. But James, who barely talked to his interim coach that season, was already out scouting candidates from other schools.

On the morning of the final UNC game, Duke's athletic council met and decided not to extend McGeachy's contract. It was announced shortly after Duke's first-round ouster in the 1974 ACC Tournament that McGeachy and the staff would not return. McGeachy went on to coach at Wake Forest as an assistant and after a number of years in private business he was named the director of athletics at his alma mater, Lenoir-Rhyne College.

smoking became the activities of choice on a campus with mostly a Northeastern student body. Waters had early recruiting victories in the New York area, but several of those key players—Don Blackman, Jim Fitzsimmons, Richie O'Connor, and Illinoisan Jeff Dawson—wound up transferring because they chafed at Waters' disciplined style of coaching.

After twice reaching the NIT (losing to eventual champion UNC in the 1971 semifinal at Madison Square Garden), Duke suffered its two worst seasons in 12 years despite upsetting the No. 3-ranked Tar Heels on the day Duke Indoor Stadium was named for retiring athletic director Cameron.

After the season, in which Duke finished 14–12 and Carolina made its fifth Final Four in six years, Waters asked the school for a new contract and public vote of confidence to quell speculation over his job security that he said was killing recruiting. He did not get it and asked again, somewhat foolishly, after Duke went 12–14 in 1973. Duke refused and told Waters to coach through the last year of his contract and that it would make a decision on his future in the spring of 1973.

Waters did not wait that long. He was offered a fund-raising position at the Duke Medical Center by his friend dean William Anlyan, and the Blue Devils suffered a September surprise when Waters stepped down a month before practice opened for the 1973–74 season. "I knew I wasn't coming back," Waters said, "so I waited until September, hoping my assistant Neil McGeachy would have a chance at the job."

McGeachy was named head coach for one season.

Waters, who still resides in Durham, spent four years as the Duke head coach with records of 17–9, 20–10, 14–12, and 12–14 for a total of 63–45. His teams were 27–25 in the ACC but did not fare well in the ACC Tournament, losing in the first round three of four years. His first two teams played in the NIT.

At Duke Medical Center, he became one of its chief fund raisers and ambassadors, and was instrumental in the rise of the Duke Children's Classic, a celebrity charity event. Waters remained a part of the health affairs team until his retirement in 2004. He also worked as a basketball television analyst for NBC, the ACC's regional network, and Madison Square Garden.

72 Coach K and the Legacy Fund

Duke basketball and world-class success are synonymous. Much of the building of the financial infrastructure of the program has been accomplished through the Duke Basketball Legacy Fund and its other development initiatives, which are imperative to continuing the success of Duke basketball.

Coach Mike Krzyzewski is the driving force behind the mission to build an everlasting basketball program, and that speaks to his desire to see the program sustained well past his coaching days. The Legacy Fund began in January 2000 with the aim to establish a comprehensive endowment fund for player scholarships, coaching salaries, operational budgets, enhancements to historic Cameron Indoor Stadium, year-round training needs, and the overall demands of the program well into the future. Each of the 41 active partners to the fund have contributed a minimum of $1 million each and contributed a total of more than $82 million to date.

In September of 2012, Steve and Judy Pagliuca gave a $2.5 million gift to endow two assistant coaching positions and to name the annual Coaches' Award for Duke basketball. One of Duke's all-time greats and one of only 13 players in school history to have his jersey number retired, Grant Hill has once again led the Blue Devils by serving as the chairman of the Duke Basketball Legacy Fund. He accepted the position, as he has everything in his life, with a full commitment to excellence. The seven-time NBA All-Star and three-time college All-American led off the fund-raising initiative with a $1 million gift to endow a scholarship in his and his wife Tamia's names.

The contributions of Legacy Fund members have also led to several facility upgrades, including renovations to Cameron Indoor Stadium, the Schwartz/Butters Athletic Center, and the building of Michael W. Krzyzewski Center for Athletic Excellence. The Legacy Fund has also funded a foreign basketball trip to London in 2003, upgraded recruiting travel with strategic use of private planes, and fully funded and outfitted the Duke Basketball Museum and Duke Athletics Hall of Fame in the Schwartz/Butters Athletic Center in 2010.

Several other programs have grown from the initial and unique Legacy Fund development plan. In 2002 Duke became just the second school to initiate a Venture Capital Co-Investment Fund within an athletic department, and that group now numbers 17 strong with each investor giving a $50,000 gift. Duke basketball's connection with the Fuqua School of Business has translated into the annual Coach K/Fuqua Conference on Leadership and five years ago established the unique Fuqua/Coach K Center on Leadership and Ethics.

Another anchor to the year-round Duke basketball efforts has been the summer basketball fantasy camp, the K Academy. Each year campers from around the country join Duke's former players for a five-day, one-of-a-kind Duke basketball experience. During the summer of 2014, 80 campers and more than 30 former Duke players came to Cameron for the experience.

As National Coach of the Decade for the 1990s and Duke's visionary leader, Coach K endeavors to secure the future of the program. With the creation of the Duke Basketball Legacy Fund, the program's heralded past as well as its future success will be forever linked.

73 Wojo

Known as a tenacious bulldog defensive player on the court, Steve Wojciechowski played a major role in the resurgence of Duke basketball over his last three years as a collegian.

During his college career, he was the "heart and soul" of the Duke basketball program and he instilled the same tenacity as an assistant coach.

Following a difficult freshman campaign in which the Blue Devils went 13–18, the 5'11" Wojciechowski helped pace the program to a 74–26 mark over the next three seasons. During his sophomore year, Wojciechowski appeared in all 31 games as the Blue Devils went 18–13 and earned a trip back to the NCAA Tournament. He started all 33 contests as the team's point guard during the 1996–97 campaign as the squad collected a 24-9 record, won the ACC regular season title with a 12-4 record, and advanced to the second round of the NCAA Tournament.

But it was the 1997–98 season that completed Duke's journey back to the top of college basketball. Wojciechowski captained a squad that advanced to the NCAA South Regional Final, finished with a 32–4 overall mark, collected 15 regular season ACC victories, and completed the regular season holding the nation's top ranking. Along with being named the top defensive player in the country his senior year, the two-time All-ACC choice also secured honorable mention AP All-American accolades.

Wojciechowski finished his career ranked in several of Duke's season and career top 10 lists. He collected the second-highest single-season steal total in 1997 with 82 and followed that by tying the 13th best figure in 1998 with 74. Wojciechowski ranks ninth in career steals with 203 and eighth in career assists with 505. Following his 1998 graduation, Wojciechowski played professional basketball in Poland before returning to Duke. He spent 1999 as an intern in the Duke Management Company and as a sideline analyst for the Duke Radio Network's coverage of the Blue Devils basketball program.

Wojo became an assistant coach for Mike Krzyzewski in 1999–2000 and was promoted to associate head coach in the summer of 2008. Wojciechowski also served as a court coach and scout for Mike Krzyzewski, assisting the USA Basketball staff with on-court duties as well as game preparation from 2006–12, including the program's gold medal performances at the 2008 Olympics and 2012 Olympics.

In his first season as an assistant coach, he was instrumental in leading Duke, with seven freshmen on its roster, to a 29–5 record,

Former Duke point guard Steve Wojciechowski, who was named Marquette's head coach in 2014, instructs the 2013–14 Blue Devils squad.

the Atlantic Coast Conference regular season title (15–1), the 2000 ACC Tournament championship, an NCAA Tournament Sweet 16 appearance, and the No. 1 ranking in both major polls following the regular season. Working primarily with Duke's inside players, Wojciechowski's second year was even better as the Blue Devils won the national championship in 2001 while also capturing the ACC regular season and tournament crowns and posting a 35–4 record. His influence was evident throughout the year from the emergence of Casey Sanders as a bona fide inside presence to Reggie Love's strong performances in the ACC Tournament to Carlos Boozer's inspired play at the Final Four after missing six games and playing a limited role in the East Regional Semifinal and Final.

Duke earned its second trip to the Final Four during Wojciechowski's coaching tenure in 2003–04. Another one of his post pupils, Shelden Williams, earned All-American recognition and was the leading vote-getter for the ACC All-Defensive team. In 2004–05 Williams was named the NABC's National Defensive Player of the Year after registering 122 blocked shots and averaging 11.2 rebounds per contest. For the 2005–06 season, Williams was again named the NABC's National Defensive Player of the Year as well as a first team All-American. Wojciechowski also saw Williams set school records for career blocked shots and rebounds while also becoming the first player in NCAA history to register more than 1,750 points, 1,250 rebounds, 400 blocked shots, and 150 steals in a career. "He was a point guard and fed the big men the ball a lot so he knows where the ball is supposed to be and where we are supposed to be posting up," Williams said. "He has done a good job giving us a guard's view of where we need to be posting our bodies in order to get the ball in good position. Also, his energy and passion for the game are unmatched."

The post play under Wojciechowski were a big reason the 2009–10 team was able to win the NCAA championship, the ACC Tournament, the ACC Regular Season, and NIT Season Tip-Off titles. Defense and rebounding were key for the Blue Devils, who held opponents to 61 points per game and ranked 14th out of 334 teams in rebounding margin. One of those post players, senior Brian Zoubek, set the school record for offensive rebounds in a single season with 143.

Because of his work as an assistant, including guiding those big men, Wojciechowski was named the head basketball coach at Marquette University on April 1, 2014.

74 Jon Scheyer

Following a brilliant college career that included All-American honors and a NCAA National Championship in 2010, Jon Scheyer joined the Duke coaching staff as a special assistant in 2013 and was elevated in April of 2014 to assistant coach when former associate head coach Steve Wojciechowski became Marquette's head coach.

A native of Northbrook, Illinois, Scheyer concluded his career at Duke as the only player in school history to record at least 2,000 points, 500 rebounds, 400 assists, 250 made three-point field goals, and 200 steals. He averaged 14.4 points per game while scoring in double figures 114 times, fifth most in school history, and leading the Blue Devils to a 115–29 record, including a 45–19 mark in ACC play.

Scheyer was a two-time team captain and scored 2,077 career points to rank 10th on Duke's all-time scoring list. He also ranks third all time at Duke in made free throws (608) and free throw percentage (.861), fourth in three-point field goals (297) and three-point field goal attempts (780), and sixth in free throw attempts (706). He played in 144 consecutive games, which is tied for the second longest streak in school history.

As a senior during the 2009–10 season, Scheyer took over starting point guard duties for the Blue Devils and averaged 18.2 points, 4.9 assists, and 1.6 steals per game to guide Duke to its fourth national championship. A great ball handler, Scheyer quarterbacked the offense while Nolan Smith usually defended the opposing team's point guard. During that season Scheyer was a consensus second team All-American, first team All-ACC, first team ACC All-Tournament, NCAA South Region All-Tournament, and NCAA All-Final Four Team selection after guiding the Blue Devils to a 35–5 record. Duke closed the season with 10 straight wins and victories in 18 of its final 19 games.

Scheyer elevated his play over the final four games of the NCAA Tournament, averaging 19 points, 4.5 rebounds, 4.8 assists, and 1.3 steals per game to lead Duke to the title. He had 18 points, five rebounds, and four assists in a Sweet 16 win against Purdue and followed with 20 points, five rebounds, and four assists in a win against Baylor to help Duke advance to the Final Four. Scheyer knocked down five three-pointers (for the second consecutive game) and finished with 23 points, six assists, and no turnovers in a 21-point victory against West Virginia before capping off his career with 15 points, six rebounds, five assists, and two blocks in a 61–59 title game win against Butler.

Scheyer started all 40 contests on the season, averaging a team-high 36.8 minutes and also leading Duke in scoring (18.2), minutes played (1,470), three-point field goals made (110), free throws made (194), free throw percentage (87.8), assists (194), and steals (65). He scored in double figures 38 times with 17 games of 20 or more points and two 30-point games.

As a junior, Scheyer averaged 14.9 points while helping lead Duke to a 30–7 record and the ACC championship. He garnered ACC Tournament MVP honors after averaging 21.7 points and 4.0 rebounds per game in wins over Boston College, Maryland, and Florida State. Scheyer was also a double-figure scorer in each of his first two seasons in Durham. As a freshman, Scheyer was named ACC Rookie of the Week three times and earned ACC All-Freshman Team honors while averaging 12.2 points and 3.3 rebounds per game. He also made 61 three-point field goals, third-most by a freshman at Duke.

Coming out of high school, Scheyer earned McDonald's All-American and first team *Parade* All-American honors in 2006 after averaging 32 points, six rebounds, five assists, and three steals for Glenbrook North High. A two-time Gatorade Illinois Player of the

Year, Scheyer had his legend grow when he scored 21 points in 75 seconds at the Proviso West Holiday Tournament as a senior.

Following his graduation from Duke in 2010, Scheyer played professionally with the Rio Grande Valley Vipers in the NBA Developmental League and overseas with the Maccabi Tel-Aviv and Gran Canaria organizations. His professional career was jeopardized in 2010 when he suffered a serious eye injury in an NBA Summer League game with the Miami Heat.

75 Nate James

A 2001 Duke graduate, Nate James scored more than 1,000 career points as a member of the program from 1996–2001. He helped the Blue Devils to a 71–9 ACC regular season record and is the only player in ACC history with five straight regular season conference titles. (He redshirted in 1998 after playing in six games.)

James, a two-time team captain, played on a pair of Final Four teams, including Duke's 2001 NCAA Championship squad. As a senior James averaged 12.3 points, 5.2 rebounds, and 1.6 steals per game while helping the Blue Devils to a 35–4 record. He earned All-ACC and ACC All-Defensive team honors during that senior season. James played in 135 games from 1997–2001 with 63 starts. He scored 1,116 points, had 500 rebounds, and shot 47.3 percent from the floor. While known mostly for defense and rebounding, he also hit 111 career three-pointers.

Following his playing career, James became a member of the Duke coaching staff beginning with the 2007–08 season, serving as an assistant strength and conditioning coach for one year and spending three seasons as an assistant coach prior to being named a special assistant on April 8, 2011. James returned to the role of assistant coach for the 2013–14 season after the departure of former associate head coach Chris Collins, who became the head coach at Northwestern.

James' championship insight helped the Duke squad make its run to the national title in 2010 along with winning the ACC Tournament, ACC regular season, and NIT Season Tip-Off titles. In the 2009–10 season, James helped guide one of the nation's top defenses, mainly due to the improvement of the post players under James and Steve Wojciechowski. One of those post players, senior Brian Zoubek, set the school record for offensive rebounds in a single season. The other starter on the inside, senior Lance Thomas, was named to the ACC All-Defensive team by the coaches and the media.

James instilled the same warrior mentality he brought to the court during his playing days. Sometimes that meant scoring, as in the 26 points he had against Texas to help Duke win the 2001 Preseason NIT or the career-high 27 that he scored at Clemson later that year on 10-of-14 shooting. James' warrior spirit usually showed in the way he went after loose balls and rebounds, the way he defended, and the way he attacked weight training workouts. ACC coaches named him to the league's All-Defensive team, while the media voted him third team All-ACC as a senior.

Three of James' most noteworthy moments were against Maryland in 2001. In the final seconds at College Park, not far from his home, he hit a pair of free throws in the face of an antagonistic crowd to send the game into overtime. In the ACC Tournament semifinals, his penchant for finding offensive rebounds led to the winning tip-in just moments before the final buzzer. And in the second half of the Final Four semifinals in 2001, James stepped up to lock down Juan Dixon, who had torched the Blue Devils for 16 first-half points. Dixon scored just three points in the second half as Duke rallied from a large deficit for the win.

One of his most significant contributions to the 2001 NCAA crown was the unselfish way he handled his move out of the starting lineup late in the year. James had started 29 straight games heading into the regular season finale against North Carolina. But Mike Krzyzewski wanted to rework his lineup after an injury to Carlos Boozer, so he decided he needed James to come off the bench. James accepted the move and played over 24 minutes per game in Duke's nine postseason victories. That team-first attitude prompted head coach Mike Krzyzewski to state that James may have been the biggest winner of all: "When he walked off the court in Minneapolis, he was not only a champion in basketball—Nate James was a champion in life."

With 117 career victories, James is among the winningest players at Duke, ranking tied for 10th in ACC history along with Danny Ferry and Andre Dawkins. Duke posted a winning percentage of .867 (117–18) with James on the court, placing him seventh on the Duke career list. Along with his five regular season ACC championships, he was also a member of three ACC Tournament championship squads at Duke.

James made his mark on the Duke record book as a player. He is one of 63 players in school history to score more than 1,000 career points with 1,116 points in his career. In 135 career games, he averaged 8.3 points and 3.7 rebounds per game while shooting .473 (387-of-818) from the field. He is one of 47 players in Duke history with 500 career rebounds and ranks 23rd all-time at Duke with 147 career steals.

Following his career at Duke, James played professionally in the United States and overseas from 2002–07. After being named the Carolinas Basketball League Most Valuable Player in 2003, James spent various parts of the next five seasons playing in Bosnia, Brazil, France, Germany, Greece, Holland, Hungary, Italy,

Japan, the Philippines, Poland, and Russia. He was also with the Philadelphia 76ers during their training camp in 2004.

76 Jeff Capel

A four-year starter from 1994–97, Jeff Capel joined the Duke staff as an assistant coach on May 6, 2011. A natural coaching hire because of his father's coaching pedigree, Capel was promoted to associate coach in July of 2013 and then named associate head coach prior to the 2014–15 season. During his successful playing career as a Blue Devil, he racked up 1,601 points, 433 assists, and 220 three-point field goals. Capel led the Blue Devils in scoring as a junior (16.6 points per game). He finished his career among Duke's all-time leaders in minutes played, three-point field goal percentage, three-point field goals, and assists. Capel helped the team to an 83–46 record. He started 28 games as a freshman for a Duke squad that lost to Arkansas 76–72 in the 1994 National Championship.

He also had some of the most memorable highlights in Duke basketball history. Most notably, with Duke trailing 95–92 at the end of the first overtime in the 1995 regular season home game against North Carolina, Capel hit a running 40-foot shot at the buzzer, which sent the game into double-overtime. Although Duke lost the game 102–100, Capel's shot was nominated for an ESPY Award for College Basketball Play of the Year.

Duke fans also remember the behind-the-back pass he dished to Antonio Lang during a critical juncture in Duke's defeat of No. 1 seed Purdue. Coach K raved about the play after Duke's 69–60 victory against the Glenn Robinson-led Boilermakers, which earned the Blue Devils a spot in the 1994 Final Four. The freshman Capel had 19 points—including three three-pointers—seven assists and just one turnover in the pivotal NCAA Tournament game.

Following his career at Duke, Capel played professionally for two years. He spent the 1997–98 season playing for the Continental Basketball Association's Grand Rapids Hoops. In 1999–2000 he played in France before returning to Grand Rapids. He began his coaching career as an assistant coach under his father, Jeff Capel II, at Old Dominion University for the 2000–01 season. In 2001 he joined the coaching staff at VCU as an assistant and was promoted to head coach of the Rams for the 2002–03 season—making him the youngest head coach in Division I men's college basketball (27 years old) at the time.

Capel guided the Rams to an 18–10 mark overall in 2002–03 to tie a school record for wins by a first-year coach. VCU's victory against George Mason in 2004 catapulted the Rams to the NCAA Tournament for the first time since 1996. The Rams lost in the first round to Chris Paul and Wake Forest but not before putting a major scare into the No. 4 seed Demon Deacons. Capel compiled a 79–41 (.658) record over four years as head coach at Virginia Commonwealth prior to being named the head coach at Oklahoma on April 11, 2006.

While at Oklahoma, Capel led the Sooners to a 96–69 (.582) record overall with two NCAA Tournament trips (2008 and 2009) and was a major factor in the recruitment and development of 2009 National Player of the Year Blake Griffin, who would go on to become the first player from Oklahoma to be selected No. 1 overall in the NBA Draft, NBA Rookie of the Year, and an NBA Slam Dunk champion.

Capel also has coaching experience on the international level with USA Basketball. In the summer of 2010, he led a USA team featuring Kyrie Irving and Austin Rivers to a 5–0 record and the gold medal at the FIBA Americas U18 Championship in San Antonio, Texas. He was also an assistant coach on a gold medal-winning USA World University Games team that featured Duke's Shelden Williams and went 8–0 in Turkey in 2005. He took over as a court coach and scout with the USA Basketball senior national team in July of 2013 and assisted the staff throughout Team USA's gold medal run at the 2014 FIBA World Cup in Spain.

77 Chris Collins

The son of former NBA All-Star and Chicago Bulls and Philadelphia 76ers head coach Doug Collins, Chris Collins was immersed in the game of basketball at a very young age.

He developed into one of the most exciting shooting guards in the history of Duke basketball, becoming a team captain as a senior and a four-year letterman from 1993–96. He ranks 11th among Duke's all-time leaders in three-point field goals (209) and 10th in three-point field goal attempts (539). Collins averaged 9.1 points, 2.0 rebounds, and 2.4 assists as a collegian. He earned second team All-ACC honors as a senior.

Collins helped lead Duke to 83 total victories, three NCAA Tournament bids, one Final Four appearance, two ACC regular season championships, an ACC Tournament title, and two in-season tournament championships (the 1992 Maui Classic and the 1995 Great Alaska Shootout).

As a senior in 1996, Collins had his most productive season, leading the Blue Devils in three-point field goals (79), three-point percentage (.441), free throws made (83) and attempted (115), assists (132), and steals (37). Collins also ranked second on the team by averaging 16.3 points per game. He was among the ACC leaders in scoring (10th), assists (fourth), field goal percentage (.467, seventh), and free throw percentage (.722, 10th). But it was his swagger on the court and ability to hit big long-range jumpers that made him a Duke favorite and loathed by opposing fans.

Following his collegiate career, Collins played professional basketball in Finland during the 1996–97 season, leading the league in scoring. He returned to the United States and began his coaching career with the WNBA's Detroit Shock for the 1997–98 season. Collins went on to serve as an assistant coach at Seton Hall for two years with Tommy Amaker, a Duke standout himself from 1984–87 and now the head coach at Harvard. In 1999–2000 Collins was part of a staff that guided the Pirates to a 22–10 record and the Sweet 16 of the NCAA Tournament.

Collins joined the Duke coaching staff as an assistant coach on July 22, 2000, and was promoted to associate head coach in the summer of 2008. Collins' resume at Duke, as a coach, includes ACC Tournament championships, ACC regular season titles, seven in-season tournament titles, and, most importantly, national championships in 2001 and 2010. Collins also served as a court coach and scout for Mike Krzyzewski, assisting the USA Basketball staff from 2006–12, including during the program's gold medal performances at the 2008 Olympics, 2010 FIBA World Championships, and 2012 Olympics.

His first season as a coach in Durham could not have been better, as the Blue Devils won the 2001 National Championship with an 82–72 victory against Arizona. Collins, who worked primarily with Duke's backcourt players, helped guard Jason Williams become a unanimous first team All-American and a National Player of the Year. Chris Duhon, a freshman under Collins' tutelage in 2001, was named the ACC Rookie of the Year. During that championship game against Arizona, Collins counseled Mike Dunleavy, who was coming off a poor shooting performance in Duke's victory against Maryland in the national semifinals. "I just talked to him about going out and being aggressive," Collins said. "If you miss a shot, so what?" Dunleavy responded, drilling a team-best 21 points, including three three-point field goals in a 45-second span in the second half to put Duke ahead by 10 points.

In the 2005–06 season, Collins aided his star pupil, J.J. Redick, register one of the most impressive scoring seasons in Duke history. Redick ranked second in the NCAA averaging 26.8 points per game while setting the Duke and ACC career scoring records and the NCAA career three-point field goals record. He was a consensus National Player of the Year and a unanimous first team All-American for the 32–4 Blue Devils. "Coach Collins has really helped my development as a player," Redick said. "He is a former player so he knows a lot of the tricks of the trade and he has taught me a few things that have really helped me, whether it is being able to pick up fouls when we are in the bonus or coming off screens."

Collins helped lead Duke to its second national championship in 2009–10 as the Blue Devils defeated Butler, 61–59, in the NCAA title game in Indianapolis. Collins coached the top scoring trio in the NCAA as Jon Scheyer, Kyle Singler, and Nolan Smith combined to score 53.3 points per game. Scheyer and Collins, who both attended Glenbrook North High in suburban Chicago, held a particularly tight bond. Collins returned to those roots in Chicago's north suburbs when he accepted the head coaching position at Northwestern University on March 27, 2013.

78 Tom Butters, the Man Who Hired Coach K

Tom Butters retired from Duke in 1998 after 30 years at the university—the last 20 as the athletic director. A former professional baseball pitcher with the Pittsburgh Pirates, Butters came to Duke in 1967 as the director of special events. He was the Blue Devils' baseball coach from 1968–70, later founded the Iron Dukes organization, and moved into the AD's chair in 1977.

Known as a champion fund-raiser, he led the way in updating several facilities that hadn't been touched since they were first erected in the 1930s and '40s. He was known as a no-nonsense administrator who, while serving on the NCAA Basketball Committee, was instrumental in negotiating its $1 billion deal with CBS.

His Duke trademark may have been his insistence on absolute integrity in every facet of the athletics operation. The 1986 men's soccer squad won the school's first ever national championship while the 1991 and 1992 men's basketball teams soon followed with the gold trophy. Duke annually graduated more than 95 percent of its student-athletes during Butters' regime.

But he is truly known for hiring the winningest college basketball coach in the history of the game.

In the spring of 1980, when the Duke administration knew that Bill Foster would be leaving for the head basketball coaching job at South Carolina, the search for a new coach was underway. The job did not attract much interest, and when it went to the little known Mike Krzyzewski, who worked one year at Indiana under Bobby Knight and also served as an assistant to Knight during the 1979 Pan American Games, it was a surprise to everyone. Krzyzewski was the head coach at Army for five years, racking up a 73–59 record, including an appearance in the NIT. He put together three winning seasons with a 20–8 record in his second year and a 19–9 mark in his third year but finished the 1980 season at 9–17.

Butters interviewed Krzyzewski before hiring him in part because of a recommendation by Knight, for whom Krzyzewski had played at West Point. But he also hired him on a gut feeling that he and assistant athletic director Steve Vacendak, a former Duke basketball player and 1966 ACC Player of the Year, had about Krzyzewski and his plan to bring a man-to-man, in-your-face defense into the ACC.

Krzyzewski was also looking at the Iowa State job at the time and made a visit to Ames, Iowa. This would place him closer to his Midwestern roots and hometown of Chicago, but the call of the ACC was stronger than the call of the Big 8 Conference. Bob Weltlich of Mississippi, however, looked to be the front-runner for the Duke job. Weltlich, a Knight protégé like Krzyzewski, served as an assistant on the NCAA championship 32–0 Indiana team in 1976. Weltlich, who would go on to coach South Alabama, Florida International, and Texas instead, was in Durham until Tuesday morning, March 19, the day Krzyzewski was named head coach. Other coaches known to have been interviewed for the job included Tom Davis of Boston College, one-time Duke assistant Bob Wenzel, and Paul Webb of Old Dominion.

It was a surprise selection, to say the least.

Krzyzewski's name had not been mentioned in a single speculative story by the local media. This seemed to delight Butters, who seemingly had snookered the media before revealing his new head coach at a press conference in May of 1980. Krzyzewski, the same coach who earned a reported $10 million in 2011, started at $48,000. Butters walked out with a funny-looking young man with a pointy nose under a jet-black comb-over and thin lips from which came perhaps the funniest line he uttered in what would be a four-decade career at Duke. "My name is pronounced Sha-shef-ski,"

Dr. Kevin White

On May 31, 2008, Kevin White was named Duke University's vice president and director of athletics and he has held an extremely prominent role in the redevelopment of Duke athletics, especially the basketball program. Guided by the strategic plan that was approved by Duke's board of trustees in April of 2008, White successfully oversaw Duke's fund-raising efforts during an economic downturn, completed partnerships with major corporate entities to enhance revenue streams, commissioned a master facilities plan to position Duke well into the 21st century, and emphasized a stronger commitment to the university's intramural, club, and recreational sports programs.

Since White's arrival, Duke has captured seven NCAA championships—women's tennis in 2009, men's basketball in 2010 and 2015, men's lacrosse in 2010, 2013, and 2014, and women's golf in 2014—and 17 ACC titles. In all, 118 Blue Devil teams advanced to NCAA postseason competition during White's Duke tenure.

Academically, Duke's teams performed strongly under White. In the 2014–15 academic year, 25 of 26 Blue Devil varsity teams earned grade point averages of 3.0 or better, and more than 217 made the Dean's List, while 479 Duke student-athletes made the All-ACC Honor Roll (leading the ACC for the 27th time in the last 28 years).

White's commitment to the overall mission of the university remains clear. In May of 2011, Duke athletics announced that a portion of ticket sales from Blue Devils regular season home sporting events will be directed to the Duke University libraries. Per White's vision the Duke Athletics Library Fund has generated significant unrestricted revenue for the Duke University libraries to support teaching and research across the institution. In the fall of 2012, Duke University announced the $3.25 billion Duke Forward fund-raising campaign to raise money for Duke's 10 schools, Duke medicine, and a range of university programs. Included in the campaign is a $250 million goal for Duke athletics to be divided three ways—for facility enhancements and support ($100 million), endowment income ($50 million), and operating funds ($100 million).

In 2013–14 several facility projects were initiated or set for execution, including numerous renovations to Wallace Wade

Stadium, modifications to the front of Cameron Indoor Stadium, and the new Scott Pavilion, which will house several of Duke athletics' administrative units, as well as new strength and conditioning and sports medicine areas. White, who holds a PhD in education, has taught graduate-level classes since 1982 and currently teaches a sports business course in Duke's Fuqua School of Business as part of Duke's MBA program.

White joined the Duke family after leading Notre Dame's athletics program to success both on the playing fields and in the classroom from 2000–08. He also has held a number of prominent national leadership roles within intercollegiate athletics, including his service in 2006–07 as president of the National Association of Collegiate Directors of Athletics (NACDA) and in 2005–06 as president of the Division I Athletic Directors Association. Given his background and success, it is not surprising that 23 current directors of athletics were mentored by White.

Prior to joining Notre Dame in 2000, White served as athletic director at Arizona State University, Tulane University, the University of Maine, and Loras College in Iowa. Before becoming an administrator, White served as head track and field coach at Southeast Missouri State (1981–82) and assistant cross country and track and field coach at Central Michigan (1976–80).

he began. "It is spelled K-R-Z-Y-Z-E-W-S-K-I. And if you think that's bad, you should have seen it before I changed it. My players call me Coach K."

Three years later, no one at Duke was amused. The Blue Devils had become the laughingstock of ACC basketball, while UNC and N.C. State had won national championships. Duke's second and third seasons under Coach K had featured insufferable seventh-place finishes in the ACC and two of the worst records in the school's history at 10–17 and 11–17. Already a group of disgruntled boosters calling themselves the "Concerned Iron Dukes" had formed. "What were they concerned about?" Krzyzewski deadpanned years later. "Me as their basketball coach."

The great start to a critical 1984 season, which started strong, was beginning to fall apart for the Blue Devils and Krzyzewski. The "Concerned Iron Dukes" were meeting regularly, discussing who would be their next basketball coach and their next athletic director. Even Krzyzewski thought it might be his last season at Duke. The morning following a 97–66 loss to Wake Forest, Butters stuck his head in the basketball office just past 8:00 AM to see if Krzyzewski was in yet. Coach K wasn't, having spent most of the evening and early morning watching film of the Wake Forest disaster. It was a Krzyzewski-coaching ritual to spend most of the evening immediately after a game going over the film with his assistants. These film sessions usually lasted until 4:00 or 5:00 AM. This meticulous preparation would eventually lead to ACC and national championships. But in 1984 he was still crafting out a program. He wanted to be ready the next day to discuss with each player what they did during the entire game and make adjustments.

Butters asked the secretary to have Mike come to his office when he arrived.

A somber Krzyzewski entered Butters' suite later that morning. Butters could tell by how thin Krzyzewski's lips looked that he was uptight about his job. The embarrassing losses of the past two seasons were supposedly behind the program, but the 31-point loss to Wake Forest rekindled that hurt, and Krzyzewski didn't know exactly what to expect in the middle of January of his fourth season as he walked into his bosses office.

Butters was about to answer that question. "I looked right at Mike and told him, 'The fans, the media, even you don't know how good of a basketball coach you are,'" recalled Butters, then in his seventh year as Duke athletic director. "'But I know how good you are.' And I opened my drawer and pulled out a new five-year contract and slid it across the desk."

When Krzyzewski realized what it was, his eyes filled up and a tear trickled down his cheek. Someone did believe in him. They did believe in what he was trying to do to make Duke basketball a power once again.

79 Make a Fist

On the side of the 2001 Duke National Championship ring is the emblem of a closed fist. That symbol has been one of the great motivational tools in the Mike Krzyzewski coaching era at Duke. The "FIST" has been a team-building tool that stands for Five Individuals Standing Together. It reflects the importance of having all five players on the court working together to achieve a common goal. No matter how strong each of the five fingers are, the lesson is that together as a fist the five fingers are much stronger.

The clenched fist was first used by the communists in the Spanish civil war as a counterpoint to the open-palmed Roman salute adopted by the fascists. The clenched fist symbolizes strength and unity—fingers that are individually fragile can together make a powerful fist. It was co-opted by many revolutionary causes, most potently the civil rights struggle in the United States and during opposition to third-world colonialism.

The notion is so significant to Krzyzewski that he has a sculptured fist in his office on his desk. One of the telling signs of the importance of the symbol is that the word "FIST" was written on the grease board in blue in the Blue Devils' locker room when they faced Michigan for the national championship in 1992.

The closed fist—symbolizing working together—is an important motivational tool for Coach K.

Krzyzewski takes the five fingers one step further as he places an important quality to each finger. Communications, trust, collective responsibility, caring, and pride represent each of the five digits.

80 Billy King

Known as one of the top defensive players during his collegiate career, Billy King was an outstanding player on the Blue Devils' nationally ranked teams in the late 1980s and received the 1987–88 Henry Iba Corinthian National Defensive Player of the Year award following his senior season. King helped the Blue Devils to a 112–27 record, an average of 28 wins per season as Duke went to the Final Four twice, won the Atlantic Coast Conference regular season, and won two ACC Tournament titles. Although he was a very solid collegiate basketball player, King has made his name in the basketball world at the professional level.

He joined the pro ranks after spending four seasons as an assistant at Illinois State University under head coach Bob Bender, a former Duke player. King also spent one year as a color analyst for ESPN's basketball coverage of the Ohio Valley Conference. His first pro job was as an assistant coach with the Indiana Pacers for four seasons under Larry Brown.

King would then move on to the Philadelphia 76ers, where he would spend 10 years with the organization, serving as the team's president from 2003–07. King joined the 76ers in June 1997 as vice president of basketball administration, a role in which he served as the point person for basketball operations.

Less than a year later, he was promoted to general manager, a position he held until being promoted to team president following the 2002–03 season. During his 10-year tenure, King guided the team to five consecutive playoff appearances (1999–2003), including the 2000–01 season in which the Sixers captured the Atlantic Division and went to the 2001 NBA Finals for the first time since 1983.

Holding several roles within the USA Basketball program throughout his career, King has served as a member of USA Basketball's program advisory panel, board of directors, treasurer, and as an athlete representative on the 1997–2000 executive committee. King has been honored and recognized by numerous organizations for his success in professional sports. In July of 2000, he was honored as the Sports Executive of the Year at the Rainbow Sports Awards, reflecting not only his accomplishments in the sports industry, but also the grace, dignity, commitment, and humanity that he exemplifies throughout his everyday life. In 2001 *Street and Smith's Sports Business Journal* named him one the industry's "Forty under 40." He was also inducted into Duke University's Hall of Honor on December 2, 2001, in its charter group. In May 2003, *Sports Illustrated* named King one of the "101 Most Influential Minorities in Sports." King also was honored as the NBA Executive of the Year in July of 2003.

King was named as the New Jersey Nets' general manager on July 14, 2010, and he oversees all aspects of the team's basketball operations. King wasted no time putting his stamp on the Nets in his first season as general manager, making a mid-season blockbuster trade to acquire All-Star point guard Deron Williams from the Utah Jazz on February 23, 2011. In July of 2012, King overhauled the (now Brooklyn) Nets roster, re-signing Williams to a multi-year pact, trading for All-Star guard Joe Johnson, and re-signing center Brook Lopez as well as forwards Gerald Wallace and Kris Humphries. He also drafted Duke's Mason Plumlee in the first round of the 2013 NBA Draft.

81 Snow Day

The February 12, 2014, renewal of the Duke-North Carolina game set for 9:00 PM in the Dean Smith Center marked just another Duke-Carolina week—until two winter storm fronts were forecast to collide over North Carolina. Travel alerts for roads and airports began on Monday more than 48 hours before the game.

To concerned media and fans who called, Steve Kirschner, UNC's director of communications, basically outlined the ACC's short-sighted policy that the game must be played if the officials and visiting team can make it safely. As it turned out, Duke being close enough to bus over two hours before the game ultimately caused the problem. Any other opponent, save N.C. State, would have already been in town the day before, staying at a local hotel.

At about 11 o'clock the morning of February 12, Kirschner walked from the basketball suite to his office in the next building and nearly got frostbite. He thought to himself, *If it does snow it will freeze right away*. The calls and emails were now flooding in at both schools. But the response was the same—the game would go on as scheduled, reciting the ACC policy if need be.

The media was having its own problems driving to the Smith Center. Several members of the press corps got close enough before hitting traffic snarls that they left their cars and walked for an hour to just get there. ESPN analyst Dick Vitale's plane was unable to land at the airport. After circling for more than an hour, a runway was sufficiently cleared and Vitale's Southwest Airlines flight from

Tampa touched down. But no one was there to get him, and no cabs were going to Chapel Hill because of the mess on Interstate 40. ESPN's Dan Shulman and Jay Bilas were staying at the Sheraton, four miles from the Smith Center, and it took two hours for them to drive there. Tim Brando and color analyst Dan Bonner of the Raycom team had a similarly arduous journey getting to the arena from their hotel. By mid-afternoon the governor had declared a state of emergency.

With schools letting out early, several members of the Duke basketball staff had ventured out to pick up their children at school. After dropping them at home they began the trek back, which now took two hours. Duke assistant Steve Wojciechowski lived just two miles from Cameron Indoor Stadium on the west side of Durham. The normal five-minute drive from his home to his office had become an adventure with cars strewn all over Morreene Road. Twice, Wojo had to drive through ditches just to keep moving forward.

By mid-afternoon on February 12, Smith Center director Angie Bitting had already been on the phone with the Duke operations' staff hourly. She was assured the Blue Devils were coming and, in fact, planned to be there by 6:00 PM, an hour early. Instead, the Duke team should have left later because by 7:00 most everyone had gotten to where they were going and the roads were icy but clear.

After governor Pat McCrory declared a state of emergency and urged everyone to stay off the roads, Kirschner put out a second statement, saying the game was still on but recommended anyone who could not walk to the Smith Center should stay home. That statement implied that any of the 28,000 students who lived on or close to campus would be welcome to come and cheer on the Tar Heels.

Around 4:00, Kirschner called Duke associate athletic director Jon Jackson, his friend for more than 25 years, and asked him for a status report. While Jackson said the team was still planning to come, Kirschner heard less conviction in his voice. Jackson told him of reports that the 15-501 highway Duke would travel to Chapel Hill was impassable with vehicles either stuck in traffic or abandoned. And that the Duke bus had yet to arrive to pick up the team, which had hoped to leave within the hour.

Finally, just before 5:00, Kirschner called Duke associate director of sports information Matt Plizga, who said that not only had the bus yet to make it to Cameron, but also half the Blue Devils and coaches were having trouble getting there for the pregame meal. Rodney Hood, a transfer from Mississippi, was scared to death driving from his apartment. "I'm not used to this snow," he said, "and there were cars everywhere."

In Durham County alone the Sheriff's Department had already reported 52 traffic accidents. And the fact that UNC was situated on a hill (with a Chapel) was not making the Duke party feel any better about the trip over. Almost any approach to the Smith Center included driving up an incline. Franklin Street, Airport Road, and Manning Drive were all littered with cars that were stuck like a scene from the movie *The Day the Earth Stood Still.* "Steve, I don't think we can get there," Plizga said to Kirschner. "And if we do, what if we can't home after the game?"

Within 10 minutes UNC athletic director Bubba Cunningham called Duke AD Kevin White, and they agreed to postpone the game. White said he would contact the ACC to get official approval. Once the decision was made, Kirschner suggested that Roy Williams be told and asked to call Mike Krzyzewski to formalize the postponement and discuss rescheduling. The reaction was immediate on sports radio shows and social media: the Blue Devils were chicken to come over and play in front of 22,000 students, the only fans who could make it to the game on foot, but both programs came to the same conclusion about rescheduling the game.

That meant only three viable options. Play the following night, when the roads would still be treacherous; do some kind of back-to-back doubleheader the day before or after the Saturday, March 8, game at Duke; or play on the following Thursday, February 20, with a slight advantage going to Carolina because the Tar Heels had a game the previous Monday at Florida State and Duke the next night at Georgia Tech. The game was played on the agreed upon February 20 date, and UNC rallied from 11 points down in the second half to defeat Duke 74–66 in Jabari Parker's only game at the Dean Dome.

82 Jim Spanarkel

James G. Spanarkel was a street-wise, pigeon-toed kid from Jersey City, New Jersey, the first piece of the puzzle put together by Bill Foster in building a nationally dominant Blue Devils basketball program in the late '70s. His high school coach, Rocky Pope, candidly described the 6'5" guard/forward to Bill Foster's assistant Bob Wenzel, "About the only thing he will do for you is win. He's not very fast or quick, can't jump, and is not a very good shooter. But when the other team presses, we give him the ball. When we need a basket, we give him the ball. If we're having trouble stopping a big man, we put him on the guy. If we're having trouble with a guard, we put him on that guy."

Spanarks, as he became known, was a hard-nosed defensive player who turned into one of the ACC's best rebounding guards, averaging more than four a game, and drove hard to the hole before settling for jumpers. As a sophomore he led the nation in free throws attempted and made. He was also a deceptively good athlete with quick hands and a lot of basketball savvy.

Compared to the streets of Jersey City, Spanarkel found Duke to be more like a paradise with pretty girls galore and plenty of parties. But he also worked diligently at his craft. Between classes he went to Cameron to shoot free throws alone, putting a bounce-back net under the goal so the ball came right back to him after every shot. He often did not change from his school clothes, using every possible minute to improve. Not surprisingly he went on to make 80 percent of his career free throws, once knocking down 52 in a row. "One of the reasons we wanted him was because he was tough," Foster said. "We wanted a tough kid because we knew he was coming into a tough situation." That tough kid was part of Foster's first recruiting class at Duke. "I know he isn't all that highly touted," the Duke head coach said. "But I think people are going to like him. I think they will appreciate the way he plays the game."

Well aware of what was expected of him, Spanarkel knew he had to get into great physical shape. As a freshman he felt so chubby that he ate Kellogg's Corn Flakes for five weeks in order to lose 20 pounds. It helped that his father was a regional salesman for Kellogg's. A slimmer Spanarkel averaged better than 13 points and four rebounds and went on to win ACC Rookie of the Year in a landslide. As a sophomore he averaged 19.2 points per game and 20.8 as a junior, hitting more than 86 percent of his free throws and leading the Blue Devils to the national championship game against Kentucky. His senior season saw a drop off in scoring to a 15.9 average but an overall improvement in his game as a leader of the Blue Devils, who spent the first month of the 1978–79 season ranked No. 1 in the nation.

Spanarkel was a first team All-American selection in 1978 and second team in 1979, while being chosen first team All-ACC in

1978 and 1979 and second team in 1977. He was selected as the MVP of the 1978 ACC Tournament and MVP of the NCAA East Region. He was the first Duke basketball player to score 2,000 points in his career, ending with 2,012.

Spanarkel was drafted 16th in the 1979 NBA Draft and spent his first season with the Philadelphia 76ers. He then played the next four years for the Dallas Mavericks, averaging a career-high 14.4 points per game during the 1980–81 season. Upon his retirement from the NBA, he turned to the broadcast booth as the New Jersey/Brooklyn Nets television analyst and additionally works CBS Sports regular season and NCAA Tournament coverage with Ian Eagle while also working as a studio analyst with NBA TV.

83 Tinkerbell

Gene Banks was the best prep player from Philadelphia since Wilt Chamberlain. Eugene Lavon Banks, a 6'8" man-child, not only had game but enough bravado to put the love of an entire city—and a college basketball program—on his broad shoulders. His coach at West Philadelphia High School, Joey Goldenberg, said he would "take Banks over any high school player I've ever seen, except Chamberlain, and that would be a toss-up."

Better known as "Tinkerbell" for how he seemingly floated above the court when taking off for one of his slam dunks, Banks was courted by most major schools in the country—from the Carolinas to UCLA—and enjoyed every minute of the attention. In all, more than 200 schools wanted Banks, who had the charm to make them all think they were in it with Tinkerbell.

With official visits limited by the NCAA, Duke head coach Bill Foster was one of the best at talking with players on the phone. He used those conversations in many different ways. On one of his early trips to see Banks play, he ended up walking right past "Tink" at the end of the game and not saying a word. Banks was offended, telling his mother later that evening that despite playing a great game the coach from Duke "must not like me" because he didn't say a word.

Foster called that night and coyly told Banks he wasn't sure his game was good enough to play at Duke. He was gambling that Banks wanted to be the final piece of the puzzle that would transform the Blue Devils from losers to winners, and, sure enough, the confident player now wanted to show Foster he could be that change agent. In later years the two laughed about the conversation, but it did exactly what Foster had intended and put Duke squarely on the mind of the kid from West Philly. "If things go well and I have God's grace," Banks said, "I think I can finish up as the most versatile, complete, exciting, flamboyant, hustling player that Duke has ever had...I really felt that once the smoke cleared, I could make them a national power."

But even with all his candor and confidence, Banks was a team player. He could be just as effective dishing out assists and pulling down rebounds as he was scoring. During his college career, both Foster and his coach for one season, Mike Krzyzewski, would implore Banks to be less selfish and shoot the ball more. Banks would end his Duke career averaging 16.8 points per game, scoring 2,079 points, and averaging right at eight rebounds per game. His best scoring year was his senior year when he averaged 18.5 per game and hit several key shots, including a jumper with no time left on the clock on his Senior Day to tie North Carolina. His outstanding play in overtime would seal the victory. He was an All-American selection in 1981 and an All-ACC selection in 1979, 1980, and 1981.

Banks was a second round selection of the San Antonio Spurs in the 1981 draft as the 28th overall pick. He played six years in the NBA with the Spurs (1981–85) and Chicago Bulls (1985–87) averaging 11.3 points per game in his NBA career. An Achilles injury in a summer All-Star Game cut short his NBA career.

84 The Alaskan Assassin

The first player from Alaska to play for the Blue Devils, sharp-shooting Trajan Langdon, earned the nickname "Alaskan Assassin." "He is the best shooter I have ever had," commented Mike Krzyzewski following one of Langdon's deadly shooting exhibitions. "He doesn't take many shots to score his points. He is an incredible efficient shooter and releases quickly. Some of his shots are made before he gets the ball because he has beaten his man. He works hard when he doesn't have the ball so he gets good looks."

Upon his arrival at Duke, the Anchorage native moved right into the starting lineup. After his freshman season, Langdon, a gifted two-sport athlete, played for USA Basketball in the Junior World Championship then went and played pro baseball for the Idaho Falls Braves on a severely sprained ankle. The ankle problem caused him to miss the entire 1996 season, including a trip by the Blue Devils to the Great Alaska Shootout. He had to watch from the bench as the Blue Devils won the title.

Following two surgeries on his ankle, Langdon returned for the 1997 season at full force as he led the Blue Devils in scoring; tied the school record for threes, nailing seven against North Carolina; and poured in a career high 34 points against Clemson. In 1998 he was selected team captain and had another 34 point-game against UCLA while leading the Blue Devils to a 32–4 record.

It was 1999 that turned out to be the two-time team captain's best. He finally got to play in the Great Alaska Shootout, averaged 17.3 points per game for the season, earned second team All-American honors, and enjoyed a third straight season as an All-ACC performer while leading the Devils to a 19–0 record against conference foes. He earned MVP honors in the East Region of the NCAA Tournament and helped lead the Blue Devils to the NCAA championship game against Connecticut. Langdon led a star-studded Duke team with 25 points during the 77–74 loss to UConn, though he turned the ball over on Duke's last two possessions of the game.

The son of a University of Alaska-Anchorage anthropology professor, Langdon was selected in the sixth round of the 1994 Major League Baseball draft by the San Diego Padres and 11th overall in the 1999 NBA Draft by the Cleveland Cavaliers. On November 2, 1990, Langdon made his NBA debut with the Cavaliers and became the first Alaskan to play in the NBA. He played three injury-plagued years for the Cavaliers with his best season coming in 2000-01.

He went on to become a stalwart on one of the greatest basketball teams in the world for CSKA Moscow. He was named first team All-Euroleague for the 2007 and 2008 seasons and was selected the Euroleague Final Four MVP in 2008 after leading CSKA Moscow to a Euroleague title. In June 2011 he retired two days after helping CSKA to its ninth consecutive Russian League crown.

85 Bob Verga

He showed up on the Duke campus in a vintage red Stingray Corvette and proceeded to set the college basketball world on fire with his incredible scoring and shooting ability. To say he was a confident young man may be the understatement of the century. He was the son of a well-to-do doctor in Sea Girt, New Jersey, and always dated the best looking girl on campus. He was a member of the Kappa Alpha fraternity and spent most of his free time on the weekend at Durham's renowned Stallion Club—home to such legendary acts as Maurice Williams and the Zodiacs, the Tams, Joe Tex, and Tina Turner. On one particular evening, when a number of the players were busted for drinking and suspended for a game, Bob Verga slipped out the back door just in time to miss getting into any trouble.

He was "Mr. Cool" both on and off the court.

From 1965 through 1967, he was as good a college basketball player as you will ever see. He made first team All-ACC all three years, one of only five players in the history of Duke basketball to perform this feat, and was selected as an All-American his junior and senior seasons. In his 80-game career, he scored 1,758 points, averaging 22 points per game. Verga's senior season scoring average of 26.1 points is one of the best in Duke and ACC history.

You could see he was going to be a great scorer in his freshman season, when he played for the freshman team and scored 51 against Virginia Tech and averaged 32.2 points per game. With no three-point line, Verga was a shooting and scoring machine. His top efforts as a varsity player were a 41-point outing against Ohio State in the Greensboro Coliseum and a 39-point effort against Wake Forest.

It was 1966 when Verga played in one of his most memorable games, an NCAA East Regional Final against Syracuse. He went 10-for-13 shooting for 21 points and led the Blue Devils to the Final Four once again and was voted the MVP of the East Region. The next week Verga came down with a high fever and illness and was sent to the Duke University Hospital just a few days prior to the No. 2 Blue Devils taking on No.1 Kentucky in College Park, Maryland, in the semifinals of the NCAA Final Four. He was released from the hospital in time to make the trip but was not at full speed as he was able to score just four points as the Blue Devils lost to the Wildcats 83–79.

In his junior season he was featured in an eight-page layout in *Sports Illustrated* titled "Lonely and Lively Hours of a Star." The spread had pictures of him all alone in class studying Latin and all alone in the gym shooting but talked a great deal about his off-campus adventures.

Verga was drafted by the NBA's St. Louis Hawks in the third round of the 1967 NBA Draft and by the Kentucky Colonels in the 1967 ABA Draft. Verga opted to play in the ABA and averaged 23.7 points per game in his rookie season for the Dallas Chaparrals. He averaged 18.8 points per game in his second ABA season with three different teams and played the next two seasons with the Carolina Cougars, averaging 27.5 points per game during the 1969–70 season, in which he made his only appearance in the ABA All Star Game, and 25.3 the following season. After averaging 21.7 points per game for the Pittsburgh Condors in the 1971–72 season, Verga finished his career with the NBA's Portland Trail Blazers in 1973–74.

After leaving pro basketball, he became a tennis pro and was named to the ACC's Silver Anniversary team in 1978 as one of the top 15 players in the league's first 25 years and was inducted into the Duke Sports Hall of Fame in 1984 and was one of 18 charter inductees in the Duke Hall of Honor.

86 Jack Marin

A pure shooter, Jack Marin had a solid grasp of every phase of the game of basketball. More than a prolific scorer, he was a winner. In his 86-game career in Durham, the Blue Devils compiled a 72–14 record, finished first in the ACC all three years, won two ACC Tournaments, and played in the Final Four twice.

A native of Farrell, Pennsylvania, Marin came off the bench his sophomore season and averaged 17.9 points per game. It would be his junior and senior seasons when he would really shine. He put together a handful of 30-point games in those two years, including a 35-point performance against Notre Dame, a career-high 36 points versus Wake Forest, and a 30-point effort in a win in Detroit against Cazzie Russell and Michigan. In one stretch of his junior season over a 17-day period, Marin tallied three games of more than 30 points and three games with more than 20 points, scoring 15 against South Carolina in the seventh game. During the stretch he hit 80-of-117 from the floor, and Duke captured all seven games. He was a two-time All-ACC performer, second team All-American, and led the team in scoring his senior year. His junior year he was second on the team in scoring while leading the ACC in field goal shooting at 54.6 percent, despite being a long-range shooter.

One of his best games came in his next to last game as a Blue Devil in the semifinals of the 1966 Final Four at Cole Field House in Maryland. Marin poured in 29 points as Duke lost a four-point decision to No. 1 Kentucky. Marin was trying to take over the scoring duties from his ill teammate Bob Verga, but he also had to guard Wildcats forward Pat Riley, whom he held to 19 points.

The fifth overall pick of the 1966 NBA Draft by the Baltimore Bullets, Marin spent 11 seasons in the NBA and from 1966–77 playing for the Bullets, Houston Rockets, Buffalo Braves, and Chicago Bulls. He was named to the 1967 NBA All-Rookie team and was a two-time member of the NBA All-Star team. He scored 12,541 points in his career and led the NBA in free throw percentage during the 1971–72 season. He was involved in a well-known trade, being sent to the Rockets for Elvin Hayes. Marin was one of the best free throw shooters ever in the NBA, hitting 84 percent for his career.

Following his retirement from professional basketball, he came back to Duke and enrolled in law school. Several years into his law practice, he started representing basketball players, specializing in helping Americans secure jobs in foreign leagues. He has also served as an outside counsel to the NBA Players Association. Along with his law practice, Marin spent three years, from 1998–2000, as the executive director of the Celebrity Players Tour, a professional golf circuit for notable ex-pro athletes and entertainers. As part of the Hope For The Warriors, a non-profit based out of Jacksonville, North Carolina, he teaches golf and other sports activities to United States Marines who have been severely wounded in combat.

87 Just Say No to L.A.

From July 1, 2004, when the news first broke that the Los Angeles Lakers wanted Duke's Mike Krzyzewski to become their head coach, until July 5, when the situation was resolved, there were a lot of nervous Dukies in Blue Devil Nation. The Lakers offered Krzyzewski enough money to make him the highest-paid coach ever in sports at the time at a reported $40 million for five years, along with the team presidency and an ownership percentage of the club.

But early on the morning of July 5, after making his decision late the evening before, Krzyzewski called Lakers general manager Mitch Kupchak and informed him he was staying for his 25th season at Duke. Then he called the school's new president, Richard Brodhead, whose first official day on the job coincided with the job offer to the university's highest-profile employee.

Later, at a news conference with athletic director Joe Alleva and Krzyzewski that was televised across the nation, Broadhead said, "I have the happy news of saying that Mike Krzyzewski, the famous Coach K, is going to be staying at Duke. I am so delighted that you decided that your real place was in the world of college basketball."

Krzyzewski first heard from the Lakers prior to the NBA draft. Before returning the call, he assumed the call was about the status of freshman Luol Deng and recruit Shaun Livingston, who eventually were selected seventh and fourth overall. "I talked with Mitch Kupchak at a time when I was taking inventory. I said, 'I'm 57, maybe I should just look.' As it went on, I took a closer and closer look. As I looked at this and myself, I found that I wanted to lead. Your heart has to be in whatever you lead. It became apparent that this decision was somewhat easier to make because you have to follow your heart and lead with it. Duke has always taken my whole heart. I didn't make this decision because of tangibles. I made this decision because of intangibles, and the tangibles were, as they always have been, so much here."

This was not the first time an NBA team went after Coach K. Former Carolina star Billy Cunningham, minority owner at the time of the Miami Heat, sat in Krzyzewski's living room talking to him about his future in the late '80s. After the 1990 season, the Boston Celtics offered a coaching position to Krzyzewski, but after meeting with former Duke assistant coach Red Auerbach in Washington, he then declined their offer. In 1994 the Portland

Trail Blazers came close to obtaining the coaching services of Krzyzewski, but after a weekend at the beach with his family, he turned down that offer as well. In 2010 the New Jersey Nets offered him between $12 and $15 million, and in 2011 the Minnesota Timberwolves also offered up their head coach spot. Each was turned down.

Though this didn't stop the NBA offers, Duke offered and signed Krzyzewski to a lifetime contract to coach after his third national championship in 2001. It also gave him the title of special assistant to the president, a position Krzyzewski said he intends to hold after he retires as basketball coach. But Krzyzewski wants to coach at Duke for a long time. "The allure of coaching in college has no price," he said. "To me, it was what was going to give me the most happiness, and I've been really happy at Duke and really fulfilled at Duke."

88 Randy Denton

It was at the ripe old age of 15 that Randy Denton burst upon the scene in basketball—January 8, 1965 to be exact. A 6'10" sophomore high school basketball player from Raleigh, North Carolina, Denton stood even taller on that evening as his Enloe Eagles took on the mighty Broughton Caps, the defending Eastern 4A State Champions and a team that possessed one of the greatest players in the history of basketball, "Pistol" Pete Maravich.

Enloe was the new school in Raleigh, taking on the flagship school in the area. After the game went back and forth, Denton scored five points in the final 26 seconds of the game to lead Enloe to a 63–61 victory. It was the first varsity win by any Enloe team against Broughton. Denton tallied 18 points on the night while Maravich scored 20 points.

But with Maravich in the game, it wasn't over until the final whistle. With one second left and Broughton down by three, Maravich was on the foul line. He made the first free throw, then tried to miss the second so that it came off the rim and could be tipped in. It didn't get tipped in. "I was sure Pete would try something," said Denton coach Howard Hurt, a former Duke basketball player. "And I could only hope it wouldn't work." Added Broughton coach Ed McLean, who went on to be an assistant at N.C. State: "Denton played a great game, a tremendous one for a sophomore, the pressure was on him, and he really came through."

It was a very special time for high school basketball in the Capital City. Both Maravich and Denton were thought of as big-time basketball players and played a lot of ball against each other. "Pete and I knew each other from a few nightclubs in Raleigh and we played against each other in pickup games at the old Hayes Barton pool courts and in summer league games at the Raleigh YMCA," Denton said. "It was a great time."

Denton developed into a very fine basketball player, and the 6'10" player garnered a great deal of attention from college coaches. Hurt and Denton's mom received more than 200 letters from colleges around the country. He was recruited by Frank McGuire at South Carolina, Dean Smith at North Carolina, Vic Bubas at Duke, and his future head coach Bucky Waters, who was at West Virginia at the time. Hurt remembers McGuire coming to town in his big white Cadillac while Denton remembers Smith taking his mom to the Angus Barn a couple of times. "My dad died in the summer of '66 suddenly. I only made one recruiting trip, and that was to Davidson, who had Lefty Drisell as the head coach," Denton explained. "My dad loved Duke, he thought a lot of Coach Bubas, and his love of Duke and Coach Hurt were the reasons I went to Duke."

At Duke he became known for his consistency. As a center for the Blue Devils, he earned second team All-ACC honors as a sophomore and junior and first team as a senior. In all three years of his varsity career from 1969–71, he led the team in scoring and rebounding and was named All-America in 1971.

His 19.7 career scoring average stands sixth in Duke history while his 12.7 rebounding average is tops in school history, and he stands fourth in career rebounding. Six times he scored more than 20 points and had 20 rebounds in a single game, and his scoring averages of 17.4 as a sophomore, 21.5 as a junior, and 20.4 as a senior show his true consistency.

It was in his senior season that Denton felt he had one of his best games of his career when he helped lead the Blue Devils to an 82–71 win against No. 10 South Carolina. Denton had 15 points and 11 rebounds, while Tom Owens of South Carolina had just 12 points and six rebounds. In 1968 Denton and the Blue Devils captured the Sugar Bowl Tournament, beating Iowa, and Denton was named the MVP of the tournament.

He takes great pride in the fact that he never lost a Senior Day game in Cameron Indoor Stadium to North Carolina, winning all three games. But it was following the 1969 season that things changed for Denton. The coach that he had come to Duke to play for, Vic Bubas, was stepping down, and Bucky Waters would become his head coach for the next two seasons. "My heart dropped. He was always kind of a father figure to me because my father thought so much of him," Denton explained. "I remember after the season, we had lost our final game to Carolina in the ACC Championship Game in Charlotte, and a week later, he called us in one by one and told us the time had come for him to move on to another job."

The Boston Celtics selected Denton in the fourth round of the NBA draft, and the Memphis Pros of the ABA selected him in the first round. "Red Auerbach called and told me I could come work with the team in the summer and try out with the team, while Memphis gave me a guaranteed three-year contract," he said. "That's why I went to Memphis."

When the ABA folded, Denton was drafted by the New York Knicks in the dispersal draft but ended up playing his final year with the Atlanta Hawks for Hubie Brown, who had been an assistant coach at Duke during Denton's career. Following his playing career, Denton settled in his hometown of Raleigh and is now director of business development for executive building maintenance. He has worked with the Duke Medical Center on building projects for years, though he is still known for his spectacular hairdo that he wore during his playing days in the ABA. "I had as good a 'fro as any of the guys in the league including Dr. J," he said with a big smile.

89 Elton Brand

Elton Brand came to Duke as part of one of the most highly touted recruiting classes in the history of the school. Brand, Shane Battier, Chris Burgess, and Will Avery were all part of the 1997 Duke recruiting class. In the two seasons Brand was a Blue Devil, Duke put together an amazing 36–2 record against ACC opponents.

Brand hailed from Peekskill, New York, where he played at Peekskill High School, averaging 40 points and 20 rebounds in high school and helping his team to two state championships. Brand was named the state of New York's Mr. Basketball his senior year.

Brand would only be around for two seasons as a Blue Devil, but he made a huge impact on the program. His freshman season

The 1999 National Player of the Year, Elton Brand, posts up North Carolina's Kris Lang.

was interrupted with a foot injury that caused him to play in just 21 games, but he still scored 281 points for an average of 13.4 points along with 7.3 rebounds per game. He upped those numbers as a sophomore, posting 19 double-doubles and nearly averaging a double-double with 17.7 points and 9.8 rebounds. He had the best field goal percentage in the ACC at 62 percent.

His size and girth allowed him to be an incredible rebounder and a very strong defensive player and was a key to the Blue Devils going 19–0 in ACC games in 1999. He was the main cog in their run to the national championship game that year. His outstanding play in 1999 earned him National Player of the Year honors.

One of his best games as a freshman was on Senior Day in 1998. Down by 17 points at 64–47 to the Tar Heels, Brand led a comeback by posting up and making inside shots and holding Carolina's Antawn Jamison to just one free throw and one tip-in in the last 11 minutes as the Blue Devils came back to capture the victory.

Selected as the No. 1 pick of the 1999 NBA Draft by the Chicago Bulls, Brand became the first Blue Devils player since Art Heyman to be a No. 1 pick. The 1999 NBA Draft saw four Duke players go in the first round with Trajan Langdon selected with the 11th pick, Corey Maggette with the 13th pick, and Will Avery with the 14th pick. As a rookie with the Bulls, Brand was named co-NBA Rookie of the Year with former Maryland guard Steve Francis of the Houston Rockets. In his first season, he averaged 20.1 points and 10 rebounds per game and followed that up in his second season with the same 20.1 scoring average and 10.1 rebounds.

In 2001 Brand was traded to the Los Angeles Clippers, where in 2002 he became the first Clippers players since 1994 to be selected to the NBA All-Star Game. In 2003 when the Miami Heat offered the restricted free agent a contract worth $82 million over six years, the Clippers matched the offer and Brand remained in Los Angeles and had his best season. In 2006 he posted his career best scoring average at 24.7 points while leading the Clippers to their first playoff win since 1976. In July of 2008, Brand signed a five-year, $82 million deal with the Philadelphia 76ers, where he played through the 2012 season, fighting injuries through most of his days in Philadelphia. In July of 2012, Brand was claimed off waivers by the Dallas Mavericks, where he played in mostly a reserve role averaging 7.2 points and six rebounds in 21.2 minutes per game. The Atlanta Hawks signed Brand to a contract in July of 2013, where he lent experience to a young Hawks team that was one of the best teams in the NBA in 2015.

90 The Landlord

Shelden Williams played in all 139 games during his four-year career at Duke. He proved to be one of the greatest big men to ever don a Duke uniform as he lived up to his nickname of "Landlord" by capturing the National Association of Basketball Coaches (NABC) Defensive Player of the Year honors twice—in 2005 and 2006—and having his No. 23 retired in the rafters of Cameron Indoor Stadium. "He's great, in every sense of the word," Mike Krzyzewski said. "We're so lucky to have him. He's going to go down as one of the greatest players in the conference and at Duke. He's broken records, but he is such a team guy. He's truly a great player."

At 6'9" and 250 pounds, Williams was a force in the middle owning the lane where he earned his nickname of "Landlord," seemingly instructing to opponents that "Thou shall not enter the paint." His size and tremendous timing blocking shots and pulling down rebounds made him a true power on the court. As a freshman at Duke, Williams averaged 8.2 points, 5.9 rebounds, and 1.6 blocks per game while earning ACC All-Freshman honorable mention honors. In 2003–04 Williams' numbers grew to 12.6 points, 8.5 rebounds, and 3.0 blocks as he helped guide Duke to the Final Four. He also received several All-American honors and second team All-ACC accolades as a sophomore. As a junior Williams became the first player on a Krzyzewski team to average a double-double (15.5 points and 11.2 rebounds). He also registered a Duke-record 122 blocks while earning national Defensive Player of the Year honors.

Williams claimed that NABC Defensive Player of the Year honor for the second straight year and set Duke records for career blocked shots and rebounds as a senior. He was a consensus first team All-America in 2006, finished third in the league in scoring at 18.8 points per game, and became the 11th player in ACC history—and the first Blue Devils player—to lead the conference in rebounding in back-to-back years.

The Forest Park, Oklahoma, native grabbed 14 rebounds against George Washington on March 18, 2006 to pass Mike Gminski as the leading rebounder in Duke history. He also became just the third Blue Devil to register a triple-double on January 11, 2006, against Maryland when he finished with 19 points, 11 rebounds, and 10 blocks against the Terrapins.

A very intelligent player, Williams learned early the importance of blocking shots and keeping them in play. "A lot of time people try to make statements by throwing the ball way back into the stands when they make a block," Williams said. "I used to do that when I first started blocking shots, but my dad always told me that while it's cool and gets the crowd going, it doesn't do any good for your team. So a lot of times, I try to tip it where I can get it or a teammate can get it, so we can start a fast break."

Williams closed his career at Duke first in rebounding (1,262 to rank sixth in ACC history) and blocked shots (422 to rank fifth in ACC history), fifth in field goal percentage (.572), and 13th in points (1,928). He also became the first player in NCAA history to register 1,750 points, 1,250 rebounds, 400 blocks, and 150 steals in a career.

Williams played six years in the NBA as well as in France and China. On November 13, 2008, Williams married former University of Tennessee and current Los Angeles Sparks basketball star Candace Parker.

91 Carlos Boozer

At 6'9", 250 pounds, Carlos Boozer was a pure force inside. With his wide body, he was one of the best Duke players ever at setting picks. Born in West Germany, he grew up in Juneau, Alaska, and became the Blue Devils' second player from the state of Alaska following Trajan Langdon. Boozer played his high school ball at Juneau-Douglas High where he earned *Parade* All-American honors and was one of the most sought-after big men in the country.

Boozer played in a lot of basketball games for the Blue Devils— 101 games, to be exact, from 2000 to 2002 and started in 93 games. The big man also played a lot of winning basketball for the Blue Devils, finishing with a 41–7 ACC record in his career with three ACC Tournament titles.

As a freshman Boozer led the Blue Devils in rebounding and had eight 20-point games. In his sophomore season, he proved to be a very powerful player for the Blue Devils on the boards with his rebounding as well as scoring. He played well until the home finale of the season when he broke his foot against Maryland. But he recovered astoundingly quick and scored 19 points in the

2001 Final Four semifinals against Maryland and 12 points and 12 rebounds in the championship game victory against Arizona. "Carlos really put together the whole package," commented teammate Shane Battier. "He really concentrated on the defensive end, and that translated into great offense. He was much more of a complete player."

After winning the national championship, he announced his next year—his junior season—would be his last as a Blue Devil and closed it out on a high note. He was named to the All-ACC first team, the ACC Tournament MVP, a third team All-American selection, and led the team to the Sweet 16 in the NCAA Tournament. The Cleveland Cavaliers selected him in the second round (35th overall) of the 2002 NBA Draft. He had a very solid rookie season, averaging 10 points per game and 7.5 rebounds and was named to the NBA's second team All-Rookie squad. He followed that with an even better second season with 15.5 points and 11.4 rebounds.

Controversy surrounded his contract after the 2003–05 season, and Boozer became a free agent. After getting released from his deal with the Cavaliers, he signed a $70 million deal with the Utah Jazz, where he would play for the next six seasons. Those six years saw the peak of his basketball career. Under veteran coach Jerry Sloan, Boozer was able to blossom not only as a defender and rebounder, but also as a scorer. In his third year with the Jazz, the 2006–07 season, Boozer was named to the NBA All-Star team. Reaching the Western Conference Finals, he averaged 23.5 points and 12.2 rebounds in the 17 playoff games for the Jazz that season. He was selected to the All-Star Game again the next season. In July of 2010, the Chicago Bulls traded for Boozer, and he played for the Bulls for the next four seasons, averaging 15.5 points. In July of 2014, Boozer signed with the Los Angeles Lakers. On the international level, Boozer has been a member of two USA Olympic teams, including winning the gold medal at the 2008 Olympics as the Mike Krzyzewski-coached team defeated Spain.

92 Mark Alarie

There are many, including his former college roommate Jay Bilas, who believe Mark Alarie's No. 32 should be retired and hanging from the rafters of Cameron Indoor Stadium. From the very humble beginnings of the team's freshman year record of 11–17, Alarie was the catalyst, along with Johnny Dawkins, for the Blue Devils' phoenix-like rise from the ashes as they went to three consecutive NCAA Tournaments, won an ACC title, and reached a Final Four season his senior year when the Blue Devils played for the national championship and put together a 37–3 record. "He was quiet on the court but had an explosive competitive fire," wrote Bilas in 2004. "His jersey should be retired along with Dawkins… He was that good."

Alarie came to Duke from Brophy College Preparatory in Phoenix, Arizona, where he earned the state's Player of the Year honor while averaging 29.9 points and 17.3 rebounds. As a Blue Devil, he scored 2,136 points in 133 games for a 16.1 per game average and had 833 rebounds for a 6.3 average. He shot over 50 percent from the floor his last three seasons and possessed a smooth long-range jumper prior to the existence of the three-point line. At 6'8" Alarie was the player you hated to guard because he could hit the jumper, or if you played up tight on him, he would just drive past you to the basket. While finishing second to a scorer like Dawkins each year in points, he led the team in rebounding for three years and topped the charts all four years in blocked shots.

His sophomore season, the year the Blue Devils returned to the NCAA Tournament for the first time in four years, was his best statistically as he averaged 17.5 points and 7.2 rebounds, earning first team All-ACC honors. As a junior he was on the All-ACC second team and moved back to the first team as a senior, also earning All-American honors and sharing the team MVP with Dawkins in 1984.

What Alarie loved doing more than anything was playing in big games against big-time rivals like Georgia Tech and North Carolina. He had 26, 24, and 17 points in three battles with the Yellow Jackets during his senior season and hit the go-ahead shot when Duke beat the Yellow Jackets for the ACC Tournament title. He led the team in scoring and played superb post defense in 1984 when the Blue Devils upset No. 1 North Carolina as well as scoring the first points ever in the Dean E. Smith Center when it opened in 1986. But his most memorable performance came when he led Duke to victory in his Senior Day game in Cameron Indoor Stadium, clinching Duke coach Mike Krzyzewski's first ACC regular-season crown. "I like the fact that the very last time we competed on that floor, we whipped a very good team," Alarie said. "When I look back, that's an important memory for me. The last time we played on that court, which is such a fantastic place to compete at and to witness a game, I'm just thrilled at the outcome."

The Denver Nuggets drafted him in the first round of the 1986 NBA Draft. He played in Denver one season and then spent four years with the Washington Bullets before a recurrent knee injury caused him to retire. His best season was his fourth year when he averaged 10.5 points and 4.6 rebounds for Washington. After the NBA, Alarie earned his MBA and became an investment banker. He took a year off in 1999–2000 to serve as an assistant coach at the U.S. Naval Academy, but then he returned to being a financier.

93 Kyle Singler

The 2010 Final Four's Most Outstanding Player, Kyle Singler owns Duke career records for consecutive games played (148), games started (147), and minutes played (4,887). Before becoming that rugged, four-year player who stepped up in the biggest of moments, he attended South Medford High School in Medford, Oregon, where he became one of the top high school prospects in the country. The McDonald's and Jordan Brand All-American led South Medford to its first-ever state basketball championship by defeating defending state champion Lake Oswego and standout Kevin Love.

At Duke, Singler immediately made an impact on a team that finished 28–6, averaging 13.3 points per game and 5.8 rebounds. He had such a strong freshman campaign that there was considerable speculation that Singler would leave Duke following his freshman year and head for the NBA, but Singler felt he wasn't ready and needed to mature both mentally and physically. He did both as he ended up the top scorer on the team as a sophomore and then led his team on a Cinderella-like journey as a junior to the national championship.

As a junior he had a career-high 30 points against Georgia Tech while lighting it up from three-point range by hitting on 8-of-10 attempts. In his breakout season, he averaged 17.7 points and seven rebounds per game while being ranked among the top 10 players in the ACC in almost every statistical category, including three-point field goal percentage, scoring, free throw percentage, and minutes played. In leading the Blue Devils to their fourth national title, Singler averaged 20 points and nine rebounds in Final Four victories against West Virginia and Butler. Against the latter he had

19 points, nine rebounds, and two blocks in the climactic 61–59 victory.

Despite ending his junior year in that fashion, Singler spurned the NBA, staying at Duke for his senior year. During that final season, Singler played against his brother E.J. and the Oregon Ducks and tied his career high with a 30-point performance. Although the Blue Devils would not win another title, being eliminated in the round of 16 by Arizona, Singler had another great season as he averaged 16.9 points and 6.8 rebounds while playing 34.8 minutes per game. He became the fourth leading scorer in school history with 2,392 points and received his second All-ACC first team selection.

Following graduation Singler was selected by the Detroit Pistons in the second round with the 33rd overall pick. Because of the NBA lockout, Singler signed with Club Baloncesto Lucentum Alicante, a professional basketball team based in Alicante, a port city in Spain. He was an MVP in the Liga ACB league, scoring 23 points and pulling down four rebounds in his first game. In November of 2011, he signed on with the Real Madrid team and helped it defeat Barcelona for the 2012 Spanish King's Cup. In July of 2012 he signed with the Detroit Pistons and captured second team All-Rookie honors in 2012–13, averaging 8.8 points and four rebounds. Singler was traded to the Oklahoma City Thunder in February of 2015.

94 The Lost Season of 1994–95

To stay in shape, one of the avocations of a 47-year-old Mike Krzyzewski was playing racquetball with former Duke assistant football coach and wrestling coach Cameron Falcone. Coach K pulled a muscle in his butt in one of those racquetball games and had aggravated his back by not getting the appropriate treatment. On October 15, 1994, the first day of basketball practice, the pain in Krzyzewski's back was so severe that he turned the drills over to his assistant coaches and watched them while lying on the playing floor of Cameron Indoor Stadium. Tests showed a ruptured disc but no nerve damage. On October 19 he met with doctors who asked him to walk on his toes when his back began to hurt. "When I stepped with my right foot, I was fine," Krzyzewski explained. "When I stepped with my left foot, I collapsed because I had lost 50 percent of the strength in my lower left leg, and my foot went numb."

Two days later Krzyzewski underwent back surgery to ease the pain enough for him to return to practice and continue getting the Blue Devils ready for the season. Once again he never gave his body time to rest, despite strong suggestions from his doctors that he stay out longer so he would be able to finish the season, if not start it. In his mind he knew they weren't delaying anything for him and that the college basketball season waits for no one.

But the problems began piling up early—from Krzyzewski's back surgery, which caused him to miss two weeks of early practices and conduct others sitting on a stool, to junior Chris Collins injuring his foot on the first day of practice, to not knowing the academic status of Jeff Capel for the spring semester, to Erik Meek giving up his redshirt year, to Joey Beard having transferred, to Ricky Price injuring his ankle.

The Blue Devils had played in the Rainbow Classic after Christmas, and Krzyzewski ignored orders from his doctor to avoid the transcontinental flight and stay home to rest. Assistant coaches Mike Brey and Pete Gaudet, Coach K's Army associate and former head coach of the Cadets, were more than capable of leading the 6–1 team while Coach K remained in Durham to recuperate further. But his military background of never leaving his troops made Krzyzewski go on the trip to Honolulu, lying on the main cabin floor of the Delta commercial flight for much of the eight-hour trip from Atlanta.

After a loss Hawaii, the Blue Devils opened the ACC season at home with Clemson on January 4. Following an implausible home loss to perennial ACC doormat Clemson, Duke faced a weekend trip to Georgia Tech. All week doctors and Mickie Krzyzewski pleaded with Coach K not to get on another bus or airplane until his back healed. His distraught wife issued what was close to an ultimatum: get on that bus and she wouldn't be there when he returned. Mickie was as stubborn as Mike in many ways, and her stance convinced him that he should stay back and get a complete examination at the Duke Medical Center.

Late Friday afternoon, the Blue Devils found out they would be without their head coach for the next game, perhaps longer. Lack of sufficient time to recover from the October back surgery had actually caused Krzyzewski to regress. Doctors say normal patients who undergo the kind of procedure he had would typically stay out of work for three months. But guess what? They weren't going to postpone the Final Four until June to accommodate Krzyzewski's problems, so he returned to practice after recuperating at home for less than a month.

As usual on this Friday, prior to flying to Atlanta to face Georgia Tech for the second time in eight days, the Duke coaching staff met in the conference room. This meeting only lasted 10 minutes. "It was Mike telling us he was leaving—doctor's orders," recalled Brey, now head coach at Notre Dame. "Luckily, we had just played Tech in the Rainbow Classic so we didn't have to go over much preparation."

Brey and Gaudet were the only members of the coaching staff traveling with the team to Atlanta; the third assistant, Tommy Amaker, was on the road recruiting and got a surprise phone call from Brey. "You're not going to believe this," Brey said to Amaker from his hotel in Atlanta, "but we're on our own tomorrow night."

Gaudet, who was handed the interim head coaching title almost by default, was the most shocked because he had known Krzyzewski for years and how strong-headed he was. It was logical for Krzyzewski to let the "next in command" take over because he thought his absence would be short term. "He was such an intense person I don't think anyone thought it was going to hold him back," Gaudet said years later. "Nothing held him back. He didn't get much sleep anyway. The combination of that, the trip to Hawaii, game after game after game, there comes a point when you don't know how much you can endure. But none of us saw him stepping aside."

Little did they know, but the chaos and distractions of the season were just beginning as the Blue Devils would drop from a nationally-ranked 9–3 team with a head coach having won two of the last four national championships to losing 15 more games, winning just four, and finishing 13–18 overall and missing the NCAA Tournament for the first time in 12 years. "He was in trouble," explained athletic director Tom Butters. "He didn't know why. I didn't know why. He offered to resign, and I said that was crazy. Let's find out what is wrong, assess the situation, and see what to do from there."

What became worse than the defeats—six in a row after Coach K left the bench and three more three-game losing streaks—were the rumors that Krzyzewski had a mental breakdown and was walking away from the game. Everyone had their version of why Krzyzewski was missing the season. The reason was simple but not very well articulated by anyone at Duke. He came back too early from back surgery and was exhausted, and a few weeks off was not going to miraculously make him better.

No one heard a word from Krzyzewski until Duke released a statement on January 16 that the coach would remain "out for an indefinite period of time expected to last several weeks." That actually stoked the speculation because a back injury wouldn't keep him from doing an interview, even if while lying in bed. It gave new life to the rumors about what was really ailing the coach who had become a national name almost overnight.

Coach K's secretary Donna Keane made occasional trips to the house, bringing correspondence and tapes, but Mickie carefully monitored how much contact her husband had with his assistant coaches and players. She demanded he have complete rest and was miffed when she caught him on the phone late at night talking to Brey or Gaudet.

Finally, Butters and the Krzyzewskis agreed that the coach would not return that season and released the news to the media without any quotes from Coach K or his doctors. That sent the speculation soaring again, as the team blew a number of early leads and lost some close games—all the signs of a wayward ship with no captain. The collapse of the program reinforced what might have been taken for granted: just how valuable Krzyzewski was to Duke basketball. Without his presence and leadership, the Blue Devils lost their leader and their edge and needed a new start.

95 Tate Armstrong

Tate Armstrong, one of the greatest shooters in the history of Duke basketball, also may have played one of the most courageous games in the school's history. In January of 1977, Armstrong, a 6'3" guard from Houston, Texas, played an incredible game. In the first few minutes of the contest, Armstrong fell hard on his right wrist but refused to come out.

The ACC's scoring leader continued to shoot the ball and fight through the pain as he played the entire 45 minutes of the overtime game and scored 33 points, leading the Blue Devils to an 82–74 win in Charlottesville, Virginia, breaking a 27-game streak of ACC road losses that dated back five years. Following the game Armstrong's wrist was examined and deemed to be broken, ending his college career. He had led the Blue Devils to an 11–3 record. They finished the year going 3–10 for the rest of the season without their scoring leader.

Armstrong was recommended to the Duke coaching staff by Blue Devils All-American Jack Marin, who had seen him play in Houston, when Marin was playing for the NBA's Houston Rockets. Armstrong went on to become one of the most prolific scorers in Duke history, scoring 1,304 points from 1974–77. He averaged 24.2 points as a junior and 22.7 points as a senior prior to the wrist injury.

It was his junior season when Armstrong really burst onto the college basketball scene as he showed off his ability to shoot the basketball. His 24.2 average that year was the highest since Bob Verga set the school record with 26.1 in 1967. It ranked second in the ACC that season to Kenny Carr's 26.6 for N.C. State. In ACC games only, Armstrong led the conference with a 28.5 average, and his average in ACC road games was an incredible 31.5 points per game.

His junior season featured his best scoring night with 42 against Clemson as well as some amazing shooting. In a game at Maryland, he made 11 consecutive shots on the way to 37 points. Later that year in the ACC Tournament, once again against the Terps, he hit his first eight shots and scored 33 points. Maryland coach Lefty Driesell called him the best one-on-one player in the ACC since David Thompson and that he held his breath each time Armstrong touched the ball.

Armstrong, though, wasn't just a shooter. He passed out 12 assists in a win against Tennessee at Cameron Indoor Stadium and was named the Defensive Player of the Year for two straight seasons. His junior year saw him selected first team All-ACC, and he was just the second player in the history of the ACC to make the All-ACC Tournament team with his team being eliminated in the first round.

The summer of 1976 was noteworthy as well as Armstrong was selected to the gold medal-winning 1976 United States Olympic team. He was one of two underclassmen selected for the team, which was coached by Dean Smith and featured seven ACC players. Despite not deeing a lot of action, he was the highest-scoring U.S. Olympian per minute played with 16 points in 15 minutes.

Following graduation in 1977, Armstrong was a first-round selection of the Chicago Bulls in the NBA Draft. In his two-year professional career, Armstrong averaged 10 minutes and 3.8 points.

96 Chris Duhon

Chris Duhon was the kind of player who always impressed everyone with his quickness, amazing ability to dish out assists at just the right time, and strong defensive play. His play was so extraordinary he was named the National Player of the Year his senior year in high school, ACC Rookie of the Year as a freshman at Duke, preseason ACC Player of the Year entering his junior year, and All-American his senior season.

During his career at Duke, Christopher Nicholas Duhon had 1,268 points, 819 assists, 489 rebounds, 301 steals, and 162 three-pointers in 4,813 minutes of playing time. He started 113 games and averaged 5.7 assists to just 2.5 turnovers, one of the best assist-to-turnover ratios in ACC history. Duke compiled a 123–21 record, making Duhon the second-winningest player in Duke and Atlantic Coast Conference history—behind Shane Battier's 131 wins. He helped lead the Blue Devils to three ACC championships and was a finalist for the 2004 Wooden Award, the Naismith Award, and Rupp Trophy awards. He left as the only Atlantic Coast Conference player to record 1,200 points, 800 assists, 475 rebounds, 300 steals, and 125 three-point shots.

Duhon played his high school basketball at Salmen High School in Slidel, Louisiana, where he was named to the McDonald's All-American team, winning the three-point shooting contest, and was voted Mr. Basketball in the state of Louisiana. He came to Duke as a backup to Jason Williams at the point guard position but moved into the starting lineup late in the season, providing a spark as the Blue Devils went on to win the 2001 National Championship.

While he could score and pass the ball very well, what he did best for the Blue Devils was on the defensive end of the court. He was considered by many as one of the best defenders in college basketball and made the ACC All-Defensive team in 2002 and 2004. He clamped down on a succession of top scoring threats to help the Blue Devils win the ACC Tournament in 2003 and did the same in the NCAA the following year to carry Duke to the Final Four.

But his offensive spurts were clutch for the Blue Devils. With time running out at Wake Forest in his sophomore season, Duhon took a pass from Williams and hit an off balance floater at the buzzer to give Duke an 82–80 win. As a senior his length-of-the-court drive and reverse layup with 6.5 seconds left defeated UNC in overtime in Chapel Hill while his three-pointer with 36 seconds left was the clinching dagger in Duke's victory against Florida State.

Following his collegiate career, Duhon was selected with the 38th pick by the Chicago Bulls in the 2004 NBA Draft. As a rookie for the Bulls, he played in all 82 games and averaged 5.9 points and 4.9 assists per game. In 2008 Duhon signed a two-year deal worth $12 million with the New York Knicks and had an incredible game in November of 2008 against Golden State when he dished out a Knicks-record 22 assists. He would end his career playing two seasons with the Orlando Magic and his final year, 2013, with the Los Angeles Lakers. He tallied a total of 3,946 points, 1,364 rebounds, and 2,690 assists in his NBA career. With his retirement from the NBA, Duhon moved into the college coaching ranks in April of 2014 when he was hired by first-year head coach Dan D'Antoni as an assistant at Marshall University.

97 Steve Vacendak

In 1966 there wasn't a national award for the best defensive player in the nation, but if there had been, it would have been awarded to Duke guard Steve Vacendak, one of the most tenacious defenders to ever play the game. He is also the only person to be named ACC Player of the Year after not making the All-ACC team. A 6'1" guard from Scranton, Pennsylvania, Vacendak had such an outstanding performance in the ACC Tournament that he was named the tournament MVP and the ACC Player of the Year following the tournament. (The Player of the Year is now named before the tournament, so any Player of the Year also will be All-ACC.)

The 1966 ACC Tournament—the last ever played in Reynolds Coliseum—was very important to Vacendak. The Blue Devils were looking forward to a rematch with North Carolina State in the title game. But they almost didn't get there as young UNC coach Dean Smith unveiled his Four Corners delay game in the semifinals. "What people don't remember about that was that really was the first stall game that I knew about," Vacendak said. "It was 7–5 at halftime. Carolina was just standing out there holding the ball, and I think [referee] Charlie Eckman was being interviewed on the sideline by Ray Reeves."

Duke trailed 17–12 late in the second half and seemed to be en route to an early exit. "I remember distinctly standing out there thinking, *This is a heck of a way to go out*," he said. "We had a wonderful team. We were able to come back and win. I made a couple of defensive plays and I think I scored a basket. I also remember then Mike Lewis hit a free throw or two and we won."

Actually, Lewis hit one of two free throws with two seconds remaining to give Duke the 21–20 victory. But the Blue Devils still had to get past N.C. State in the title game. And with four minutes left, Duke was down five and seemed to be in trouble. Vacendak hustled and hit a couple of key baskets down the stretch to give the Blue Devils the victory and the title. Although all five Duke starters hit double figures, Vacendak led the way with 18 points in the 71–66 victory.

His selection as the Everett Case Award winner (for tourney MVP) was no surprise. But that was just the start. A week earlier Vacendak had finished ninth in the All-ACC voting. But when the Player of the Year poll was taken after the tournament, the Duke senior got 51 votes, easily outdistancing his roommate, Jack Marin, who finished second with 29 votes.

He was known on the court for his so-called dirty work where he would dive on the floor for the ball, hustle after loose balls, compete on every single play, and was a legitimate scorer playing on teams with scoring machines like Bob Verga and Marin. During his junior year, Vacendak averaged 16.2 points per game and then 13.2 as a senior. During his three-year varsity career, Vacendak led the

Blue Devils to a 72–14 overall record, a 36–6 record in the ACC, and two trips to the Final Four.

Following graduation he was selected in the fourth round of the NBA draft by the San Francisco Warriors but never played in the NBA, opting to play in the ABA. Following his retirement from basketball, he went to work for Converse and came back to Duke in 1980 as the associate athletic director. Vacendak was instrumental in the hiring of Mike Krzyzewski as basketball coach. Vacendak had been introduced to Krzyzewski by Vacendak's high school coach Jack Gallagher when Krzyzewski was coaching at Army. Vacendak went to an Army-Navy game in the late '70s, sat in on Krzyzewski's scouting report prior to the game, and left very impressed.

In 1980 when Bill Foster left as head coach at Duke and headed to South Carolina for the same position, Vacendak had been hired to be the associate athletic director. Though he had not come to work yet, he was still involved directly the process, urging athletic director Tom Butters to hire Krzyzewski. "Let me get this straight," Butters asked Vacendak. "You're pushing me to hire a man whose name I can't pronounce—and certainly can't spell—and who has a losing record?"

98 Tommy Amaker

Following the recruitment of one of the greatest classes in the history of Duke basketball in 1982 with the signing of Johnny Dawkins, Mark Alarie, Jay Bilas, and David Henderson, the 1983 class consisted of the point guard who would be the catalyst for the Blue Devils' success. A native of Falls Church, Virginia, Tommy

Amaker played his high school ball at W.T. Woodson High in Fairfax for legendary coach Red Jenkins. Amaker's mother was a schoolteacher, and under high school rules at the time in Virginia, Amaker could attend whatever school he wanted in the county and he headed for Woodson, where he started on the varsity as a freshman. Amaker went on to become a McDonald's and *Parade* All-American by his senior season.

At Duke he quickly moved into the starting point guard position, supplanting Johnny Dawkins, who moved from playing the point as a freshman to the shooting guard slot for the remainder of his All-American career. As a freshman in 1983–84, Amaker was able to help lead the Blue Devils to their first NCAA Tournament appearance since the 1980–81 season with strong play at the point on offense and great on-the-ball defense as well, bringing havoc to teams trying to get into their offense.

During his junior year of 1985–86, Amaker was key to the Blue Devils' drive to the national championship game. One of the best defensive players in the game, Amaker stole the ball from North Carolina guard Jeff Lebo and converted the theft into a layup that gave the Blue Devils a three-point halftime lead that they never surrendered in the regular season finale against the Tar Heels. The victory gave the Blue Devils the 1986 ACC regular season title— their first outright since 1966—and they would win the ACC Tournament as well.

In the Elite Eight against Navy and All-American center David Robinson, Amaker and Dawkins combined for a great defensive effort as they kept the Navy guards from being able to pass the ball to Robinson where he wanted it and made Navy change their offense. In doing so it helped Jay Bilas, who was guarding Robinson, play tougher defense on the big man, and the Blue Devils won the game to head to their first Final Four since 1978. In the 1986 Final Four, the Blue Devils defeated Kansas in the semifinal match 71–67 behind two clutch free throws by Amaker with five seconds to go in the game before the Blue Devils lost in the championship game to Louisville.

During his senior season, he was able to lead the Blue Devils back to the Sweet 16 of the NCAA Tournament before losing to eventual champion Indiana. During that year he was honored for his incredible defensive play with the first Henry Iba Corinthian award given by the National Association of Basketball Coaches. He also was named well second team All-ACC.

Following his graduation from Duke, Amaker was drafted in the third round of the 1987 NBA Draft by the Seattle SuperSonics. His size at just six feet hurt him, and he was cut from the Sonics prior to the season. He had been drafted in the USBL Draft by the Staten Island Stallions and ended up having a short stint with the Wyoming Wildcats of the CBA before deciding to return to Duke and pursue an MBA degree at the Fuqua School of Business. He met and talked with Duke head coach Mike Krzyzewski about getting into coaching and became a graduate assistant and then a full-time assistant coach for the Blue Devils for nine seasons. During his first four years as an assistant, he was part of four consecutive Final Fours and two national championship teams in 1991 and 1992. He took his first head coaching job in 1997 at Seton Hall and took the Pirates to postseason tournaments in 1998, 1999, and 2001 in the NIT and the NCAA Tournament in 2000. In 2001 he became the head coach at the University of Michigan and dealt with the turmoil of self-imposed sanctions by the school. He was able to build a team that eventually won the 2004 NIT Tournament and finished as a runner-up in 2006. His coaching tenure at Michigan lasted from 2001–07.

In 2007 Amaker became the head coach at Harvard and took the Crimson basketball program to an incredible new level of success. In his third year as the head coach in Cambridge, Massachusetts, his club set the record for most wins in school history with 21. The 2010–11 season was another record-setting year as the Crimson made their first ever appearance in the AP poll and posted another victory mark with 26 wins. Harvard has captured the Ivy League title and made a trip to the NCAA Tournament four consecutive years—2011–12, 2012–13, 2013–14, and 2014–15. The 2012–13 team gave Harvard its first NCAA Tournament victory as the Crimson defeated New Mexico 68–62 while the 2013–14 team posted another record 27 wins and upset No. 5 seed Cincinnati.

99 Mike Dunleavy

The son of an NBA player and coach, Mike Dunleavy Jr., possessed an understanding of the game of basketball that most players coming out of high school didn't have. He used that knowledge and his skills to help propel the Blue Devils to a national championship in 2001. He came out of Lake Oswego, Oregon, as a high school All-American in 1999, joining a Duke team that had just played for the national championship in April but was now depleted after several players left early for the NBA.

As a freshman for the Blue Devils, Dunleavy came off the bench as a sixth man, was named to the All-ACC Tournament team, and was selected as the reserve contributing the most to Duke's team morale. As a sophomore he became one of the Blue Devils' top scoring threats and was the spark in the Duke offense in the 2001 NCAA Championship Game against Arizona. During one stretch of the game, he scored 18 of the Blue Devils' 21 points to open up a double-digit lead. Part of an 11–2 run, his trio of three-pointers put the Blue Devils up 50–39 four minutes into the second half. He was an easy pick for All-Final Four team and had shown his prowess for explosive scoring just a month earlier when he hit a team-high 24 points against North Carolina in the ACC Championship Game victory.

As a junior he was captain of the team along with Carlos Boozer and Jason Williams. He averaged 17.3 points and 7.2 rebounds per game for the 31–4 Blue Devils. Against Wake Forest he had his career-high scoring game as he hit for 30 points, shooting 11-of-15 from the floor. A second team All-American selection and an Academic All-American selection, Dunleavy would have been a favorite for National Player of the Year honors as a senior but learned from his father that it was the best time for him to go pro and decided to forgo his senior season and head for the professional ranks.

Dunleavy appeared in 104 games as a sophomore and junior and scored 1,371 points for a 13.2 average, had 601 rebounds, and dished out 225 assists. At 6'9", 220 pounds, he was a smooth player who could score inside as well as hit jumpers from the outside and handle the ball. In each of his three seasons at Duke, the Blue Devils finished the year ranked No. 1 in the nation.

Dunleavy began his professional career with the Golden State Warriors after being selected as the third overall pick in the 2002 NBA Draft. He played for the Warriors from 2002–07 with his best season coming in 2004–05 when he averaged 13.4 points per game. He was traded to the Indiana Pacers in January of 2007 and in his first full season with Indiana he started 82 games and averaged a career-high 19.1 points, shooting 48 percent from the floor.

Following the NBA lockout of 2011, Dunleavy signed a two-year, $7.5 million contract with the Milwaukee Bucks. He played two years for the Bucks and then signed with the Chicago Bulls in July of 2013 for a reported $6 million for two years. In the 2014 NBA playoffs, he had a career-high 35 points, including a franchise playoff record eight three-pointers against the Washington Wizards.

100 Chris Carrawell

Chris Carrawell grew up on the tough side of north St. Louis and attended Cardinal Ritter College Prep, where he led the team to an 80–13 overall record. A fourth team *Parade* All-American, he set the school's record for points, rebounds, and assists. When he arrived at Duke, he became a player who could play several positions and score, rebound, and defend. He was named All-ACC twice and accumulated 1,455 points. During his career the Blue Devils forward compiled a 133–24 record, including a remarkable 58–6 mark in ACC play.

As a freshman he shot 57.6 percent from the field, averaged 5.5 points, and led the team in slam dunks with 22. One of the most intriguing games came when the Blue Devils took on Wake Forest, and Carrawell, at 6'6", was asked to guard one of the premier big men to ever play the game in Tim Duncan. Carrawell battled Duncan and the Deacons' other big man, Loren Woods, his former high school teammate at Cardinal Ritter. With 1:18 left in the game, Wake guard Tony Rutland drove inside, and Carrawell pinned his shot against the backboard, enabling the Blue Devils to win the game 73–68. "Chris was unbelievable," said his teammate Trajan Langdon following the game. "He was giving up four or five inches and he just battled."

As a sophomore Carrawell started in just 10 games, coming off the bench to provide the Blue Devils a spark either offensively or defensively. He started off slow after having shoulder surgery prior to the start of the year but ended the season scoring in double figures 22 times and finishing fourth on the team in scoring with a 10.1 average as the Blue Devils put together a 32–4 mark and reached the Elite Eight. He started every game his junior season,

Versatile, gutty forward Chris Carrawell drives against Maryland's Laron Profit during Duke's 82–64 road victory in 1999. (Getty Images)

averaging 9.9 points per game on a team loaded with NBA talent that went undefeated in the ACC and played in the 1999 National Championship.

But it was his senior season when he truly blossomed as a great player. He averaged 16.9 points, 6.1 rebounds, 3.2 assists; shot 49 percent from the field and 78 percent from the free throw line; and recorded 35.6 minutes per game in his senior season. He led the Blue Devils to a 29–5 record, the ACC Tournament title, a No. 1 seed, and a Sweet 16 berth. He was rewarded as the 2000 ACC Player of the Year and a first team All-American.

A second round draft pick by the NBA's San Antonio Spurs, Carrawell never played in the NBA and headed overseas after graduating from Duke. He played a year in Italy before returning to the United States to play in the inaugural season of the D League with the Asheville Altitude. Over the next six years, he played in Lithuania, Germany, Australia, and the Philippines. After playing in the Netherlands, he spent four years at Duke in a variety of administrative roles. After being hired in 2007–08 as Duke's athletics outreach coordinator, he became a graduate assistant and head team manager from 2008–10 and then became an assistant video coordinator and assistant strength and conditioning coach in 2010–11. After serving as a special assistant to the Duke women's team and as an assistant coach for the New Jersey Nets' D League team, Carrawell was added to Marquette's coaching staff by his former Duke teammate, Steve Wojciechowski, in 2014.

Acknowledgments

My first visit to Cameron Indoor Stadium came when I was six years old, when my dad was able to obtain tickets from a business associate and I had the chance to get my first feel for big-time college basketball. While I never attended Duke University, I have been a fan for well over 50 years and worked either for or with the school for the past 38 years.

I graduated from Guilford College in 1977, after having served as the sports information director there for three years as a student. During that time there were a couple of pretty good basketball players, namely Lloyd "World" B. Free.

Following graduation I went to work as the assistant sports information director at Duke beginning in May of 1977, working under the talented Tom Mickle. I went on to serve as director of promotions and marketing for the Blue Devils until starting my own communications company and purchasing the rights to the Duke Radio Network and the Duke coaches' radio and TV shows. Through those mediums and publishing *Blue Devil Weekly* for over 18 years, I have had the privilege of interviewing hundreds of Duke players and coaches throughout the years.

I am especially grateful to the late Mickle and former Duke director of athletics Carl James for hiring me at Duke and for the incredible belief that John Roth has placed in me for over 35 years of working together and developing some truly outstanding publications, radio broadcasts, and television shows. Thanks to John for editing so many of my stories over the years and making me look good. His *Encyclopedia of Duke Basketball* was tremendously valuable research material for the publishing of this book.

To Amy McDonald, assistant university archivist, and the staff of the Duke University archives at the Rubenstein Rare Book and

Manuscript Library in Perkins Library for all of their tremendous support and being the keepers of the "Holy Grail"—the files of past Duke basketball games.

To the guys at Duke—Art Chase, Matt Plizga, Mike Sobb—who have always provided incredible support and help in all of our endeavors with the Blue Devils over the years.

Special mention to Chase and Plizga for the excellent work they do with the Duke basketball press guide, making it a wonderful source of accurate information.

Thanks to Jeff Fedotin and Noah Amstadter of Triumph Books for their editing and guidance in putting this book together.

Thanks, as always, to the people who have always believed in and supported me—Barbara and Sammy Rigsbee, Jim Pomeranz, Temple Sloan, Scott Yakola, Charlie Smith, Tommy and Betty Saunders, my cousin Terry Moore, Rev. Brian Gentle, Rev. George Johnson, Tim Kent, Anthony Dilweg, Will Hedgecock, Tom Drew, and Dr. Jim Urbaniak.

To the guys in the office, Pat Streko, Lane Cody, and Ian Haynes who make it fun to go to what we call "work" each and every day.

And to my family, my wonderful high school sweetheart who became my wife, Robin, and the loves of my life, my daughters, Beth and Sarah.

My special thanks to my friend and one of Duke's greatest student-athletes, Mike Gminski, for bringing special meaning to the foreword.

Sources

Brill, Bill. *Duke Basketball A Legacy of Achievement.* Champaign, Illinois: Sports Publishing, LLC, 2004

Brill, Bill. *Duke Basketball, an Illustrated History.* Dallas, Texas: Taylor Publishing Company, 1986

Home Court—Fifty Years of Cameron Indoor Stadium. Durham, North Carolina: Phoenix Communications, Ltd., 1986

Roth, John. *The Encyclopedia of Duke Basketball.* Durham and London: Duke University Press, 2006

Moore, Johnny and Chansky, Art. *The Blue Divide.* Chicago, Illinois: Triumph Books, LLC, 2014